FEAR AND LOATHING

FEAR AND LOATHING

THE STRANGE AND TERRIBLE SAGA OF HUNTER S. THOMPSON

PAUL PERRY

THUNDER'S MOUTH PRESS
NEW YORK

Copyright © 1992 by Paul Perry
First edition
First Printing, 1992

Published by
Thunder's Mouth Press
54 Greene Street, Suite 4S
New York City, NY 10013

Library of Congress Cataloging-in-Publication Data
Perry, Paul, 1950–
Fear and loathing: the strange and terrible saga of Hunter S.
Thompson / an unauthorized biography by Paul Perry.—1st ed.
p.   cm.
Includes bibliographical references and index.
ISBN 1-56025-012-7 (cloth): $22.95
1. Thompson, Hunter S.   2. Journalists—United States—20th
century—Biography.   3. Thompson, Hunter S.—Literary art.
I. Title.
PN4874.T444P47   1992
070′.92—dc20
[B]   92-23397
                                        CIP

Book design and composition by The Sarabande Press
Set in Bodoni Book
Printed in the United States of America

Distributed by
Publisher's Group West
4065 Hollis Street
Emeryville, CA 94608
(800) 788-3123

For Joseph A. Longo, III, M.D.,
a friend indeed

CONTENTS

PREFACE

R eader, beware. This is a violently unauthorized biography.
It is not privy to all of Hunter Thompson's secret thoughts or
vile intimacies, but to a hell of a lot of them, nonetheless.
Which is why he is against it.

Here are reports of provocative escapades, legendlike tales from
the life of the one true Prince of Gonzo. Who is the man behind
them? Whence comes his love of fun, his apocalyptic drive, his
grim paranoia? Is it possible that a mere mortal could survive what
he has survived?

This wasn't intended to be an unauthorized biography. I wanted
the full faith and cooperation of Hunter in producing this book. We
had worked well together in 1980 on a piece Hunter wrote on the
Honolulu Marathon. Surely, I thought, we could work on an autho-
rized biography together. Wouldn't one be done someday anyway?
With or without his blessing?

I wrote, called, and faxed Hunter in his mountain lair. There
was never any reply. Finally, I consulted the man who knew him
best: Ralph Steadman.

"He's afraid of biographies," declared Ralph. "But just go ahead and write it anyway. When you start researching it he'll come on board. He likes you."

To show his support, Ralph agreed to be the first interviewed for the book. We spent three days together at a Tucson, Arizona resort, talking about their strange, and yes, *terrible* relationship. I even have two hours of the interview on videotape. "Send it to Hunter," said Ralph. "It will drive him crazy."

I never did send him the video. Instead, I pressed on with the research, gathering material from all over the globe. Many of Hunter's oldest and best friends spoke at length about their enigmatic friend. All told I interviewed more than 100 people whose paths had intertwined with the man called "Duke" in the *Doonesbury* comic strip.

But Hunter himself never came on board.

I think the book is better as a result. Biographies by their very nature pry into a person's private life. With Hunter's cooperation, many of the stories related here would have remained untold.

During our work on the marathon piece, Hunter shared with me many confidences about his life and art. I took copious notes. Hunter even allowed me to tape a lengthy interview in which he discussed frankly his drug use, divorce, desire to get off the treadmill of journalism, and even intimate details of his health. All of that is here, straight from his own mouth.

Res ipsa loquitor is what he says. *The thing speaks for itself.*

INTRODUCTION

"My soul and my body chemistry are like that of a chameleon, a lizard with no pulse," Hunter notes at the end of *Songs of the Doomed*. "They call me 'Lizard Man,' and I laugh smugly. . . ."

Yes, may he not call his lawyers, may he laugh smugly at our blundering and piecemeal attempts to capture his shifty tale.

Annie Leibovitz photographed Thompson for three days in 1976. She took him, in his Colorado retreat, from every angle: eating, altered by substances, in deep sleep, abruptly wakened. For the final pictures, he posed in front of a hearth fire in his living room like a demented version of Ozzie Nelson. When she was through, he emptied all the undeveloped rolls of film from her bag into the flames.

When all the anecdotes have been taken, the quotes quoted, and the tales told, any biography of Thompson has, in the end, to be at least metaphorically burned.

Thompson has created himself as one of the most fascinating and complex characters in American literature. He rides the edge at high speed while engaging in a mix of raucous verbal and

gestural antics: hoax, legerdemain, gargantuan exaggeration, buf-
foonery, consciousness alteration, threat, insult. He plays, all at
once, the roles of friend, trickster, "chemotherapy" doctor, clown,
and prophet—to name only a few of the most conspicuous and
mythological of his personae. He gets people hooked on him
because he's fun, irresistible, liberating, infectious. As he said of
his friend Oscar in *The Great Shark Hunt*, he's "too weird to live
and too rare to die."

He says in *Songs of the Doomed*, "To get along, go along." But no
one can keep up with him, no one can get a whole take on a man
who changes "constantly. . .with the total, permanent finality of a
thing fed into an atom smasher."

His writing, at its top pitch, achieves the constant intensity of
apocalypse, "total, permanent finality" happening all the time.

In his note at the beginning of *Generation of Swine*, he quotes
Revelation: "And I will give him the morning star." He says, "I
have stolen more quotes and thoughts and purely elegant little
starbursts of *writing* from the Book of Revelation than anything
esle in the English language." It's partly, he goes on to explain,
because he's on the road without his library, and there's Gideon.
Also, what he sees on the road in America is Apocalypse and Hell,
instead of Paradise on Earth, the American Dream.

Thompson's theme, the Death of the American Dream, began in
the sixties and it is serious, political, and personal, a prophet's cry.

To the extent that it is political, it is about the decay of liberal
hopes. Of the 1988 presidential election, he writes in *Generation
of Swine*, "1968—the Death Year. . . . The Democratic Party has
never recovered from that convention. It is a wound that still
festers, and these people are not quick healers. He quotes himself,
from *Fear and Loathing: On the Campaign Trail '72:* "How long, O
Lord. . . . How long? Where will it end?"

Thompson's personal story follows the cresting and fragmentation of the American Dream. He starts off as an American success story: An underprivileged kid from the provinces, a problem boy who never graduated from high school, makes it to the big time as a journalist on his own highly individual terms. He is the quintessential rebel hero, a good guy under a bad rep, thriving on liberal freedoms. His fame peaks with his classic 1971 reportage on the death of the national dream, *Fear and Loathing in Las Vegas,* and his 1972 campaign coverage for *Rolling Stone.* His subsequent article collections, from *The Great Shark Hunt* (1979) to *Songs of the Doomed* (1990), become food for all those Americans who share his cry "How long, O Lord. . . . How Long? Where will it end?"

In the mold of an apocalyptic prophet, he laments, rails, terrorizes, harangues, and joins the suffering of a doomed generation, but he never stops scouting around for signs of Hope and tidings of the promised Dream. Just before this biography went to press, a *Rolling Stone* article appeared in which he endorsed Clinton for president: "Another four years of the Reagan-Bush bund will mean the Death of Hope and the Loss of *any* sense of Possibility for a whole generation that desperately needs that fix and will wither on the vine without it."

Earlier in the article, he does his "chemotherapy" act as foreplay for his endorsement. (He administers sixteen Advils to Bill Greider, who had ripped his knee tendons.) "I can't stand pain," Thompson explains. "Not even to be *around* it." Even if the American Dream is a snake-oil idealism against pain on a grand scale, the article implies, it's better than straight pain.

Persistently, he hands out this old-time idealism along with the apocalyptic visions, the wit, the speed, the booze, and the rest of the mix in his medicine bag.

His photograph on the back cover of *Songs of the Doomed* shows a no-longer-young writer, without his trademark cigarette or even a hat to cover his bald spot, with an American flag hanging around his neck like a scarf of honor or an albatross. On the front cover, in a field of Colorado snow, still without a cigarette, he's shooting his electric typewriter with a shining gun at close range.

The more pictures, the more images, the more voices, the more substances, the more mischief he lets out, the more he makes a fool of any of us who think we're on to him. The only conclusion to this dilemma of an impossible biography is his: "Let us Rumble," or "Let the good times roll."

FEAR AND LOATHING

1

LOUISVILLE (1939–1955)

Louisville, the cultural center of the Bluegrass State and home to the Kentucky Derby, is famed for its production of cheeseburgers, cigarettes, gin, half the world's bourbon, and Hunter Thompson.

Virginia Ray and Jack R. Thompson, an insurance agent, lived at 2437 Ransdale Avenue near Cherokee Park, a green expanse of woods, trails and open fields designed by Frederick Law Olmstead. Their middle class two-story wood-frame home was much like the others in their neighborhood. Hunter Stockton, the first of their three sons, was born on July 18, 1939.

Hunter's boyhood pal was Duke Rice. They were crazy about sports. They used to watch the Louisville Colonels through holes in the outfield fence at Parkway Field. Rice recalls that Hunter's idol was a young player named Jimmy Piersall, who later left the Colonels to play for the Cleveland Indians. Famed as the wild man of the major leagues, Piersall couldn't take the pressure of the big leagues and went around the bend numerous times. "Hunter loved him," said Rice. "After a game, he talked about wanting to be a ball player just like Jimmy Piersall."

When they were eight, Hunter and Rice decided they wanted a

baseball field in their neighborhood. The site they settled on was a vacant lot owned by a man named Butcher, hence the name "Butcher's Field." The boys mowed the field, marked the foul lines with lime, and put in whitewashed rocks for bases. The lot sloped uphill to first, downhill to second and third, and level to home plate.

More ambitious projects followed Butcher's Field. Organized sports weren't played in the Louisville school system until tenth grade, so there were athletic clubs all over the city. Hunter and Duke wanted to join the prestigious Castlewood Athletic Club, but members had to be between ten and sixteen. Since they were only eight, they started their own club, the Hawks AC.

With city facilities already scheduled for use by the regular athletic clubs, the two boys arranged to borrow the basketball court of a neighbor named Red Speed. They pulled together a rag-tag team from the neighborhood and invited teams from other parts of the city to play in weekend "tournaments." To lure the better teams, they instituted the "Hawks Invitational." Their approach to marketing was so successful that registration tables sometimes lined Speed's court, and games were scheduled to run all day.

Hunter and Rice received their widest acclaim as the two reporters listed on the masthead of the *Southern Star*, a mimeographed newspaper founded in September 1947 and edited by a ten-year-old, Walter Kaegi, Jr. It cost three cents a copy and consisted of two pages of local news, opinion, and advertising. Hunter's sports and stamps columns for the *Star* are his first published journalism. The paper caught the attention of the *Louisville Courier-Journal*, which commented that the reporters' pay of ten to fifteen cents an issue "is somewhat below the national salary level for reporters." The *Star* lasted for five issues.

Hunter's partnership with Duke Rice took a back seat when a

new boy, Gerald Tyrrell, moved into a house around the block from the Thompsons. Nicknamed "Ching" because he had been born in China where his father worked for the state department, Tyrrell was a world traveler in a place where few of his ten-year-old peers had ever been across the Ohio River. He and Hunter hit it off right away.

They shared a delight in amassing great armies of lead soldiers. After digging trenches and tunnels and building elaborate fortifications in the Thompson's backyard, they lined up their battalions and played war. When Hunter wanted to increase the size of his army, they built and hollowed out large tanks from wooden blocks and challenged a neighborhood boy to a "guest war." "We hid this poor kid's soldiers in the hollow tanks and walked away with them," recalled Tyrrell. "Kind of a reverse Trojan horse trick."

When Hunter and Tyrrell were twelve, they began to be on the lookout for girls. They went to the Highland Presbyterian Church basement for the weekly meeting of the youth group "League." In what was supposed to be a supervised environment for dancing and socializing, recalled Tyrrell, Hunter led a move toward close dancing in the dark.

Hunter and Tyrrell also attended dance classes in the oak-paneled rooms of the Louisville Country Club, where their dancing partners were from the rich Louisville upper class. Hunter made himself conspicuous by livening up the required semiformal attire with a Confederate flag tie.

Because of the organizational skills he had displayed in forming the Hawks AC, Hunter was nominated for membership in another upper-crust Louisville institution, the prestigious Castlewood AC he had wanted to join four years before. He was very proud of his Castlewood letter sweater with its big white "C," and wore it almost daily. "We envied Hunter for that sweater and the looks it got him from the girls," said Tyrrell, who was nominated into the club a year after Hunter.

Hunter directed notoriously theatrical hazings for the younger boys he pledged into the club. David Wood, a Castlewood initiate, recalls having to go into a drugstore with other boys and stand behind several little old ladies who were eating lunch at the soda fountain. On cue from Hunter, who was watching through the window, the boys fell to the ground and faked epileptic fits. The women went down on their knees to help the boys, who then jumped up and ran from the store. On another occasion, Hunter, again watching through the window, had a couple of boys go into the drugstore and spin the paperback book racks until centrifugal force caused the books to fly off.

Society girls fraternized with the Castlewood boys by holding sorority open houses at the Louisville Country Club. In suit and tie, Hunter and Tyrrell pedaled their bikes to the club slowly to avoid getting sweaty. According to Tyrrell, they went because, at the end of the evening, in accordance with an old Louisville tradition, the girls went behind a closed door and kissed the boys on the lips.

Hunter had a neighborhood admirer in a little blonde girl named Susan Peabody, who found him sweet but difficult. "Hunter was always where the action was, even if the action wasn't the nicest kind," said Susan. "He was always excessive, highly sensitive, highly experimental. Everything was excessive. Hunter was never ho hum from day one. He was always interesting and bright, as well as jerky and nervous."

By Susan's account, the two of them "kind of fell in love." For a Christmas present, Hunter bought Susan a bracelet that had "Susan" engraved on one side and "Hunter" on the other. As Hunter rode his bike to deliver the bracelet, Susan's older brother and a friend intercepted him. They made Hunter explain what he was doing, then grabbed the package and hung his bicycle from a tree. When he protested, they pulled off his pants and hung them in the tree too.

Despite his organizational virtues and charisma, Hunter had a bad reputation around Louisville. He was off-limits for many children. His first run-in with the law was at around the age of eight. He and a group of boys were hiking around Cherokee Park when one of them had to stop at a men's room. While the boy was in the stall, Hunter and the other boys soaked paper towels in tap water and threw them at each other. Before long the spitball fight escalated into a full-scale battle. They threw garbage cans and wrote on the bathroom walls. The boys were later caught by the police, taken to the police station where a report was filed, and returned to their homes.

When Hunter was in eighth grade, his previous vandalism made him a prime suspect in a series of church and school break-ins committed by a group who, in notes taking credit for their crimes, called themselves "the Wreckers." The break-ins escalated to serious vandalism. The Wreckers tore up classrooms, broke windows, splashed paint on the walls, and even started a couple of small church fires. They were never caught, and it was never proven that Hunter was involved in their crimes. "They had us down at the police station several times, taking fingerprints and asking questions, but they never did lock us up for it," said Sam Stallings, a new buddy, the son of a prominent Louisville attorney who was president of the local Bar Association.

Hunter had often expressed to his friends dreams of becóming a professional athlete, and early on he showed a lot of promise. He had matured faster than the other neighborhood boys and was able to dominate them by size alone. According to Duke Rice, by eighth grade other kids were more able to compete with Hunter. They, too, had Castlewood sweaters and played hard to honor the Castlewood tradition. Hunter lost his position as starting end on the Castlewood football team. Although he played for both the Highland Junior High School basketball team and the Castlewood basketball team, he was second string on both.

According to Tyrrell, Hunter got slowed down by extra weight. He worked behind the candy counter at a local drug store and ate the product when the owner wasn't looking. "It was a jolt for Hunter," said Tyrrell. "Here was a leader of a bunch of guys who were very heavily oriented toward sports. But as he grows up he finds that he's not very good at them. And then what? If you can't be a sports figure, what are you going to be?" As Rice sees it, wildness took the place of sports.

When Hunter was fifteen and a sophomore in high school, his father died suddenly of a heart attack. Friends say there was no control on his wildness after that. According to Duke Rice, "His dad was a nice and quiet man who kept him on the straight and narrow the best he could. When he died there was no one to do that. His life got turned upside down from that point on."

Hunter's mother went to work in the circulation department of the Louisville Free Public Library to support her three sons. With her out of the house, Hunter often ditched school. He pretended to leave with the other kids, walked around the neighborhood until his mother was gone, then returned home and had the place to himself.

His bedroom was his castle. There were plaques and trophies from Castlewood games covering the dresser and the wall above it. Another wall bore a flag from one of the holes at a local golf course. It was the first hole he had parred; he refused to leave the green without the pin. Around his bed, paperback books were stacked about two feet high, just high enough so that, if they didn't have another stack next to them, they would topple over.

Like his mother, he had become a voracious reader. It wasn't uncommon for him to have a wild night on the town and then sit up reading until three or four in the morning. "I went on to be an English major at Princeton," said Ralston Steenrod, a high-school friend, "and one thing I remember was that Hunter was better read as a high school student than most of the people I graduated with from Princeton."

Hunter's bedroom retreat also included a hi-fi. "He would be up in his room with his player going as loud as it could," said one friend. "You could hear it three counties away. He lived in an old, quiet neighborhood and I can't understand why he never got busted."

Another item was a .22-caliber rifle. One day he and Tyrrell set up a target in his window and fired bullets through it and out into the neighborhood. They had to reload the rifle after each shot by pulling a bolt and dropping a fresh bullet into the chamber. Hunter was in the process of doing this when the gun fired and a bullet went through the floor and the china cabinet below, just missing a stack of heirloom dishes. Hunter's mother never noticed the damage.

Drinking seemed a natural thing to do in Louisville. "I don't know of anyone who was not profoundly affected by drinking, if not themselves then somebody else in the family," said Judy Booth, another of Hunter's friends. "All the boys started drinking in eighth grade and the girls would hold on a little longer. Whether he picked it up from his mother or not doesn't really matter. Drinking was right around the corner for Hunter one way or the other."

According to Tyrrell, Hunter had his first drink in the spring of his sophomore year. The two of them were at a social-club dance with David Porter Bibb and Jimmy Noonan. After the dance, Noonan had the idea of getting some liquor and heading for Cherokee Park. The boys bribed one of the waiters to get them a half pint of gin and a bottle of ginger ale; then they drove to the park in Hunter's two-tone Chevy and spent the rest of the evening drinking and carrying on. "He took to it like a duck to water," said Tyrrell. "And off we went."

From that point on, drinking had a place in almost everything Hunter did. When he ditched school, he often drank in his room with Sam Stallings. "Hunter and I had a thing, a sort of chemistry," said Stallings, who admired Hunter's quick wit and intellect. "When we got together, we just partied all the time. That isn't to say that Hunter wasn't good in school, because he was. He could whip things up right out of his head that would impress the hell out of our English teacher. But he was interested in a social life as well as going to school. And nothing was going to get in the way of that."

Hunter also hung out at the house of Bobby Butler, a wealthy friend whose stepfather was the president of a tobacco company. When Butler's parents were away, the boys raided the liquor cabinet.

Another friend was Norven Green. Short, unathletic and unpopular, Green was Hunter's gofer. He was particularly adept at obtaining Hunter a five-finger discount by stuffing cigarettes or whiskey into his jacket.

If there is one thing all these friends agree on, it is that Hunter was the leader of the pack. The stories of his drinking and carousing are legion.

For example, Hunter and Tyrrell were once at the home of a wealthy East End girl for a summer party. Hunter stole a bottle of Yellowstone Whiskey from the liquor cabinet and slipped it into his car. After the party, he and Tyrrell went to Cherokee Park and drank the bottle dry. Tyrrell threw up on himself in the front seat. Hunter drove Tyrrell home, hosed him off in the front yard and snuck him upstairs without waking his parents or any of the other three children.

Hunter's most notable nights on the town were with Sam Stallings. "Hunter and I were creatures of the night," said Stallings. "We lived for darkness."

Hunter and Stallings partied three to four nights a week at 100 proof bacchanals that sometimes ranged over several counties. A typical night started at a school dance or sporting event or someone's private party. There, as Stallings put it, they got "juiced up" and ready to roll. The next stop was often Louise Reynolds's house, which had the largest liquor cabinet. If the mood was right, they stayed there until daybreak. Otherwise they drove on, sometimes setting up car bars in Louise's huge Cadillac. Using fake IDs, they went to hot spots like Brady's or the Old Kentucky Tavern, near downtown, where they sipped Kentucky whiskey until 2:00 a.m. and listened to a dance band. At closing time, they bought more whiskey at a liquor store. If they couldn't find a party to crash, they ended up in the park or took off down the highway. Sometimes they had the car jammed with as many as eight friends as they sped down country roads, weaving across the center line and swilling booze.

Their destination was Lexington, the next-largest town. Usually they didn't make it. Small town police across Kentucky were on to them, and often they were stopped and jailed for drunk driving. At first Stallings's father bailed out all the kids and brought them home. After a while, he just bailed out his own son and left the others to stew in jail until court the next morning.

"At four in the morning, there were only three things out there: booze, broads, and cops," said Stallings. "When we went out, we always ended up with two of them. Unfortunately it was usually the combination that brought my dad with it."

If Hunter showed up for school on Monday, he usually hadn't changed clothes since Friday. Once he showed up in the tuxedo he had rented for a Friday night dance. On most Mondays he didn't show up at all. That was his day of rest, to recover from the weekend's hangover. The next day he brought in a forged note.

Archie Gerhardt, his economics teacher, recognized the fake note and the signs of hangover. Gerhardt gave the class thirty minutes to study before discussion; Hunter always fell asleep for the last half of the study time. Once Gerhardt woke Hunter up and took him outside the room, where he made Hunter promise to at least be honest with him about where he was when he was out. Hunter agreed. After that he gave Gerhardt a blow-by-blow account of his weekends, but Gerhardt was never able to get through to him about school. "I feel bad about Hunter because I think I stumbled some way or another. He was making C's in most of the classes when he should have been making A's. School was easy for him and he could have been brilliant if he had tried."

Juvenile authorities had their eyes on Hunter and his crowd. One night in their junior year, Hunter and Tyrrell went to a liquor store with Bobby Butler and Bobby Walker, whose father was a district attorney. The usual routine on these trips was to have Tyrrell put on glasses and comb his hair so he looked old enough to buy booze. This time police had staked out the store. When Tyrrell made his purchase, they arrested him and took all the boys to the police station for possession of alcohol.

The district attorney was furious that his son had been arrested. Tyrrell's parents ordered their son to stay away from Hunter. After that, in defiance, Hunter and Tyrrell decided to go to a party every night. They managed to pull it off for twenty-six straight nights before running out of places to go.

Another time Hunter got drunk with Stallings and some other boys. They stopped at a filling station on Eastern Parkway and, in a fit of rage at the attendant, destroyed the men's room, smashing the mirror and shattering the toilet. The police came and Hunter was arrested. Flagrant vandalism was a serious offense. Hunter was sent to the Louisville Children's Center. While there he acquired a real fear of jails. Not only did incarceration mean a loss of personal freedom, it also presented the threat of physical violation.

Although nothing suggests that Hunter was sexually violated, he talked fearfully of his time in juvenile detention. "I think it was his first exposure to homosexuality," said Steve Isaacs, who played pickup games of basketball with Hunter. "He told me how he tied his arms and feet to the bed posts to keep the big kids from turning him over and buggering him. He said that these big kids would come in after lights-out with bottles of vaseline and flip the little kids over and corn hole them."

Hunter told Tyrrell, "Children's Center is something you want to avoid. The people who run it aren't nice and you might run into somebody who wants to take advantage of you sexually."

To imply that Hunter was little more than a carousing party boy would be to simplify a complex man. Even in high school he had many faces and was capable of adapting to a variety of groups. "He always fit in well with the upper-class kids in town," said one classmate. "He never had any money like we did, but he fit in."

There were many literary associations in Louisville in those days, associations with names like Delphic, Halleck, Chevalier, and Dignitas, all of which pledged members from the various high schools each year. Like fraternities, they required a special blend of qualifications, not the least of which was money. The one with the biggest reputation, the toniest of them all, was the Athenaeum

Literary Society. In it could be found the kids most likely to succeed, for whatever reason. Most members of the Athenaeum were intelligent, and also the scions of Louisville's wealthiest families.

Hunter didn't have a plug nickel. He hung out with the rich, but that could not change his address. The frustrations of this social situation may have been partly responsible for the rage and erratic behavior that seemed to permeate his being.

"Hunter really resented being on the outside looking in," said T. Floyd Smith, one of Hunter's wealthy friends. "He was an outsider not because of who he was, but because he didn't have the family money and connections behind him to allow him to do some of the things that his friends did."

Hunter felt a bond with the rich kids of Louisville and pursued them avidly. Their social status gave them a level of freedom that the members of the middle class could never attain. They were free of the need to find nine-to-five jobs. They took real vacations, not just two weeks in the summer, and traveled to exotic spots.

Some of the wealthy kids thought Hunter was too wild or too lower-class for their circles, but many more liked him. In 1953, they invited him to join the Athenaeum.

The society began in 1824 as the "Athenaeum Club," its name derived from the Greek temple named after Athena, goddess of wisdom. Its members were people distinguished for their literary or scientific achievement. The *Athenaeum,* the club's journal published by James Silk Buckingham, contained the works of such local writers as Etrich Sheppard, Leigh Hunt, and William Roscoe. In 1862 a group of students from Male High School formed the "Athenaeum Association" for the purpose of debating questions of the time; at the end of each month they published a newspaper filled with the topics and results of their debate. In 1898 the name was changed to the Athenaeum Literary Association and a constitution and bylaws were drawn up. An annual literary journal contained the works and musings of members.

The society had changed considerably by the time Hunter was a member. His mother called it "primarily social" and Steve Isaacs described it as "an Animal House fraternity." According to Ralston Steenrod, "Whether it was literary in more than name is subject to some debate."

The "Athenaeum Pledge" sums it up nicely:

Come pledge to the Athenaeum
Our love of wine and song.
The bond of high school friendship,
A bond full soft yet strong.
Then raise high and drain your glasses
And fill your hearts with praise,
For high, and the Athenaeum,
And friendship's sunny days.

Members met every Saturday night so as not to conflict with Friday-night high-school sports. Their discussions of literature and club plans lasted from 7:30 to 9:30. During these discussions a side of Hunter emerged of which many of his fellow students were not aware. Here was a Hunter who read good books and was capable of discussing a wide variety of literature, though he liked the works of F. Scott Fitzgerald the most and considered him "a spokesman for his generation."

Athenaeum members were expected to contribute poetry and prose to the *Spectator*, the annual literary journal. It was here, writing for this literary journal, that Hunter was first able to channel his rage and talent onto the printed page. He contributed to a comical advice column under the name "Harried Hunto." His piece, "Open Letter to the Youth of Our Nation," signed by "John J. Righteous-Hypocrite" and mockingly decrying his own raucous lifestyle, took third prize essay in the Athenaeum's Nettleroth

Contest. Another essay, "Security," seriously summed up the kind of life he did not intend to lead.

SECURITY
by Hunter Thompson, '55

Security . . . what does this word mean in relation to life as we know it to-day? For the most part, it means safety and freedom from worry. It is said to be the end that all men strive for; but is security a utopian goal or is it another word for rut?

Let us visualize the secure man; and by this term, I mean a man who has settled for financial and personal security for his goal in life. In general, he is a man who has pushed ambition and initiative aside and settled down, so to speak, in a boring, but safe and comfortable rut for the rest of his life. His future is but an extension of his present, and he accepts it as such with a complacent shrug of his shoulders. His ideas and ideals are those of society in general and he is accepted as a respectable, but average and prosaic man. But is he a man? Has he any self-respect or pride in himself? How could he, when he has risked nothing and gained nothing? What does he think when he sees his youthful dreams of adventure, accomplishment, travel, and romance buried under the cloak of conformity? How does he feel when he realizes that he has barely tasted the meal of life; when he sees the prison he has made for himself in pursuit of the almighty dollar? If he thinks this is all well and good fine, but think of the tragedy of a man who has sacrificed his freedom on the altar of security, and wishes he could turn back the hands of time. A man is to be pitied who lacked the courage to accept the challenge of freedom and depart from the cushion of security and see life as it is instead of living it second-hand. Life has by-passed this man and he has watched from a secure place, afraid to seek anything better. What has he done except to sit and wait for the tomorrow which never comes?

Turn back the pages of history and see the men who have shaped the destiny of the world. Security was never theirs, but they lived rather than existed. Where would the world be if all men sought security and not taken risks or gambled with their lives on the chance that, if they won, life would be different and richer? It is from the bystanders (who are in the vast majority) that we receive the propaganda that life is not worth living, that life is drudgery, that the ambitions of youth must be laid aside from a life which is but a painful wait for death. These are the ones who squeeze what excitement they can from life out of the imaginations and experiences of others through books and movies. These are the insignificant and forgotten men who preach conformity because it is all they know. These are the men who dream at night of what could have been, but who wake at dawn to take their places in the now-familiar rut and to merely exist through another day. For them, the romance of life is long dead and they are forced to go through the years on a tread-mill, cursing their existence, yet afraid to die because of the unknown which faces them after death. They lacked the only true courage: the kind which enables men to face the unknown regardless of the consequences.

As an after thought, it seems hardly proper to write of life without once mentioning happiness; so we shall let the reader answer this question for himself: who is the happier man, he who has braved the storm of life and lived, or he who has stayed securely on shore and merely existed?

Athenaeum friends gave Hunter the persona "Dr. Hunto." Some say it was in reference to his near medical abilities to anesthetize himself with alcohol, others to the way he babbled like an academic when he drank. "He became extremely verbal after midnight," said Steenrod.

Hunter's passion for alcohol was well satisfied in the Athenaeum. Parties always followed the weekly meetings. When the weather was right, the meetings took place around a campfire on "Athenaeum Hill," a special area set aside for them in Cherokee Park—a privilege granted their society because their membership roll included senators, congressmen, and mayors.

"Hunter's joy at these hill parties was gathering up great quantities of different kinds of beer and other drinks and arranging them nicely in his trunk," said Tyrrell. "He got great pleasure describing what the different drinks were and how the evening was going to be high times because there was so much to consume."

Ralston Steenrod remembers a get-together at someone's house to complete poetry and short stories for the journal. Soon the free-pouring of alcohol took the edge off the deadline. By four in the morning, more members were asleep than awake. Despite their alcoholic haze, Hunter and Steenrod were the only ones still functioning. "We typed until daybreak, finishing up other people's stories and editing much of the journal." Such a mess was made of the house that the housekeeper quit when she arrived the next morning.

There were wild nights without liquor as well. Hunter had a penchant for shocking street theatre, the kind that bordered on the illegal and dangerous. One night he and Paul Semonin, another member of Athenaeum, staged a fake kidnapping. The plan was to drive up to the Bard Theatre in downtown Louisville and grab a co-conspirator who was pretending to wait in line for tickets. They were going to rough him up as he screamed for help, and then drag him across the sidewalk and into the back seat of their waiting car.

Everything went as planned, but the one thing they didn't count on was the quick response of a civic-minded judge who was sitting in a restaurant across the street. When the screaming started, he jumped up from his table and began chasing the car down the street. The boys thought they had finally lost the judge, but when they stopped a block away at a streetlight, they were horrified to see the judge still huffing down the street, trying desperately to read their license plate. They got away, but the next day a short article appeared in the *Courier-Journal* with a statement from the judge and a description of the car under a headline about a "possible kidnapping."

Once Hunter and Semonin stuffed a gunny sack with cotton in such a way that it resembled a human being and then stood on an overpass and threw it in front of a passing car. On another occasion, Hunter pretended to lash a friend with a bullwhip in the middle of a downtown street. As horrified passersby scrambled to call the police, Hunter and his partner disappeared.

Eleven days before high school graduation, in June 1955, Hunter was cruising Louisville with Ralston Steenrod and Sam Stallings at 1:00 A.M. Steenrod was a high-school football star with a distinguished academic record. For these combined talents and his financial need, Steenrod was awarded full-ride scholarships to both Yale and Princeton. Stallings was the antithesis of Steenrod. The problem child of a rich and well-connected family, he was only interested in raising hell.

The three boys got into some serious trouble that night, and they were hauled down to the Jefferson County Jail. The incident became a watershed for Hunter that propelled him out of the community. The boys were brought before the courts with unequal results. Stallings, who was eighteen at the time, was tried as an adult. His father, past president of the Kentucky Bar Association, defended him and was able to win an acquittal for his son. Hunter and Steenrod were seventeen and tried as juveniles. At that time in Kentucky, juveniles were treated as wards of the court. Under that system, the defendants were not allowed to have legal counsel. The judge assessed the case and decided what course of action would be best for the child.

Steenrod got off without a jail sentence or probation. Although Yale revoked his scholarship, he was able to attend Princeton.

Hunter wasn't nearly as lucky as his fellow defendants. Although, according to Steenrod, Hunter had been innocent, his past had caught up with him. Underage drinking, buying liquor as a minor, destruction of property—all these charges came pouring out of the files of the juvenile social workers who had dealt with him over the years. Juvenile Court Judge Louis H. Jull rejected Mrs. Thompson's plea, "Please don't send him to jail," and sentenced a tearful Hunter to sixty days in the Children's Home, to begin immediately, and to reform school or the military when he got out of detention. Hunter and Stallings were not allowed to take final exams or graduate with their class at Male High School. Hunter never did officially graduate.

"All of this had a great impact on the guy," said T. Floyd Smith. "He was a sensitive person, essentially insecure, who wanted to be admired. Now all of his friends were going off to Ivy League schools and he was going to jail and then to the military. All of this made him extremely resentful."

There were other things fueling Hunter's resentment. Although most people in his circle supported him or at least tolerated his wild behavior, many just didn't like him. In the Athenaeum, for instance, the more serious members resented his untamed nature and strong penchant for drink. On previous occasions they had tried to oust him from the literary society for missing meetings or stealing liquor at the homes where parties were held. The same was true in the Castlewood AC, where his antics didn't always define good sportsmanship. But majority ruled, and Hunter was popular with the majority. When motions were raised to eliminate him from the rolls, his friends came to his rescue.

With Hunter's new criminal record, his friends became less vocal. New calls were made for his impeachment from the Athenaeum. A trial was called by a majority of the leadership and charges of "insufficient morals" were leveled against him. To be a member of Athenaeum, one had to uphold a triad of qualifications: academic superiority, athleticism, and good social graces. The tribunal argued that Hunter had already folded on the first count. How could they keep him as a member when he failed so miserably in "social graces" as to end up in jail on an armed robbery rap?

"Everything he did was outside the convention," said one of the members who wanted him thrown out of Athenaeum. "Among writers, that attitude is saluted. But for us he had gone over the edge and none of us were delighted to be in the same club with him. We didn't want to be outside the convention. We wanted to belong."

About forty members convened to decide the fate of Hunter's membership. As he sat in juvenile jail, fearful of the inmates who now surrounded him, the impeachment trial was carried on to the disgust of the members who felt he had been wronged. He was impeached.

"I was horrified," said T. Floyd Smith, one of the few who bravely stood up for him. "It was a kangaroo court. Talk about being thrown out of the pack. He was thrown out by the wolves."

Hunter did have his supporters while he counted his days in detention. A group of young debutantes led by Louise Reynolds delivered a cake that one of her servants had baked especially for Hunter. The girls swooned over Hunter as he graciously accepted the cake and promised to eat it all himself.

Other friends, too, felt he was a victim of circumstances. Semonin wrote Hunter letters expressing disbelief at what had happened. He knew Hunter had, over the years, been guilty of many things that probably should have landed him in jail, but not this. Like most of the people who knew the real story, Semonin felt Hunter had been sacrificed by the system.

Gerhardt, Hunter's teacher, unsuccessfully spoke up for him at Male High School when the decision was made not to let him have a diploma. "The one good thing I can say for Hunter is that his sentence was totally unfair," Gerhardt protested.

But people who knew him also believed he had been courting disaster for some time. He was an angry young man filled with resentment at the world around him. His father had died, leaving his family with little money or guidance. His best friends were well ahead of him on the social ladder, if indeed he was even on the social ladder. No matter how hard he tried, he would always be an outsider in Louisville's world of debutante balls and future Ivy Leaguers.

"Because of all the resentment, he made a living out of twisting the tiger's tail," said Smith. "This time the tiger just bit him and no one could really say he didn't deserve it."

Hunter spent only thirty days in jail, getting half his original sentence lopped off for good behavior. Back on the streets again, one of the first things he did was buy a case of beer and toss the bottles one by one through the school superintendent's living room window. "That'll teach the bastard for suspending me from school," he declared.

A few days later, Hunter went to the army recruiting office to fulfil the other part of his sentence. He picked up a few brochures, then brazenly approached the recruiting sergeant. "I want to join the Army right now," he announced.

"Six week wait," said the recruiter.

Hunter cursed and went to the air force recruiting office next door. The master sergeant at the desk told him he could be out of Louisville in a few days if he passed the entrance exams. Hunter breezed through them and hit the streets.

With a few friends he went on a drunk, swilling whiskey and talking about the good old days, down by the Ohio River. Early in the morning someone produced deer rifles. Taking careful aim, the boys fired bullets that hit some boats just below the water line. "Just for old times' sake," Hunter muttered as the boats filled slowly with water and sank to the muddy bottom.

Within a few hours he was on an airplane bound for Kelly Air Force Base in San Antonio, Texas.

2

"TOTALLY UNCLASSIFIABLE" (1956–1961)

On the flight to boot camp, Hunter found himself sitting next to a recruit who was desperately trying to calm his fear of the military by drinking whiskey straight from the bottle. Hunter soon joined in, chugging booze while insisting that military life would be a breeze and fun, too. "Where else are you going to learn to fly jets?" he muttered.

When the plane arrived at Kelly Air Force Base, Hunter was so drunk he had to be assisted off the plane by his fellow recruits. The heat and humidity of San Antonio gagged him as he stumbled down the steps and found his place in a low row. As the ranking officers shouted out roll call, he vomited.

Boot camp didn't exactly go downhill from there, but it didn't get much better. He had to wake up at dawn and eat bad food. He got constant abuse from drill sergeants. The tests he took at the end of boot camp showed a strong aptitude for electronics. "Don't they know I'm afraid of electricity?" he complained to a woman in personnel. "Of course," she shot back cynically. "Why do you think they assigned you to it in the first place?"

At least he couldn't complain about where his training would take place. He was assigned to Eglin Air Force Base in Florida. Given the hundreds of hellholes that he could have been sent to, it was truly a stroke of luck to be sent to northwestern Florida where he could unwind in the balmy tropical air when not being forced to attend class on electronic warfare and high frequency radio maintenance.

But that was just it. Hunter didn't like to be forced to do anything. He wanted an air-force career with some excitement in it. "Flying those fucking jets would be fine," he complained to his superiors. "Fly them on your own time," they barked back. "Your aptitude tests say you are a perfect electronics technician."

His only way out of the less-than-exciting world of electronics would be to take a dishonorable discharge. But he didn't want such a heinous label following him the rest of his life. That isn't to say he didn't tempt fate.

In a letter he wrote to Judy Booth, his brother Davidson's former girlfriend, he described an incident that would have gotten most airmen drummed out of the service. After a night of drunken revelry, he was driving back to the base, an open half bottle of gin between his legs. As he sped up the long drive to the guardhouse, dislike of the military and its rigid authority boiled up inside him. Instead of stopping at the front gate to flash his ID badge, he angrily tossed the bottle of gin into the guardhouse as he drove by. He was seriously reprimanded by the base commander, but he didn't get discharged. And he was still in electronics school.

After a few months, a glorious thing happened. The sports editor of the base newspaper was busted in Pensacola for urinating on the street. Without warning, the *Command Courier* found itself in desperate search for a new sports editor. Hunter, also desperate, decided to try for the job.

A quick reading of some journalism textbooks in the library gave him such shoptalk as "feature lead," "inverted pyramid style," and "headlines." Armed with copies of the Athenaeum *Spectator*, Hunter made his pitch at the Office of Information

Services. They could tell by the way he talked that he could get along in the newsroom. And his work on the *Spectator* showed that he knew his way around words and pictures. Hunter landed his first journalism job.

The Eglin electronics staff was furious when they discovered that Hunter was the new base sports editor. They had assured him the only way out of electronics was through the door marked "dishonorable discharge," but he had slipped through a side door they didn't know existed and walked away to something he really wanted to do. No matter how much his master sergeant complained, there was no bringing Hunter back to electronics school.

Being a member of the press gave Hunter freedom. All of a sudden he was living the life of a sportswriter, which is the journalistic equivalent of being a dilettante. His days were spent covering waterskiing tournaments at the beach, where he could jot a few notes and indulge his love of Hawaiian shirts and khaki shorts. Pacing the sidelines at base football games, he shouted at players and got the game down on paper to the best of his abilities. He played golf in the afternoons. He even found time to write a sports column for a little newspaper called *Playground News* in Fort Walton Beach.

When Hunter couldn't find legitimate sports to write about, he covered illegitimate ones like cock fights or professional wrestling. Rather than write about the fakery, he played it completely straight, writing as actual fact the broken arms, separated shoulders, gouged eyeballs, and ripped-off ears that the wrestlers were faking.

Through it all he wrote letters to his Louisville friends and packed the envelopes with clippings of his stories. Duke Rice, then a student at Virginia Tech, got letters describing "the constant hell of the structured military life." With the letter was "this beautiful story about Adolph Rupp, the coach of the University of Kentucky basketball team."

Gerald Tyrrell, on his way to Yale, got letters that, as he remembers, "described the horseshit food and bullshit hour that they had to get out of bed." With his letters came copies of columns bylined "Thorne Stockton," a pen name Hunter used when writing for *Playground News*.

Paul Semonin, Hunter's old friend from Athenaeum, now at Yale, received a letter thanking him for his friendship and support, and expressing sadness over being made to testify against their friend Abe, who ran the liquor store where they got their booze. Hunter goes on to tell Semonin that he has decided to turn over a new leaf.

Whatever his intentions, Hunter couldn't keep himself out of trouble. Even the relative freedom of military journalism was not enough. He was frequently reprimanded for leaving the base without permission, and was even threatened with a transfer if he didn't stop pushing the boundaries of appropriate air-force editorial policy.

It was not bad behavior but a journalistic act that finally got him ousted.

A source in the base commander's office informed Hunter of a remarkable act of special dealing that was about to be conducted. In order to let the quarterback for the base football squad sign with a professional team, the air force had agreed to give him a medical discharge.

Hunter was beside himself. Late one night, he slipped into base headquarters and rifled the files for the player's medical discharge. The next day, just before the *Command Courier* went to press, Hunter pulled a photograph off of its front page and replaced it with the football star's medical discharge.

The result was anger and chaos. According to an eight-page memo that was included in *The Great Shark Hunt*, the base commander's rage was felt throughout the chain of command.

Written by Col. W.S. Evans, chief of the Eglin Office of Information Services, to the base staff personnel officer, and dated August 23, 1957, the memo concluded, "In summary, this Airman, although talented, will not be guided by policy or personal advice and guidance. Sometimes his rebel and superior attitude seems to rub off on other airmen staff members. He has little consideration for military bearing or dress and seems to dislike the service and want out as soon as possible." It was requested that Hunter "be assigned to other duties immediately."

More than ever, Hunter wanted to start over again as a civilian. "I got a letter from him saying that he just wanted a normal life," remembers Tyrrell. "He was definitely tired of being hassled."

Hunter's wish was granted by the kindly master sergeant who edited the base newspaper. He liked Hunter and recognized the spark of creativity and anger in Hunter's writing. He made a pitch to have Hunter honorably discharged. By the early fall of 1957, Hunter was a free man.

Of course he couldn't leave quietly. As a parting shot at the air force, he penned a tale of rebellion and riot on the base. In this story, a group of enlisted men sneak into the officers' quarters and begin drinking great quantities of whiskey and wine from the officers' bar. The enlisted men get wild and begin fighting and pillaging. Other enlisted men join them. Soon a full scale riot rages over the entire base. Reinforcements of military police have to be flown in from other bases. Women are raped, airplanes are set on fire.

Hunter placed the story on the editor's desk and wired a copy to the Associated Press for national distribution. Then he drove at top speed for the front gate.

Hunter also penned a bogus news release "from the Eglin Office of Information Services," offering the "official" version of his departure. Dated November 8, the release told how air police-man Manmountain Dense had been badly hurt by an exploding wine bottle "hurled from a speeding car which approached the gatehouse on the wrong side of the road. . . ." The release, later published in *The Great Shark Hunt*, traced the incident to Hunter S. Thompson, who had been discharged on that day. "According to Captain Munnington Thurd," says the release, Thompson is "'totally unclassifiable' and 'one of the most savage and unnatural airmen I've ever come up against.'"

Hunter was free, but free to do what? He wasn't entirely sure. He considered going to school, but the thought of the structured life of a student made him twitch. And besides, would he want to go to any school that would have him? University of Kentucky was a possibility, but all of his friends were off in the Ivy Leagues.

His second option sounded better. He liked being a working journalist. Where other professions might doom him to life inside a cubicle, journalism let him earn while he roamed. It was a poor man's trust fund, a real ticket to ride.

His first foray into civilian journalism was a disaster. He worked for only a few weeks for a newspaper called the *Jersey Shore Times* in Pennsylvania. Hunter describes his experience there in "Tarred and Feathered at the Jersey Shore," in *Songs of the Doomed*.

According to Hunter's piece, he and a local feature writer became friends. One night, Hunter borrowed the writer's car to take his daughter for a ride through the countryside. In the course of the evening's adventures, one of the car's doors and the front bumper were practically torn off. The following morning Hunter and the other journalists watched as the writer, furious, drove the car into the newspaper parking lot, door and bumper grinding on the asphalt. Fearful that the publisher would deduct repair costs from his salary, Hunter immediately left the office, drove home, packed, and headed for New York City.

.   .   .

New York City was like a homecoming for Hunter. Here he could truly be himself. No behavior was too strange for the New York of the fifties. He could roam the streets drunk if he wanted to, and no whispering campaigns would start up the way they did in Louisville. No one even noticed drunks in this city.

Many of his friends from Louisville were there. T. Floyd Smith was working on an undergraduate degree at Columbia College. Paul Semonin was in the city studying art. Gerald Tyrrell was nearby, at Yale.

Hunter took up residence on Perry Street in Greenwich Village, in a place a friend described as "looking like a Hollywood set for hell.

"The apartment was below ground. The way you got down to it was to walk in off the street through a side entrance, down a rickety flight of stairs and into the backyard of the building. Then you had to duck under the clotheslines to get to his door. When you opened the door you were immediately hit by heat and ahead of you there were flames dancing off the wall. This was the boiler room for the building above. You would walk along this catwalk next to the burner with a broken door and go into the first door after the burner. This was Hunter's apartment. Needless to say, he never needed heat."

The apartment's insides were painted black. It was a fairly large railroad flat with a domed ceiling; the entrance was through the kitchen, behind which was a living room and bedroom. There were no windows, so the only way you could tell if it was day or night was by lying on your back and peering up into an airshaft. If it was daytime, a tiny patch of blue was visible.

In this "cave" Hunter and his friends enjoyed long drinking

bouts. "This place really had a beat feel to it," said Semonin. "And we were doing our best to at least drink like the beats."

New York was going to be a new leaf for Hunter. If he couldn't match the education his friends were getting, he decided he would at least try to come close. He registered for night school classes at Columbia University.

He also applied for a job at *Time* magazine and was hired as a copy boy. It was not a prestige position, but at least it paid a livable sum of about $85 per week.

For a brief period Hunter adhered to a tight schedule. He arrived in the morning at *Time* for his daily eight hours, and then he caught the subway up to Columbia at 116th Street and Broadway for evening classes.

It didn't take him long to discover that school was not his destiny. Friends from that period said he complained about having to sit still in class while, as he put it, he was not learning anything valuable anyway. "Hunter liked to be in the action, not just read about it," said Smith, "which made him poor student material."

Within a few months of starting at Columbia, Hunter quit school, never to return. Always greatly influenced by the books he read, he soon found himself under the spell of Sebastian Dangerfield, the main character in *The Ginger Man*, the wild and picaresque novel by the Ireland-based writer J.P. Donleavy. *Time* magazine called Dangerfield "one of the most outrageous scoundrels in contemporary fiction, a whoring, boozing young wastrel who sponges off his friends and beats his wife and girl friends." The reviewer goes on to say that the reader will love Dangerfield anyway "for his killer instinct, flamboyant charm, wit, flashing generosity—and above all his wild, fierce, two-handed grab for every precious second of life."

Hunter loved this book like no other. To be sure, he felt a

kinship with the outsiders in F. Scott Fitzgerald's books. The writings of Jack Kerouac, especially *On the Road*, had aspects that he would soon act out in his own life. A friend recalls a time in which they both sat in Hunter's apartment and read magazine pieces written by Tom Wolfe out loud to each other. But *The Ginger Man* gave Hunter a role model for New York City life.

"Hunter read and reread that book," said Semonin. "This book and the spirit that Donleavy put into it really jelled his personality. He may have been enamored with the writing of Fitzgerald, but *The Ginger Man* fit him like a glove."

Hunter quoted chapters and verses, read passages aloud, and talked about scenes from the book almost incessantly, especially ones in which Dangerfield beats the system or demonstrates with some kind of flair that he is unable to be domesticated in any way.

"The guy in *The Ginger Man* feels that society should take care of him," said T. Floyd Smith. "Hunter has a big swath of that in him. He wanted to beat the system, not destroy it. He loved the system. He just wanted to reform it so it took care of him."

As his friends pursued lives that would allow them to become a part of the system or at least peacefully coexist with it, Hunter never stopped testing the bounds of acceptable behavior.

"Usually he was just on the border of good taste," said Semonin. "But sometimes he bordered on criminal behavior. And sometimes we were right there with him."

With his old friends and Gene McGarr, a fellow copyboy at *Time*, Hunter was constantly prowling the taverns of Manhattan. One evening, when they couldn't find action in the bars, Hunter and McGarr decided that the LeRoy Park pool was a place to get some relief from the oppressive summer heat. They organized a group that included McGarr's wife Eleanor, a prep-school guy who lived down the hall from Hunter, and Hunter's girlfriend from *Time*, Connie Dibble.

The five walked down to the pool and climbed the ten-foot high cyclone fence that surrounded it. Once inside, they took off their clothes and dove in. After about ten minutes of swimming, Connie Dibble came up from underwater to see five Italian boys staring at her. "What the fuck are you doing here?" one of the boys yelled. "This is our fucking turf. You'd better get the hell outta here!"

A boy ambled over to the pile of clothing and began kicking it into the water. Eleanor McGarr became furious. "What are you doing, throwing our clothes in the water!" she shouted, standing on the pool deck in front of the five locals. "What's the matter with you?!"

When McGarr came out of the pool to defend his wife, all five of the "guineas" (as the Irish McGarr called them) began swinging at him. As they started to get the best of the big Irishman, Hunter grabbed two of them and threw them into the pool. McGarr hammered the remaining three.

"We better get the hell out of here," said McGarr, watching the five boys retreat over the fence.

They pulled their clothes from the pool and wrung them as dry as possible. But they didn't move fast enough. More boys showed up, and this time ten came over the fence. The prep-school boy panicked and ran, leaving McGarr and Hunter to face the angry horde. McGarr stood shoulder to shoulder with Hunter, who wasn't quite sure what to do, but was willing to do it anyway. "Hunter didn't know how to fistfight, let alone fistfight against overwhelming odds," said McGarr. "But he wasn't running away. He was very brave."

McGarr decided to inflict the most damage he could on the fewest number of people. When the first three toughs reached him, he pummeled them with everything he had learned in his Bronx upbringing. Hunter was in there too, swinging hard at a couple of the boys who quickly backed off, heading for the safety of the cyclone fence.

"Now let's get the hell out of here," said McGarr.

Suddenly McGarr's wife screamed. Outside the cyclone fence stood about fifty more of the local toughs, many armed with sticks and bottles. "We don't want the women," shouted one of them. "Just you guys."

Slowly they got dressed and Hunter and McGarr helped the two women over the fence. "Don't look back," McGarr told his wife. "Hit the ground running and don't stop until you find a policeman."

There was nothing left for McGarr and Hunter to do but climb the fence. The gang on the other side backed away to let their prey get over and onto the ground. Then they moved in. McGarr kept his back to the fence to keep the attackers in front of him. Hunter pulled away and was surrounded by boys who were throwing bottles, slugging, kicking, and beating him with sticks. Before long he was in a fetal position on the ground, trying desperately to protect his soft spots.

And then it was over. The toughs disappeared, leaving Hunter and McGarr dazed and bleeding as police rushed the scene. One of the policemen wrote up a report while others cruised the neighborhood rounding up suspects. One by one the suspects were paraded in front of Hunter and McGarr. All told, about a dozen boys were loaded into the paddy wagons and taken to the precinct jail.

"We're taking you to a hospital," said one of the cops, leading Hunter and McGarr to an ambulance. "Come by the precinct house when the doctors get finished."

At St. Vincent's, Hunter and McGarr were placed in a tiled room and hosed down with warm water to get the big pieces of glass out of their skin. Then the small pieces were picked off with tweezers by a nurse. McGarr got several stitches in the back of his head. Hunter's eyes were so bloodshot that the examining doctor suspected concussion and wanted to keep him in the hospital overnight for observation. "No thanks," said Hunter. "I'll take care of my own concussion at home."

Back at the precinct house, the police presented the options to the injured warriors. "If you press charges against them," said a harried cop, "they'll press charges against you and you will have to spend the night in jail, too." Hunter and McGarr conferred for a few minutes and decided to drop the charges.

When Hunter got home, the prep-school boy down the hall came by to apologize for leaving the fight so soon. Hunter growled and then noticed the boy's girlfriend, who was looking at Hunter with a heightened level of interest. Later that night she returned to Hunter's apartment to check on the patient. Her services were in such demand that she visited for several days, a move which did not please her boyfriend. He complained to McGarr "that he had invested all of this money in her, and now she was fucking him over for Hunter."

The LeRoy Park pool incident was only one of a variety of trouble-making episodes. On another night, Hunter and McGarr went to the Living Theatre on 14th Street to see Gregory Corso and Jack Kerouac, who was to read from *Dr. Sax*, then a work in progress. They smuggled in a couple of six packs of beer beneath their trench coats. Throughout Kerouac's reading, they silently sipped the beer and put the cans on the floor next to them. Although Kerouac was extremely drunk and his reading almost incomprehensible, the two remained silent out of respect for him.

When Corso came on it was another matter. They had read some of his work and found it to be very macho. For some reason, they expected the same of its author. "We thought Corso was about six-foot nine and wore hobnailed boots," said McGarr. What they got instead was the real Corso, all 5'6" of him. It was more than they could bear. As Corso read, Hunter and McGarr took turns kicking empty beer cans down the aisles of the theatre. By the end of the reading, Corso was furious.

Hunter eventually took his "Ginger Man" attitude to work. After almost two years of experience, he was humiliated at the low-level job foisted upon him at *Time*. He tried to convince the editors that he should be made a reporter and, after six months or so, a foreign correspondent. The editors pointed out the intricacies of the bureaucracy, as indicated by their masthead. They had Hunter look at the complex maze of desks, cubicles, and tiny offices he had to work through before making it out into the field where he could roam the world and file copy from pay phones.

Hunter became sullen and uncooperative. When editors asked him to pass copy along to other editors or to take copy over the phone from some foreign bureau, he dragged his feet. Before long he was involved in pitched battles with the editors. Finally *Time* could tolerate no more. He was dispatched to personnel, where he was shown the door.

"This kind of behavior was a pattern for Hunter," said Semonin. "He would hold a job for a short period of time and then it would be terminated because of some kind of incident or incidents filled with retribution and accusations. He just couldn't work with people."

It was the summer of 1959 and Hunter was out of work. His life was in a state of turmoil, but he was in good company. Semonin had just finished a six-month stint in the marine corps reserves and was living in a room on Charles Street in Greenwich Village. Gene McGarr had been let go by *Time* at the same time as Hunter. Smith was around, enjoying his summer vacation away from Columbia, and Don Cooke, an acquaintance from Louisville who would later become a good friend, was in the city as well.

With this group Hunter mulled over the unfairness of life and planned his revenge against the editors of *Time* magazine.

Don Cooke remembers one Sunday morning at McSorley's, where they used to go to drink half and halfs for breakfast and read the *New York Times*. Hunter and Cooke were sitting quietly in a booth, cigarette smoke curling upwards from their ashtrays, when Hunter suddenly slammed his open hand on the table. "Hell of an idea!" he shouted.

"Where?" asked Cooke, trying to see what story Hunter was reading.

"Not in the paper, goddamn it. Listen." The two leaned toward the center of the booth as Hunter plotted his revenge on a particular *Time* editor.

"They ship the magazine to the printer tomorrow, so today is their heaviest work day of the week," said Hunter. "I want to fuck with this guy's head. Cooke, I want you to call him up and tell his secretary that the shipment of Siamese sperm he ordered has arrived from the Orient and is being held for him at the Fourteenth Street piers."

Without hesitation, Cooke eased himself out of the booth and placed the call from the phone next to the bar.

"The secretary was appalled," he said when he got back. "She believed it completely."

"Great!" said Hunter. He spent the next few hours writing postcards that he sent to this editor over the next few weeks. They were signed by "Dr. Bloor," a persona Hunter temporarily adopted. One of them, for example, mentioned sheep that the editor had ordered for his particular needs. All contained references to homosexual liaisons.

"We read these with the greatest joy," said Cooke. "Then we made our way to the White Horse Tavern on Hudson Street where Dylan Thomas had his last drink and wrote another card or two over there. All of this was aimed at just getting vengeance on the people who did him [Hunter] in."

Hunter kept looking for a job, but the search was an exercise in futility. The jobs he could have, he didn't want, and he had not yet put in the kind of apprenticeship that would land him a good job. His termination from the jobs he had held gave him a low respectability factor. He had established himself as an outsider by choice, a person who was constantly angry at the establishment. "Hunter always thought of himself as a noble person with noble instincts," said Smith. "Unfortunately he never had the money to live like nobility."

One night he was mulling over the job situation with McGarr in a Village bar called Stefan's when McGarr hit upon a plan. He now worked at an advertising agency and knew of a job opening in the copy-writing department. Why not cook up a resume he could give to the director of copy writing? Although they were looking for someone with a little more experience than Hunter had, he could embellish the facts of his life to fill in the gaps. Since the resume would reach the director's desk through McGarr, they would never check his credentials anyway.

"Great idea," declared Hunter.

In his resume, Hunter S. Thompson was an Ivy League honors graduate and a world traveler with foreign correspondent credentials. His references included a university president and a United States senator. He was published in newspapers like the *New York Times* and the *Washington Post.*

When the director of copy writing read the resume McGarr put on his desk, he called Hunter immediately and set up an appointment.

The first thing to strike the director was the fact that Hunter was so young. He could not imagine that someone so experienced could be in his early twenties, as this man across from the desk from him clearly was. He also could not imagine that someone with such extensive writing credentials was not making a stab at writing fiction.

"Mr. Thompson, I'm amazed to see you," he said. "Based upon your credentials, I really thought you were going to be much older. Tell me, have you ever tried your hand at fiction?"

Hunter could contain himself no longer. "What the hell do you think that is right in front of you?" he laughed, pointing to the resume. "That's the most convincing fiction I have ever written."

The interview was terminated immediately. In desperation, Hunter sought a job outside New York City.

The name of the paper was the *Middletown Daily Record* in Middletown, New York. He was told about the job by Bob Bone, a photographer friend who had just been hired there. Bone knew they were searching for a new reporter and recommended Hunter. With his clips and previous employment at *Time*, plus the fact that the hiring editor never bothered to call any previous employers, Hunter got the job.

The night before Hunter left for Middletown, McGarr, his wife, and Connie Dibble went over to Hunter's apartment for a little going-away party. After a few drinks, Hunter became giddy about leaving New York. He stood up and began dancing around the room, whooping and howling as if performing a kind of tribal dance. Bounding around like a medicine man, he brought out a canister of flour from the kitchen and scattered the white powder around until everything in his black-walled apartment appeared dusted with new fallen snow.

"It was either that he was trying to wipe away the sins of the past or cover them up," said McGarr, interpreting the incident. "He wanted to leave everything pristine. Everything looks better after it is covered with new fallen snow."

The next event of the evening, recalled by McGarr, is partially recounted by Hunter in "Saturday Night at the Riviera," published in *Songs of the Doomed.*

The two couples put on raincoats, left the freshly floured apartment, and headed down the catwalk past the flaming boiler. Suddenly Hunter stopped. Next to the boiler was a fifty-pound sack of cement with its top torn open. "Great idea," he mumbled. He hoisted the sack onto his shoulder and followed the other three up the stairs.

"What are you going to do with that?" asked a concerned McGarr.

"I need it," said Hunter. "I need it."

They headed up Tenth Street to Sheridan Square, past a bar called the Riviera. During the week it was occupied by students, writers, and artists, many of whom used it as a workspace and even had their mail sent there. But on weekends, like this Saturday night, the place was mobbed with people from uptown, all living it up in the Village.

"I need stamps," said Hunter. "I've got to have stamps!"

"Where are you going to get stamps?" asked McGarr.

"The Riviera," declared Hunter, heading across the street. "They always sell me stamps."

McGarr, worried, handed his watch and ring to his wife, told her to stay across the street, and ran after Hunter.

"Are you going in there with that bag of cement?" McGarr shouted.

"Of course," said Hunter. "I've got to have stamps."

The Riviera was mobbed. Tables were full, the floor was packed, and people stood five deep at the bar. Into this scene stormed

Hunter. Without slowing down, he bullied his way to the bar and slammed the bag of cement down. A mushroom cloud puffed upward from the open end of the bag.

"You can't do this," said the bartender.

"What do you mean?" shouted Hunter. "Beer! We want beer!"

At that moment two other bartenders came around the far end of the bar and headed for Hunter. McGarr grabbed his friend by the arm.

"Let's get the fuck outta here," he said.

Hunter grabbed the bag of cement and tossed it onto his shoulder. A stream of the powder poured out of the bag and down his back.

"My suit!" shouted a man behind him. "You've ruined my suit!"

The melee began. The crowd began pushing and shoving, trying to get away from the leaking powder. Some of the people pushed to get out the door and jammed up like cattle in a chute.

Hunter pushed for the door, too, and as he did, the bag split open. Half of the load spilled down his back, the other half down his front. A cloud of cement filled the air and puffed out the front door. With the smoke and the tangle of arms and legs, it looked to McGarr's wife as though people were being shot from cannons.

Then out came Hunter and McGarr. Hanging onto their coattails were a couple of guys who were trying desperately to hit them. With some well-placed elbows, Hunter and McGarr managed to break loose and run down Tenth Street.

"Let's keep going," said McGarr, falling in beside Hunter. They ran up Perry Street and then west on Hudson, up to Christopher Street and then east until they reached the corner of Sheridan Square. There they peeked around the corner.

Cement dust still lingered in the air as police took statements from the well-powdered crowd. McGarr saw his wife and Connie Dibble just a few doors down from where they stood. "Hey," he shouted. Eleanor saw him and grabbed Connie. Soon the four walked calmly into Stefan's bar, just a block away from the Riviera.

They had just settled down and ordered drinks when a black man approached their table. He looked at Hunter as though he recognized him and then he shook his hand.

"I know you! I know you!" he said, pumping Hunter's hand. "That was the greatest thing I ever saw in my life!" He handed Hunter an epaulet that had been torn from his raincoat by one of the angry patrons at the Riviera. And then he bought all four a round of drinks.

The next day he left for Middletown. He only lasted about two months at the *Middletown Daily Record*. He tells the story in *Songs of the Doomed*, in "Fleeing New York."

According to Hunter's piece, he had trouble conforming to the workplace standards. His first major brush with office authority occurred when his complaints about the lasagna served at a restaurant across the street landed him in a fistfight with the restaurant's owner. It ended up that the owner was one of the paper's advertisers, and Hunter was reprimanded for his behavior. About a week later, he broke the office candy machine after he couldn't get it to work; all of the candy disappeared from the machine and Hunter was blamed. He was fired—and the cost of the candy was deducted from his salary. For the fourth time in just over two years, Hunter was unemployed.

His last paycheck in hand and anticipating a few months of unemployment compensation, Hunter headed for the woods outside Middletown, near Goshen, where he rented a tiny cabin and began writing a novel.

The cabin was sparse and simple. A woman who visited him there several times called it "little more than a shack, but a pleasant shack nonetheless." Hunter used the living room as an office, covering the desk in the corner with manuscript pages that he ground out on the portable manual typewriter. The combination bedroom and kitchen made up the other room. The rest of the place was strewn with newspapers, empty beer bottles, and half-downed drinks. He smoked a pipe in those days, so the sweet smell of its tobacco permeated the cabin and drifted out into the fresh air of the Catskill Mountains.

While working on his novel, Hunter went through long private periods during which he did nothing but write, eat, and sleep. Sometimes late at night he took a run down a country road just to get his juices flowing again. Other than that, these were periods of great concentration.

His novel, titled *Prince Jellyfish*, never published but eventually excerpted in *Songs of the Doomed*, explored the life of a hell-raiser from Louisville who finds himself floating arrogantly through life in much the same way that a jellyfish is forced to float on the sea's currents.

The main character is Welburn Kemp, a hybrid name Hunter created from those of two boys who'd attended Male High School in Louisville. Welburn Brown died in a sports car crash, while Kenny Kemp was seriously brain damaged after another automobile accident. Although the two were about five years older than Hunter, he and his friends thought very highly of them, mainly because they spent time with the younger boys in the community. Their tragedies had a great effect upon Hunter. Perhaps this was his idea of a tribute, although the character most closely resembled Hunter himself.

Welburn Kemp is a struggling young journalist who runs from his past and finds himself in New York City, where he searches for fun and profit, in vain. Many of the novel's stories read like flashbacks from Hunter's past: Kemp being offered a job as a copyboy for minimal pay; Kemp inviting a girl to attend a gathering of Columbia students; Kemp driving through Cherokee Park reminiscing about his childhood.

Throughout *Prince Jellyfish*, Hunter draws upon people from his childhood. David Porter Bibb, a pal from Athenaeum, makes an appearance as a Columbia law student. In another section, Kemp takes a sentimental vacation to Louisville, where he is invited to the country club by "Billy Porter," another hybrid, from Billy Noonan and David Porter Bibb.

Paul Semonin, who had a cabin in New Jersey and visited Hunter frequently in Middletown, thought that Hunter was writing about his life in order to come to terms with it. "A lot of his writing was being drawn from things that I could see were yesterday's news. He needed to put the events of his life into some kind of context."

Semonin and Hunter were becoming ever-closer friends. Although he came from a wealthy Louisville family, Semonin was rejecting that lifestyle for that of a bohemian. When he wasn't attending the Art Institute in Manhattan, he was reading Kerouac and other beat writers. He and Hunter saw the rebel in one another.

During one of Semonin's visits to Hunter's cabin, the two tossed back several glasses of whiskey, then snuck across a moonlit field and into a neighbor's horse barn. They bridled two horses, quietly walked them out to the field, then jumped on and rode them bareback "like gypsies in the night," remembers Semonin.

They rode for hours through the countryside, some of the finest horse country in the United States, with plenty of trails to explore and wide alleys beneath the canopy of massive trees. Spent at last, they tied the horses to a fence post not far from the barn so the owner would be sure to find them.

"Doing things like taking those horses was part of a pattern that Hunter had developed," said Semonin. "It was the kind of act that was not criminal but very close to it. It was part of his edge philosophy in its early stages."

That edge philosophy extended to women, too. "Hunter tried to take it to the limit in everything he did," said a friend from this period. "He drank himself to the edge. He wrote himself to the edge of his abilities. He tried to drive his car faster than it should go, and when he had women around he usually tried to make them go faster than they wanted to go. That was how he got the most out of life."

At one point, breaking an old Southern taboo, Hunter began dating a black woman.

In Manhattan, a reluctant Hunter had been propelled uptown by McGarr and another friend, John Clancy, to Columbia's law school to hear Thurgood Marshall, then head of the NAACP Education and Defense Fund. Marshall delivered a stirring speech about the aims and goals of the civil rights movement. By the time he was finished, the eight hundred law students were completely silent. Then he leaned his 6'4" frame over the lectern and said, "Now give me some questions, some tough questions!"

Hunter was stirred by the sight and eloquence of this charismatic black man. He told McGarr later that he had never seen the likes of such a "powerful negro." It was no wonder that this was a new experience for Hunter. The South he grew up in was a segregated one, where blacks kept to themselves and didn't speak up or mingle. They were a shadow population who didn't go to school, eat, swim, bowl, watch movies, or do anything else on the white man's turf. Hunter's high school was segregated until 1956, a year after he left.

"Hunter was just another redneck bastard," said McGarr. "But that Thurgood Marshall speech transformed him. After that he got interested in blacks and decided to experiment with a black girlfriend."

The sight of Hunter and the black girl driving around Middletown in his Jaguar was a shocking one. Northern cities weren't much more liberal than Southern ones in those days. "Let's just say that there was a certain blue collar element in Middletown that didn't appreciate Hunter's version of racial diversity," said McGarr.

Hunter was involved in breaking other sexual taboos as well. He began seeing the wife of a prominent resident, who would sneak out to his cabin for long visits. "It was a relationship that made Hunter nervous," said Smith, a frequent visitor at the cabin.

By April 1959, Hunter finished a first draft of *Prince Jellyfish*. With his possessions crammed into the Jaguar, he headed for Manhattan.

Paul Semonin had moved back to the city. Like Hunter, he was trying to soothe a restless spirit. He was considering a sailboat trip to Europe, or a lengthy visit to Africa.

Hunter and Semonin drank with McGarr and his wife Eleanor in a bar on Christopher Street. A school friend of Eleanor's, Sandy Dawn, who had moved to New York after graduating from Goucher College, began to hang out with them. At first Sandy was attracted to Semonin and the two dated frequently, though the relationship never became more than platonic. One day she spent an afternoon talking to Hunter. She was attracted to his vigorous personality and wild sense of humor. She began to date Hunter instead of Semonin.

Judy Booth, Hunter's brother Davidson's ex-girlfriend, had also tried to establish a relationship with Hunter. Although Hunter had dated Judy off and on, he didn't want to get serious. According to a friend, he defined himself as a short-term boyfriend. "But I don't think it was short-term in their view. It was a romantic fury that left many women hurting."

For example, a woman who lived with Hunter in his Perry Street apartment was trying to decide whether or not to maintain a relationship with her boyfriend across town. When the boyfriend found out where she was living, he demanded she choose him or Hunter. The woman wanted Hunter, who immediately saw this as an opportunity to get rid of her. When she asked him to make a commitment, he told her to go to the other guy.

Other friends said that women often found his machismo overbearing. One woman called him a "strutting matador, constantly flaunting his machismo."

There was something different about Sandy. She appeared to understand Hunter. She didn't hassle him about his escapades. As a friend put it, "It was clear that she was a woman who knew what she was getting into and elected to get on this particular surge anyway."

Meanwhile Hunter was looking at ads in *Editor and Publisher*, the bible of the out-of-work journalist. He was through with small town weeklies. He found a notice from a Puerto Rican publication called *Sportivo*:

WANT TO WORK FOR THE SPORTS ILLUSTRATED OF THE CARIBBEAN?

Now is your chance. Ambitious publisher is looking for journalists who know and love sports and who wouldn't mind living in the tropical paradise of Puerto Rico.

He sent a letter and resume, and got the job.

Semonin, who was restless to travel anywhere, followed Hunter to Puerto Rico. Together they rented a shoe box of a beach house in Loiza Aldea. The rent was only $50 a month, which had something to do with the town's location. Surrounded by swamps and reachable only by dirt roads, it was almost an hour from San Juan, which was only seventeen miles away. Furthermore, of the three hundred people who lived in this village, Hunter and Semonin were the only whites.

Hunter wrote Sandy letters and called to say how much he missed her. Finally he asked her to join him, and she moved into the beach house.

According to Semonin, her relationship with Hunter was in its "honeymoon stage." "They were completely enamored of one another. Sandy was like an angel in certain ways. She was very tolerant of Hunter's routine. She had this innocent attachment and a willingness not to take him on face value or to judge him by his tantrums or behavior."

The living arrangements were close, perhaps too cozy. The strong "physical charge" between Hunter and Sandy frequently made Semonin uncomfortable. The lovers had their time alone when Semonin went to work five nights a week as a proofreader for the *San Juan Star*.

Hunter worked at *Sportivo* only as much as he had to. The magazine wasn't the *Sports Illustrated* of the Caribbean. Puerto Rico was in the midst of a bowling boom, and *Sportivo* was founded to take advantage of that boom. Hunter's assignment was the alley scene. He had to hang out at the alleys and jot down quotes, scores, and names. The names were especially important since, according to the editor, the only thing the readers were interested in was getting their names in the magazine. "Names sell magazines," he told Hunter. By Hunter's estimate, about half of his job was seeing that every bowler in San Juan got his name in print.

Hunter found extra income and pride of authorship in free-lance assignments. He took a fancy to calling himself "the preeminent journalist" in the Caribbean. He wrote tourist brochures for the Puerto Rican News Service and became a stringer for the *New York Herald Tribune*, a position that gave him some visibility and prestige on the island. He also wrote articles on such subjects as cock fighting for the *San Juan Star*, then edited by William Kennedy, later the Pulitzer Prize-winning author of *Ironweed*.

Kennedy had earlier refused to hire Hunter, who'd applied for a job there when he was still in New York. Hunter had been infuriated by the rejection and sent off a scathing letter to Kennedy, telling him he'd been nothing less than a goddamn fool not to hire him and that someday, somewhere, Hunter would meet this scoundrel and bash his head in.

Face to face, Hunter and Kennedy became fast friends, although when Hunter went to Kennedy's house for dinner, Mrs. Kennedy burst into tears, fearing that Hunter would carry out some of the threats he'd made in his letter.

In addition to journalism, Hunter was working on another novel, *The Rum Diary*. Like *Prince Jellyfish*, it was later excerpted in *Songs of the Doomed*, but never published in its entirety.

While he was in Puerto Rico, Hunter also wrote some features for the *Louisville Courier-Journal*, one of which was titled "A Louisvillian in Voodoo Country," followed with the heading "Paul Semonin, working to perfect his painting in Puerto Rico, admits he was uneasy at first."

The piece infuriated Semonin. He felt that his privacy had been invaded by the story, especially since it was being run in the hometown paper where his friends and family would read it. But on top of losing his privacy, Semonin had a greater problem: He claimed the article included blatant falsehoods. As far as he was concerned, Hunter had taken a grain of what he had said and then fabricated quotes around it. (Today Semonin takes a more philosophical view of this story, considering it one of Hunter's first full-blown Gonzo pieces.)

Semonin felt the story was a violation of their friendship. He confronted Hunter, saying that the piece was the sort of lie he shouldn't write about a friend. Hunter simply shrugged.

"It wasn't something that broke our relationship," said Semonin, "but it was something that started to rupture it in a way."

Despite the hard feelings, Semonin stayed on with Hunter and watched Hunter's actions and writing become more and more theatrical. If Hunter didn't like quotes the way they were, he made up new ones. If he didn't like events or their surroundings, he was likely to create others. If he wanted to get a point across he was happy to turn it into an action that attracted attention, often unwanted.

Even more disturbing to Semonin, who had no interest in breaking the law, was Hunter's need to beat the system—and his willingness to go to any length to do so. Semonin was with Hunter at a restaurant one night when Hunter decided to leave without paying the bill. As a result, the two ended up spending several hours in a filthy jail cell before they were rescued by William Kennedy and one of his columnists. Hunter included a fictionalized account of the story in *The Rum Diary;* it appears in *Songs of the Doomed.*

In *The Rum Diary*, which could be called *Welburn Kemp Redux,* a clear-thinking journalist (Kemp) has decamped to Puerto Rico, where his closest friend, an uptight beach boy named Yeamon, lives with Chenault, a beautiful blond tart. Chenault drives Yeamon to distraction by bathing in the nude on the beach all day, the better to stir the loins of the natives, who hide in the bushes and watch. "One of these days they'll get you, by God," says Yeamon, "and if you keep on teasing the poor bastards, I'll damn well let them have you!"

In a particularly searing scene, Chenault performs a strip tease among a rowdy group of dancing black men and is whisked away naked, presumably to be gang banged. Semonin regards this scene as the purest fiction to be found in *The Rum Diary*. Hunter knew a girl named Chenault in high school; as for the character's heavy drinking and loose behavior, "there were plenty of women in Hunter's life who, when combined, would equal a tease like Chenault," said Semonin.

The gang bang, said Semonin, had its roots in Hunter's Southern upbringing, where there was a sense that racial harmony was impossible and a sort of racial Armageddon was inevitable.

"This never happened in Puerto Rico," said Semonin. "But Hunter has this fantasy embedded in his subconcious. It is a racial nightmare that exists from all the racial stereotyping that went on in his childhood."

Whatever the relationship between *The Rum Diary* and reality, Semonin got tired of being a third wheel at the beach house. He and a friend, Harvey Sloan, made a plan to go island hopping, from Saint Thomas to Saint Martin to Saint Kitts to Antigua, in a fifteen foot boat. He didn't tell Hunter and Sandy until he'd left his job at the *Star*. Hunter said he, too, was tired of Puerto Rico and might join Semonin.

Hunter and Sandy caught a plane to Charlotte Amalie on Saint Thomas, where they met up with Semonin and Harvey Sloan. The cautious and inexperienced sailors had had their fill of rough seas and were ready to jettison their itinerary and sell their boat. Semonin wanted to catch a freighter to Europe with Hunter. Then Hunter met Donald Street, a charter boat captain, in a bar. Street was a published author whose charter business made up for his meager royalties. Hunter introduced Street to Sandy and Semonin. Before long the three were asked to crew on Street's fifty-five foot sailboat, *Isle Aire*, on a long sail to Bermuda.

They loved the idea. For Hunter and Sandy, it was a chance to resume the honeymoon. For Semonin, the trip would be a learning experience. If he learned well, maybe he could crew on a boat in an upcoming trans-Atlantic race, and finally get to Europe. The three signed on.

Sandy and Semonin pitched in and did what the skipper said. Hunter would have none of it. When Street asked him to do something, Hunter dragged his feet or asked why it had to be done at all. It soon became clear that *Isle Aire* wasn't big enough for Street and Hunter. As tension mounted, Hunter sat at the bow while Street was at the stern; if Street moved forward for any reason, Hunter moved aft. They even ate at different times.

Always uncomfortable, the situation grew unbearable when, for two days, they lay dead in the water, becalmed in the Sargasso Sea. Hunter refused even to talk to Street, and behaved as if the captain didn't exist.

When they reached Bermuda, Sandy flew back to New York, while Hunter and Semonin rehatched their plan to jump a freighter bound for Europe. The problem was that few ships bound for Europe stopped in Bermuda and, of the ones that did, none would hire Hunter or Semonin as able-bodied seamen. Semonin joked that the ships' captains must have checked their credentials with Donald Street.

After three weeks of waiting, their money ran out. In desperation, Hunter wrote to Gene McGarr, who was living in Malaga, Spain with his wife. He told McGarr that he and Semonin were so destitute that they were living in a cave on the outskirts of town, stealing cabbages out of gardens in order to eat, and likely to get thrown in jail. He asked McGarr to send him $150 so he could fly back to New York.

McGarr, although strapped for cash himself, felt it was his duty to bail out his old friend. He sent Hunter the money with the proviso that Hunter had to pay him back in a year or he couldn't get back from Spain. Several months later, Hunter wrote McGarr that he couldn't afford to pay him back. In a panic McGarr wired Sandy in New York. She had no money to send him, but contacted McGarr's mother, who, to his humiliation, sent him the money to fly home.

Back in New York City, Hunter and Semonin fine-tuned their travel plans. They stayed at Judy Booth's apartment while Semonin contacted an agency that hired students to transport cars across the country in exchange for gas money. The agency arranged for them to drive a new Ford Fairlane. For Hunter and Semonin, it was a chapter right out of Kerouac's *On the Road*. They headed west.

Their first rule of the road was to pick up every hitchhiker. In western Kansas, Semonin stopped for a man carrying a five-gallon gas can. When the hitchhiker got into the backseat, he flipped the latches on the can to reveal that it was stuffed with clothes. "No one will pick you up if they think you're a hitchhiker," he explained. "You have to be a motorist in distress."

Hunter smelled a story and interviewed the man about the difficulty of getting rides. When they neared a signpost that proved they were in the middle of nowhere, Hunter made Semonin stop and take a picture of the interviewee with his thumb out, looking forlorn.

After delivering the car to its owner in Seattle, they hitchhiked to San Francisco. There they stayed with some girls they'd known in New York who had an apartment on Telegraph Hill, handy to North Beach and the beat scene immortalized by Kerouac. They hung out at the Grant Street bars and at Lawrence Ferlinghetti's City Lights Bookstore, where they listened to beat poets read.

Within a few days Hunter was ready to leave San Francisco. He had read some Henry Miller and wanted to see the rocky Big Sur coastline that had captivated the controversial author. He asked

Semonin if he was ready to hit the road again, but this time his partner wouldn't budge. Hunter, he said, had worn him out.

There was no freer place to be in 1960 than Big Sur, or so the locals claimed. There were few policemen, guns were worn openly, marijuana was making a serious comeback, and total nudity was possible at almost any time of day or night. While many citizens of Big Sur were running from their lives, some were running for their lives, staying just a step or two ahead of the law. People came here to get away from broken marriages, ruined careers, and tormented psyches. Some residents of Big Sur even lived in trees.

The only way to reach Big Sur from the north was on Highway 1, a narrow two-lane that was made to look even smaller by the towering Santa Lucia mountains plunging into the Pacific. The dizzying perspective at times seems to defy the laws of nature.

Hunter hitchhiked from San Francisco to Big Sur, where he secured a place at the Murphy Ranch, a sprawling house at the edge of the cliffs overlooking the ocean. Within a few years, Michael Murphy was to turn this piece of paradise into a retreat called Esalen where, for a hefty price, guests could eat vegetarian meals, dig potatoes in the nude, and soak their cares away in natural hot springs.

Functioning as a sort of caretaker for $25 a month rent, Hunter set up his typewriter in the Murphy house. He was serious about working on his novels. *Prince Jellyfish* had failed to find an interested publisher, though he was far from shelving the manuscript. He wrote a letter, later published in *Songs of the Doomed*, to Angus Cameron, an editor at Knopf, who'd written him a long and thoughtful rejection. He asked Cameron to locate the address of an agent named Elisabeth McKee and send her the manuscript.

Once Hunter was settled in, Sandy flew out to join him. Their relationship was puzzling to some of the local residents. "He was chauvinistic to the point of embarrassment," said a member of the community. "The only thing that kept many of us from commenting to them in person was the fact that they seemed to work it out. We didn't want to interfere in someone else's business."

Here was an angry young man paired with a flower child; she waxed on about peace, love, and understanding, while her lover smacked her around. "She was really sweet and motherly," said a resident. "She took care of him and didn't give him any shit. I'm afraid that's what it might have come down to."

Hunter did most of his writing at night. This meant he slept during the day, which is when Sandy's duties began. She kept visitors away until he got up, then fixed his breakfast of bacon, eggs and toast while he sat outside and read the *New York Times*. He still dreamed of becoming a foreign correspondent; he hoped that, once he'd completed The Great American Novel, he'd have his entree.

Sometimes he sat there for a couple of hours, drinking coffee, smoking, and reading his output from the night before. Frequently Sandy read his work, not so much for criticism as for moral support. As one friend from that period said, "He leaned on her very hard for criticism of his work. But as far as I know, she never provided it. She was there to prop him up. And besides, it was too dangerous for her to say that there was something she didn't like in his work."

Hunter was increasingly angry at the publishing world. He was boiling mad at *Playboy* magazine for rejecting some of his stories, and for months wrote letters dripping with vitriol to that publication.

Sandy bore the brunt of this anger. Joe Hudson, a new local friend, remembers being there at breakfast when Sandy failed to retrieve something, possibly his newspaper, quickly enough. Suddenly, Hunter reached out and slapped her in the face. Tears came to her eyes as she retreated into the house.

"I was shocked by it," said Hudson. "Hunter was wound so

tight that little things would set him off. You have to remember, this was 1960. He wasn't doing drugs, not even much pot. And he wasn't drunk. He had a lot going on inside that made him very uptight. He wasn't anybody yet. He was just a writer who was trying very, very hard to produce good work and was having a hard time getting published." Verbal attacks were more frequent than physical ones.

Hudson was a Big Sur native who had just returned from art school to live on his family's ranch. Although Hudson worked on his sculpture during the day and Hunter wrote at night, their free time overlapped. At least twice a week they shared a few drinks at dusk.

Hudson was a blood-sport veteran and regaled Hunter with tales of deer and pig hunting in the mountains. Before long Hunter was caught up in the mystique of tracking game over the steep terrain and felling it with one deadly shot.

Although he'd had a .22 caliber rifle while growing up in Kentucky, Hunter had never gone hunting. His weapons training had amounted to shooting bottles and cans off his windowsill. One day Hudson crossed the canyon to Hunter's house to find his friend loading a brand new .22 Ruger pistol.

"Check this out," Hunter said, walking to the edge of the cliff. In the distance, some three to five hundred yards away, floated large chunks of bull kelp. Hunter took aim and squeezed off a shot. The bullet splashed down at least one hundred yards short. "Shit!" muttered Hunter, and they both laughed. He took careful aim again, this time raising the barrel a couple of inches. The shot fell short and a little bit to the side. "Fuck it," he grunted, and put the gun down.

Over the next few days, the gunplay continued. Hunter used the marine flora for target practice, popping off a box or more of ammunition each day. After several days he was able to put his bullets into several pieces of kelp. "He was elated," said Hudson. "It was as though he had finally made the grade."

One day Hudson arrived at Hunter's place with a tale he hardly believed himself. His mother, who lived at Partington Ridge, about six miles from the Murphy Ranch, had a house that overlooked Partington Canyon, a massive notch in the earth that was heavily wooded with oak and choked with dense underbrush. At 5:30 on a recent afternoon, she'd noticed a large animal standing in a field below her in the canyon. Through binoculars, she saw that it was a wild boar of massive proportions, perhaps five hundred pounds. For the next few days, she kept watch. The boar appeared daily at 5:30 sharp.

Hudson took Hunter to his mother's place. At 5:30, the hog lumbered into view. Hunter wanted to go get him immediately, but Hudson proposed they go down early the following afternoon and ambush him.

On the day of the hunt, Hunter and Hudson went to Mrs. Hudson's house and had a couple of drinks before setting out. A difficult trail led to the bottom of Partington Canyon. They had to use their rifles like canes, and in several places the trail was so steep they were forced to sit down and slide. The trail then rose at such a pitch that the rifles had to serve as walking sticks. It took them at least two hours to reach the field, an hour and a half longer than they had expected.

Exhausted, Hudson set down his gun and wiped his forehead. But before he could take a breather, the enormous boar was in front of him, charging straight at him. There was a blast. Hunter's bullet passed right under Hudson's armpit, singeing his shirt and making his ears ring. The boar grunted, turned, and disappeared into the bush. Hudson looked around and saw the smoking barrel of Hunter's gun. It was clear from the way Hunter was holding his rifle that he had fired from the hip. It was also obvious from the terrified look on Hunter's face that he wasn't sure until then that he had missed Hudson.

They hadn't stopped trembling when they heard little grunts. Up the trail came a dozen tiny piglets, confused and looking for their mother. "That was no boar!" shouted Hudson. "That was a great big sow with a bunch of babies!"

The two threw down their guns and began chasing the piglets all over the field, hoping to catch one and bring it back to the ranch so they could put it in a pen. The piglets were fast, however, and the men were soon exhausted. They picked up their rifles and fired them, "culling the herd" by one.

The new plan was to leave the dead piglet in the field and climb a tree to wait for the mother to return. Then, as she mourned the death of her offspring, the hunters could pump her full of lead. But before they could put their plan to work, they heard the sound of a truck coming toward them. "We're on private land," whispered Hudson. "That must be the caretaker! Let's get the hell out of here!"

The two climbed down from the tree and ran to the trail. Hunter stopped and scooped the dead piglet into his knapsack. That night the bounty was skinned and barbecued.

A few months later, Hunter and Hudson had another chance at wild boar when they were hunting with Paul Semonin, who was visiting from Aspen. The three were drinking beer in a truck while Hudson, looking for signs of deer, scanned the mountainside with a telescope. Suddenly he pulled back and looked again. Three boars were walking in a straight line down a path about two miles away.

Hudson gunned the truck and they jolted along a narrow fire road, through one canyon after another, until they spied a boar rushing into the bushes.

"You go after it from here!" shouted Hudson, slamming on the brakes and ordering Semonin to jump out. Hudson, with Hunter, sped off, hoping to cut the animal off from the front.

Semonin charged through the brush after the boar. Breathing heavily, he climbed a short hill and found himself at the edge of a field. There, in the middle of the field, stood the boar, looking straight at him.

Semonin brought his carbine to his shoulder and fired. The boar went down with a thud. Lowering his rifle, Semonin advanced. Suddenly the boar stood, dazed but ready to charge. Semonin looked around wildly for a tree to climb. There was a shot and the boar dropped. Semonin could see blood oozing from its bristly hide, just behind the ear. On the hill was Hunter, his face suffused with pride.

Back at Hudson's place, Hunter and Semonin skinned the boar. Hunter had great hopes of having a wild boar pelt to hang on his wall, and was disappointed to discover how gnarly the skin was and how difficult to remove. He cut off the head and the testicles.

He had a plan. Hanging out in the hot springs at the Murphy Ranch and irritating Hunter were members of a religious sect called the First Church of God of Prophecy (the locals called them "Holy Rollers"). Hunter took the boar's head and marched, under cover of darkness, to the springs, where he flipped the boar's head into the steamy froth. That night screams from the springs pierced the calm of Big Sur. The next morning the sect's leader found a set of boar testicles wrapped around her rearview mirror. "I don't know if they saw this stuff as a message from the devil or what," said Hudson, "but they were gone within a few days."

Another group Hunter didn't like in the hot springs were the homosexuals. On weekends, dozens of expensive cars packed the parking area and disgorged forty to sixty gays, who took over the baths from Friday until Monday. It shocked Hunter to see men holding hands or kissing naked in the moonlight.

One night Hunter strapped a small billy club to his wrist and stormed down to the baths with Hudson. A group of men sitting in one corner of the springs, surprised and unnerved by Hunter's approach, brought their hands out of the water and eyed Hunter nervously as he perched on the edge of the tub.

"You know I didn't mind it when there were just a few of you guys," Hunter said, slapping the water with the short stick, "but now there's too many." He took the club and tapped the bony part of one young man's shoulder, hard enough to make the man squeal with pain. "Frankly, I think you guys should just get the fuck out of here," he growled. "No one wants you around here. It's time for you to realize that and beat it."

Another man was tapped soundly on the shoulder until he moved across the tub. Hunter immediately found another victim. "Personally, I don't think this is a safe place for you guys to be hanging out anymore. Some of the locals are getting pissed off and when they do, you might end up on the other side of that fence, down on those cliffs."

There was an immediate exodus to the other side of the springs, out of range of the billy club, which only made Hunter speak louder as he found other shoulders to rap.

"I guess what I'm saying is that it's time for you guys to get the fuck out of here. Something nasty could happen if you don't." Hunter's voice was low and his temper controlled throughout, but Hudson was unnerved by the level of anger he had witnessed. "He didn't like gays," said Hudson, "but what he didn't like even more was someone encroaching on his space."

A few nights later the scene was repeated. Hunter stalked the baths with the billy club, delivering a painful lecture about territorial rights and the fact that he wanted them out of his territory right now.

The number of gays in the springs diminished rapidly, but

Hunter continued to carry his club, just in case. One time, as he approached, four men burst out of the bushes. They could have been linemen for the Oakland Raiders. Hunter flailed with his club. The people in the baths erupted with excitement. "Kill him! Pull his arms off! Throw him over the cliffs!" Two of the hulks tried to drag Hunter toward the cliffs, but he managed to thwack his way loose and escape.

Vengeance was swift. The next evening Hunter, Hudson, and another friend gathered on a hill overlooking the hot springs. Hunter brought his aged German shepherd, and Hudson and his friend each had Doberman pinschers. Below them some forty men were in the baths. Some sat naked on the edge, dangling their feet in the hot water.

"Party's over," growled Hunter. He pulled a .44 Magnum from his waistband and fired a shot into the air. The bathers fell silent.

"Let's go," ordered Hunter. The three men charged down the hill, the dogs tugging at their leashes and barking, then lunging at the naked men frantically climbing out of the baths. "Get to the cars!" someone shouted. Everyone, naked or not, bolted for the parking lot.

Few homosexuals came around after that. In their community the event is remembered as "the night of the Dobermans."

Hunter and Hudson went back to hunting boar, deer, and birds. For Hunter, hunting had become survival. He wrote infrequent articles for the *Louisville Courier-Journal* or anyone else who would take his work. Although their rent was only $25 a month, he and Sandy had little left over for food and clothing. In a letter to Semonin he complained about selling $40 stories while the big score eluded him; his total income for 1960, he said, was $970.

Sandy found a job in Monterey, and drove the treacherous road three or four times a week to make beds in a hotel. Gene McGarr remembers a visit he made in 1961, when he found Hunter "crushingly poor," although Hunter would never have admitted it to him. "We don't have a cent," Sandy confided to her old friend Eleanor McGarr. "We hardly have enough money to buy bread with." By this time, Sandy had lost her job.

Hunter, on the other hand, painted a fairly rosy picture of their finances. He'd had a couple of "near misses" in selling his fiction to magazines, and was certain that a big sale was right around the corner. *Playboy*, which had strung him on for months before deciding to nix his article idea about Big Sur, said they liked his clips and wanted more ideas. In the meantime, Hunter declared, "I like to live off the fat of the land."

When asked what he meant, Hunter picked up a crowbar and led McGarr down the cliffs to the jagged rocks by the sea. He shoved the crowbar under an abalone and pulled the clinging mollusk from the face of a rock. He went on to gather a dozen or so into a burlap bag, which he and McGarr lugged back up the cliff. At his house he took a sharp knife and removed the tough meat from the shells, which he threw on a pile with dozens of others. He brought the meat into the house and beat it with a hammer until it was tenderized.

Over the next several days, the McGarrs were treated to a veritable smorgasbord of abalone. Hunter and Sandy barbecued it, sauteed it, marinated in fruit juice, made sandwiches with it, roasted it, and skewered it for "abalone on a stick." "My favorite way of eating it was the curry," said McGarr. "We got that curry in a can and put it right on the abalone as we cooked it. Curry will help anything."

One day while the McGarrs were visiting, Hunter pulled open his *New York Times* and gasped. There was a dashing photograph of Hemingway in full beard with headlines proclaiming that he had committed suicide at the age of sixty-one.

Hunter was devastated. He idolized Hemingway. The king of the short story and the master of the good life had killed himself. "I think he killed himself because he couldn't write anymore," Hunter said. "He couldn't write, he was too sick to hunt. He just didn't have it anymore, so he decided to end it."

Hunter had wanted to be just like Hemingway. His appearance seemed a caricature of Papa himself. He wore a hunting cap with fold-up ear flaps, flannel lumberjack shirts, khaki shorts that revealed knobby knees, and hunting boots with wool socks. He accessorized the outfit with his billy club and/or a hefty buck knife worn on his belt.

According to McGarr, Hemingway's death forced Hunter to look closely at his time in Big Sur. Things hadn't worked out as he had planned. His fiction projects were going nowhere. In a letter to Semonin, he declared that *The Rum Diary*, "the great Puerto Rican novel," was officially dead. Although editors and agents had declared it well written, nobody would buy it. Repeatedly the only writing jobs he could score were feature pieces for newspapers that paid next to nothing. Out of desperation he had tried to get a job on a state road crew that was repaving parts of the coast highway, but he was passed over.

Things were changing around Big Sur too. Joe Hudson and his girlfriend had built a boat and left for a six-month cruise. Hunting wasn't nearly as much fun without Hudson. And Big Sur had become too Wild West, with too many people carrying guns and drunks firing off shots in the center of town. Michael Murphy called this element the "Big Sur Heavies." There were artists, dope growers, and others who had become social misfits. They were too rowdy, even for the likes of Hunter.

But it wasn't the rowdies who drove Hunter Thompson out of Big Sur. It was Bunny Murphy, the woman who had hired Hunter to take care of her ranch. Mrs. Murphy became furious when she read the article he wrote about Big Sur for a men's magazine called

Rogue. Entitled "Big Sur: The Tropic of Henry Miller," the impressionistic article insulted Mrs. Murphy with its reference to Big Sur as a place where "deviates" could live because, "nobody cares what they do as long as they keep to themselves." Of the women who lived in the hot springs, the article continued, only two were "legitimate wives." The rest, wrote Hunter, were "mistresses, 'companions,' or hopeless losers." Many of the people who live here, wrote Hunter, "defy description—sexually, socially, or any other way."

Mrs. Murphy was so furious when she read the article that she made a rare trip to the ranch from her home in Salinas. When she found Hunter, she told him that he was fired and would have to leave the property immediately. If you don't, she said, "I will call the sheriff and have him throw you off."

Hunter's Big Sur period was over.

By the end of 1961, Sandy returned to New York and Hunter went back to Louisville. Home was the cheapest place for him to live, and his mother was there to provide moral support.

Virginia Thompson was not the type to badger her son about his lack of personal progress. According to friends of the family, she was extraordinarily tolerant. One of her coworkers at the Louisville Free Public Library said, "She knew about young people and their needs in ways that most parents in those days had no idea of."

Hunter lived on what little money he had brought with him. He spent his time either at the typewriter composing query letters on story ideas for magazines and newspapers, or reading from the vast paperback library that had been in his room since high school. He found a sympathetic companion in Don Cooke.

Cooke's father, a prominent and wealthy Louisville car dealer, had been sent to prison. Fresh out of the marine corps, Cooke had been forced to return to Louisville to support his family. Against his wishes, he worked in a Ford Motor Company assembly plant. Although he and Hunter had known one another only slightly in high school, they now shared the frustration and anger of coming back to a place where they had not intended to return.

When the whistle blew at the auto plant, Cooke headed for Hunter's house where, more often than not, he found Hunter slaving over a batch of homemade beer. Having gone to great lengths to assemble the proper equipment, Hunter delivered mini-lectures to Cooke about the importance of proper fermentation time and storage temperature.

Cooke drank very little of Hunter's home brew, but what little he sampled made an impression. "It was the highest octane beer I have ever had," said Cooke, "but we didn't drink much of it because there was better tasting stuff in the saloons."

The two malcontents threw themselves into Louisville's night-life, their carousing accompanied by endless conversations on a wide range of topics, from literature to personal angst. As Cooke remembers it, "I can be fairly certain that one constant drumbeat behind everything we talked about was our determination to get away from this cesspool of social encrustation known as Louisville. Hunter easily outdistanced me in the level of his fury. He was coming out of a well of bitterness that I was a newcomer to. For him, Louisville was a place where the old guard clotted up with each other and left other people out. Hunter was one of those people who got left out."

Cooke says that Hunter would talk about the entree that journalism provided. "Without any question, fiction was the consummate form of writing, the only valid form. In the meantime, he just had to do what he had to do in humping articles out. It was understood this was the way he would eventually come up through the ranks to become a novelist."

Hunter managed to land a couple of minor assignments at the *Louisville Courier-Journal,* but they were small potatoes. His big score came from the travel section of the *Chicago Tribune,* which asked him to cover the Old Kentucky Barn Dance in Renfro Valley.

Renfro Valley was a summer hot spot for bluegrass music. As many as fifteen thousand people had at one time descended upon the tiny hollow for weekend music festivals that featured musicians from little towns like Shoulderblade, Preachersville, and Crab Orchard. During the winter, however, there was plenty of seating inside an old country barn where the locals tuned up their instruments and gave it their best effort for the radio show that was broadcast every Saturday night.

On an afternoon in February, Hunter and Cooke, swigging whiskey from an open bottle, headed for the hills of Southeastern Kentucky. They made a stop at the penitentiary, where Cooke spent some time with his father.

By the time Hunter and Cooke reached Renfro Valley they had drunk up all their whiskey. This being a dry county, they were forced to tough it out, listening to bluegrass music in the barn for nearly three hours.

By the end of the evening, Hunter had taken several rolls of film with the box camera that hung around his neck. When the last act was over, he charged to the stage and asked the director of the festival for an interview. As Cooke watched, Hunter duly filled his notebook with information and quotes.

It was nearly midnight when Hunter and Cooke headed for the car. Both had worked up a huge thirst. Looking for booze, they drove to Lexington but found nothing. Finally they arrived parched and exhausted in a tiny town called Nicholasville. When Hunter saw a motel, he slowed and let the car drift into the parking lot. The office was dark and there were no lights anywhere. They banged on the office door, to no avail. Hunter walked down the row of motel rooms, banging on each door. No one answered. "The place is ours," he announced to Cooke as he pulled one of the windows open and unlocked the door from the inside. Their departure late the next morning was as clean as their arrival; they never saw anyone in Nicholasville.

Starved by now, they pulled over in Shakertown, a worn-out town populated by Shakers, a religious sect with a firm belief in celibacy and community property. Although it was Sunday and the streets of Shakertown were empty, Hunter went to a house where a wooden sign advertised "Family Style Dinners" and began rapping on the window until a nervous woman cracked open the back door. With his best manners, Hunter convinced her to fix them a hearty breakfast of ham, eggs, coffee, and thick slices of homemade toast. Then they drove as fast as they could back to Louisville, where they spent the rest of the day watching football games and drinking in a favorite saloon.

"I have had many days and nights out with Hunter," said Cooke, "but this one stands out in my mind because he was flying so high after the Renfro trip. His story ["Traveller Hears Mountain Music Where It's Sung," republished in *The Great Shark Hunt*] was eventually published in the *Chicago Tribune* [Feb. 18, 1962] and it was his first real shot at national media. He was very excited. In a lot of ways that story made him feel like he had finally broken into the big time."

Having tasted success, Hunter made a new career move. He had heard that Dow Jones Publishing was starting a new paper in New York. He calculated that, of all the places he wanted to go to get out of Louisville, South America was the least covered and most wide open for an enterprising freelancer. He sent off a bunch of clips and a letter.

3

THE *NATIONAL OBSERVER* (1962-1964)

The *National Observer* was the brainchild of Barney Kilgore, president of Dow Jones Publishing and an eccentric media genius who wanted a publication that promoted understanding, not reportage. "The flow of news is vast," he said. "What we need in our national media is understanding."

"What Barney had in mind was a publication like the *Economist*," explained Roscoe Born, an editor at the *Observer* for its entire sixteen years. "It was his idea to hire a few of the best minds in American journalism and they would sit there and read newspapers and read wire copy and process this all through their minds." Most of the editors, like Born, were drawn from the *Wall Street Journal*, Dow Jones' flagship publication.

The notion of newspapers as an interpretive medium was a unique one in the 1960s. It challenged the market niche of *Time, Newsweek, U.S. News and World Report*, and the editorial pages of many newspapers around the country. The idea that a newspaper, even one owned by a company as large as Dow Jones, could come in and take market share was daringly absurd.

The *Observer* began publishing practice editions in November 1961, and hit the streets in February 1962. "We were looked at derisively by others in the media," remembered Born. "It was similar to the way the media panned *USA Today* when it came out. Only where they were greeted as being 'postage stamp' journalism, we were considered unbelievably prolix." Media critics at the *New York Times* and the *Washington Post* called the *Observer* "wordy" and "verbose." It was a feature salad, lacking even the structure of departments.

In late February, Cliff Ridley, the editor responsible for reading unsolicited free-lance queries, ripped open a thick envelope. Out spilled a fistful of clips and a single-page letter in which Hunter Thompson introduced himself as a veteran journalist headed for South America and looking for a place to hang his byline.

Why not? thought Ridley. Everyone at the paper was depressed and scrambling because of the bad initial reviews. They were weak in South American coverage. Here was someone with fairly impressive clips and a willingness to travel on his own tab. Ridley banged out a note saying he would gladly look at any stories Hunter might send.

A few weeks later another thick envelope arrived on Ridley's desk. It was postmarked from Aruba, and looked as if it had been worked over by many postal systems. It contained a finely crafted piece about politics on the island. To illustrate the animus between the two major parties, the Patriotic and the People's, Hunter drew on verbal sparring between prominent members of each group as they drank tall glasses of beer in the Trocadero Bar in Orangestad, Aruba's capital.

Ridley found Hunter's approach refreshing. It read like a short story, yet was full of hard information—the who, what, when, where, how and why. Ridley even found it Hemingwayesque, right down to the final quote from a Dutch politician, who said he would stay on the island if it weren't for the politics.

"The piece was wonderful," said Ridley. "I remember reading it a couple of times and then passing it on to a fellow named Jack Bridge, who was another *Observer* editor. He read it and all he said was, 'Cliff, you've got to run this stuff.'"

Enclosed with the story were photographs taken by Hunter of Aruba and a side view of himself drinking and writing with a view of the Aruba Caribbean Hotel in the background. The newspaper ran his photo with a caption identifying him as a tourist.

The piece was accompanied by a letter in which Hunter told Ridley he was about to set out for Colombia in a smuggling boat. He also mentioned that he was suffering from dysentery.

Before Ridley could walk the story through the system and into the newspaper, another piece came in from Hunter. This one, about smugglers in the Colombian village of Puerto Estrella on the northern tip of a peninsula called La Guajira, was even better than the first. "A Footloose American in a Smuggler's Den," reprinted in *The Great Shark Hunt*, came out in the *Observer* on August 6, 1962.

"In Aruba," wrote Hunter, "the Guajiro Indians are described as 'fierce and crazy and drunk all day on coconut whisky.'" He tells how he was confined to a room in a vacant hospital where he was forced to adapt to the local custom of drinking whiskey all day.

There is nothing to do but drink, and after 50 hours of it I began to lose hope. The end seemed to be nowhere in sight; and it is bad enough to drink Scotch all day in any climate, but to come to the tropics and start belting it down for three hours each morning before breakfast can bring on a general failure of health. In the mornings we had Scotch and arm wrestling; in the afternoons, Scotch and dominoes.

At the end of the article, Hunter flees to Barranquilla, where the locals treat his trip to Puerto Estrella like a dream.

Ridley loved the piece. While he briefly considered the possibility that it didn't really happen, that Guajiro really didn't exist and that, if it did, it was not the smuggling capital Hunter made it out to be, he rejected that notion, realizing that any journalist who fabricated such a story would certainly be placing his career on the line. "In light of all of Hunter's subsequent journalism, I look back on some of this stuff and wonder how much of it was true," said Ridley, "but the stuff was wonderful and quite impossible to check."

Having banished his doubts, Ridley wrote a letter accepting both pieces, telling Hunter that the work was magnificent and encouraging him to keep writing. "Please send more," Ridley wrote. "Work this good doesn't come in all the time."

As Hunter had requested, the payment for the pieces was sent to his "secretary," Sandy Dawn, in New York. Ridley paid top dollar for the stories, $125 each.

Hunter continued to move around Latin America covering the scene for the *Observer*. He communicated with Ridley by telephone or letter, and suggested most of the stories he produced.

"Brazilian Solidiers Stage a Raid in Reverse," a piece published by the *Observer* on February 11, 1963 and reprinted as "Brazilshooting" in *The Great Shark Hunt*, gives a frightening account of an "administration of 'justice'" Hunter encountered below the equator.

The article tells how "an American journalist" in Rio de Janeiro witnesses the army's destruction of "the Domino Club," a "clip joint" frequented by American tourists and wealthy Brazilians. "The journalist" sees blood smeared on the road, and learns that the dead and wounded are being loaded into the back of a truck.

"After the Domino attack," the article concludes, "the *Jornal do Brasil* ran a follow-up story, headlined: 'Army Sees No Crime in Its Action.'"

Sometimes Ridley and the other editors would suggest story

ideas, especially when wire service copy alerted them to upcoming elections. It was these stories that proved the most problematic for the editors. Hunter had a tendency to overlook some of the basics of a news story, focusing instead on local color.

"His political stuff was the only writing of his that we had to add to," commented Ridley. "We would almost always have to write in a few facts just to establish who the president was or what an election was about. Other than that, we could usually edit his stuff with a pencil."

Hunter presented a bleak tourist's view of South America. For example, in "The Incas of the Andes: He Haunts the Ruins of His Once-Great Empire," a piece published under a shorter title in the *Observer* on June 10, 1963 and reprinted in *The Great Shark Hunt*, he describes the way Incas tapping on the window of a hotel bar in Cuzco, Peru to get money "generally ruin the tourist's appetite for his inevitable Pisco Sour."

Today, the Indian is as sad and hopeless a specimen as ever walked in misery. Sick, dirty, barefoot, wrapped in rags, and chewing narcotic coca leaves to dull the pain of reality, he limps through the narrow cobblestone streets of the city that once was the capital of his civilization.

In another story, "Why Anti-Gringo Winds Often Blow South of the Border," published in the *Observer* on August 19, 1963 and reprinted in *The Great Shark Hunt*, Hunter writes about the disdain many South Americans feel for gringos. He quotes several Anglos, who offer detailed stories of the Latinos' disrespect for how Anglos are over-charged in markets, cheated by maids and forced to drink several hours a day in order to avoid rush hour traffic jams. In that piece, Hunter describes a golfer in Cali, Colombia, hitting balls from a penthouse terrace.

He was a tall Britisher, and had what the British call 'a stylish pot' instead of a waistline. Beside him on a small patio table was a long gin-and-tonic, which he refilled from time to time at the nearby bar.

He had a good swing, and each of his shots carried low and long out over the city. Where they fell, neither he nor I nor anyone else on the terrace that day had the vaguest idea.

This piece is considered by *Observer* editors to be among the best ever to appear in the paper.

"His South American dispatches read like Hemingway writing from inside a tour bus," said a friend who, following Hunter's pieces, felt that "the language barrier made him a perpetual outsider."

In the year Hunter wrote about Latin America, he published sixteen dispatches in the *Observer*, earning approximately $2,000 plus expenses. He covered elections in Peru and Brazil, mining strikes in Bolivia, and the rise of democracy in Ecuador.

The letters Hunter wrote Ridley from Latin America reveal sides of his experience there that are not featured in his articles. [Excerpts from these letters were published in the *Observer* on December 31, 1962. Entitled "Chatty Letters During a Journey from Aruba to Rio," the article was reprinted in *The Great Shark Hunt*.] He continually mentions his need for money and his chronic dysentery. He writes from Lima, Peru that he is down eighteen pounds from the 189 with which he began in Aruba. From LaPaz, Bolivia he tells about a poison insect sting he got in Cuzco that has paralyzed his leg. He complains that he's not allowed to drink because alcohol makes the medications that cure dysentery or bites impotent.

With no booze to soothe the savage beast, Hunter experimented with other substances. A number of his friends feel that it was in

South America that he began using amphetamines on a regular basis. He certainly tried a variety of stimulants while there, including the coca leaf that the Incas used to "dull the pain of reality." His doctors gave him injections of cortisone to combat the ravages of dysentery and help rebuild strength. The combination of drugs, exacerbated by the stresses of living in a third-world country, probably caused much of his hair to fall out. *Observer* editors noticed changes in his physical appearance from the photos he sent them.

After a year in South America, said Ridley, Hunter was "close to going around the bend. The phone calls were beginning to sound more and more desperate. Then one day he just said, 'I've got to come home.'"

Sandy had joined Hunter in Rio at the end of 1962. The *Observer* advanced the money for them to return to the States. They flew to Miami, where Hunter bought an ancient Nash sleeper, a car with seats that folded down into the trunk.

They drove to Kentucky to retrieve Agar, Hunter's Doberman, which Sandy had left with his mother. After a few days in Louisville they drove to Washington, D.C. When they reached the *Observer* home office in White Oak, Maryland, they made the rounds, visiting editors and chatting about Hunter's stories. Hunter felt like a returning hero. It was as close to being a celebrity as most journalists ever get, and he loved it.

Roscoe Born suggested they go to the National Press Club for lunch. They all sat at a big table and peppered Hunter with questions about South America and his current plans, the most oft-asked question being "do you want to work in Washington?"

"No fucking way!" Hunter snarled. "We want to go back to California. A friend of mine says that California is the new 'home of the uprooted,' which is what Malcolm Cowley used to call New York."

The next question was "do you want to become a staffer?"

"I don't think so," said Hunter, sweat beading on his brow. "There's something about working for a company that feels like a tarantula crawling up my back."

He regaled them with stories of gunfights and drug smugglers, of ugly Americans and beautiful senoritas. All the while they drank copiously. "This was a celebratory lunch," said Born. "We were very pleased with him and we wanted him to be entertained."

Finally the attention and booze took their toll on Hunter. Several of the editors noticed that he became very jittery and palpably fatigued. "I think he was still worn out from South America," said Ridley. "He had been sick down there so much of the time that he still wasn't up for a lot of socializing."

Dave Hacker, an editor who admired Hunter, offered to put Hunter and Sandy up at his house in Silver Springs. He and his wife worked, so the house was empty all day. Hacker noted Hunter's expression of relief. "They clearly had no place else to stay," he recalled.

That evening the Hackers were sitting on the porch when Hunter and Sandy arrived. The first one out of the car was Hunter. He charged across the lawn waving a lighted cigarette in one hand and carrying a lacquered wooden box containing a pair of .357 Magnum pistols under his other arm. He was followed by Agar the Doberman, who reached the porch ahead of him, surprising the Hackers, who hadn't known about the dog. It was left to Sandy to open the trunk and lug the two suitcases out and up to the porch. "Those fucking pistols and that goddamn dog were his whole world at that moment," said Hacker. "That was all he cared about."

After Hunter and Sandy were settled in the guest bedroom, Hacker called Cliff Ridley and invited him over for a drink. The two *Observer* editors were serious martini drinkers in those days, but they soon realized that they were minor league compared with their South American correspondent.

As they sipped their drinks, Hunter plowed through tumbler after tumbler of Wild Turkey, which he prepared in a somewhat unorthodox fashion. First, he filled a tall glass to the brim with ice cubes. Then he tipped the gallon bottle of 120-proof and poured slowly, so the amber liquor trickled over the ice. When the glass was filled almost to the rim, he covered it tightly with his hand and turned it upside down for a second. "It gives the booze that snow cone effect," he explained.

Ridley and Hacker were impressed. They drank until one in the morning, when Ridley stood up and stumbled for his car. "Another workday," he mumbled. As Hacker said good night to Hunter, he noticed that the gallon bottle of Wild Turkey was half empty, and that Hunter was still going strong. "It was like he was drinking iced tea," marveled Hacker. "He was as straight when we finished as when we started drinking."

The next night, the drinking continued, and so did Hunter's South American tales. At one point the subject of drugs arose. Data from the government had been released showing that drug use in the United States was on the rise. Ridley and Hacker argued that drugs were largely the province of the lower class, certainly not available outside the ghetto. Hunter disagreed.

"Shit, man, you put me out on any street corner in Washington and I'll guarantee that within ten minutes I'll get something," he insisted. "I'll score from any street corner even though I've never been there."

The *Observer* editors considered assigning him an article in which he did that very thing, but in the end they scoffed at the notion. "We thought it was just the booze talking," said Hacker.

"But sure enough, he turned out to be right, as anyone in Washington could attest to in just a few more years."

When Ridley left, Hacker decided to mention that some *Observer* editors suspected Hunter of making up some of his quotes, and possibly even some of his stories. Some editors doubted, for example, that the smuggler's town, Puerto Estrella, existed, while others assumed he'd fabricated the idea that its economy was based upon smuggling. They also wondered whether the story about the Englishman driving golf balls into the city of Cali, Colombia really happened, whether Hunter had really seen this, as he claimed, or had just heard about it and made the story his own.

"They've just been in the cubicles too long," Hunter countered. "A good journalist hears lots of things. Maybe I heard some of these stories and didn't see them. But they sure as hell happened."

Hacker accepted the explanation. He knew a good story overheard at a hotel often found its way into foreign correspondents' copy. He also knew that many of the best correspondents were writing half truths anyway, if not total fiction. "A toast to truth in journalism," he offered, clinking glasses.

Hunter and Sandy spent three days and four nights with the Hackers. During that time, as far as Hacker remembers, Hunter always referred to Sandy as his secretary. He doubts that lack of commitment prompted Hunter to do this; it was, he thought, Hunter's way of protecting Sandy's honor and preventing people from talking about them. "It was best to keep relationships a little vague. Back in those days, morals were different and people didn't live together like they do now. They were very careful not to be seen as live-ins."

Their next stop was Hunter's mother's house in Louisville.

Virginia Thompson wasn't fooled by the secretary routine. She had known for some time that Hunter and Sandy were living together, and had protested to Hunter that they should get married, that he should do the "decent thing." While there was nothing she could do about the relationship as long as Hunter was on his own, she could dictate terms if they were going to stay together in her house.

One night Hunter took his dog and went to see Gerald Tyrrell, who had embarked on a career in banking. The two reminisced about their wild high school days. When Tyrrell brought his life up to the present, all he had to talk about was the youth basketball team he was coaching and his life at the bank. Hunter talked for a couple of hours about everything from Big Sur to South America, touting Agar as the best deer hunter on four legs and telling how he'd used the dog in California to put meat on the table. At the end of the evening, Hunter told Tyrrell that marriage to Sandy was imminent. "My mother is pushing me to do it," Hunter said, sounding somewhat resigned. "I guess this is it."

Tyrrell sensed regret in Hunter's admission, but he also knew Hunter couldn't be forced into anything he didn't want. Hunter, he sensed, really wanted to tie the knot with Sandy; in his own way and for the time being, he was ready for marriage.

"That's great," said Tyrrell, slapping Hunter on the back. "We'll throw a wedding party for you."

On May 19, 1963, Hunter and Sandy were married at a wedding chapel in Jeffersonville, Indiana, just across the Ohio River from Louisville. They would have married in Louisville, but it required several days of waiting for the blood test and license, and they were impatient. "If he'd waited to get married in Louisville, he probably wouldn't have," said Tyrrell.

That night, Hunter and Sandy and about eight other couples gathered for the party in Tyrrell's apartment. Hunter seemed apologetic about his loss of bachelorhood. As his friends congratulated them, he shrugged and denied any responsibility for what had just happened. "We only did it because my mother wanted me to," he explained.

The people at the party noticed changes in Hunter, particularly in the way he spoke. He mumbled, firing words rapidly from his mouth. "He sounded like a machine gun," said Tyrrell, "except his voice was so deep that it was practically baritone." According to Tyrrell, most of the people at the party couldn't understand him at all.

"What gives, Hunter?" Tyrrell finally asked. "You sound like you have a mouthful of marbles."

"Really?" said Hunter. "It must be those drugs I was doing down in South America." He launched into a detailed description of the wide variety of pharmaceuticals he had sampled abroad, from smoking "the best grass in the world," to chewing coca leaves to get a buzz, to eating peyote.

Hunter's old friends were at once horrified and intrigued. Although, at the end of the evening, they toasted the couple and expressed hope that they would see much more of them, most of them felt that Hunter had moved beyond them into the fast lane.

Hunter and Sandy left Louisville and headed to New York City to visit Don Cooke and Judy Booth. While Hunter was in South America, Cooke had left Louisville for Vermont. He, too, was going to take a crack at writing a novel. On his way up to New England Cooke had stopped in New York for what he thought would be only a few days. He'd run across Judy Booth, and decided to stay a while longer. Before long, the Louisville couple was engaged to be married.

Cooke had heard that Hunter was about to get married, too, in Louisville and called to congratulate him. "Come up and stay with us after your wedding," Cooke offered.

Cooke and Judy were house-sitting in Greenwich Village. Some family friends had contacted Judy's father to see if he knew any worthy Louisville youth who might like to care for their brownstone while they traveled for the summer. Cooke was his only recommendation. Cooke told the owners that he was working at a hardware store in the Village for minimum wage, but that his true aspiration was to write the Great American Novel. Their house, he said, would provide the setting he needed for his writing. They handed him the keys. The two-story townhouse, on Downing Street, had four bedrooms, an enormous living room, and a courtyard in the back that was surrounded on all sides by apartment buildings.

Hunter arrived one afternoon with his finely cased .357 magnums, his Doberman Agar, and Sandy, carrying the suitcases. It didn't take long for him to get settled and take charge. He had Sandy put the luggage in a bedroom and began calling old friends. Within hours the house was teeming with activity, none of which would have been approved by the owners.

Gene McGarr came over. McGarr had been to Europe and come back, and was looking for work. He sat in the living room and drank Scotch while expounding on his continental adventures.

Paul Semonin had been to Africa and was back. He had always been serious, but now he discussed the ever-changing political scene in Africa with great fury. Cooke was astonished at his knowledge of even the smallest principalities of that huge continent. It amazed him that a boy from Louisville could have so much passion about a culture that was so different from his own.

Hunter held his weight in discussing the people and geography of South America. Unlike Cooke, Semonin was not impressed with Hunter's view of South America. It amazed Semonin how little Hunter seemed to care about South American politics; Hunter's so-called political pieces, Semonin thought, only scratched the surface of the story. In private Semonin called Hunter's South

American writings the work of "a tourist out of his depth." Semonin had experience with Hunter's temper, and mentioned his opinion only to people he could trust to keep quiet.

According to Cooke, Hunter paced nervously around the townhouse and seemed to be on his own wavelength. He talked about a variety of things, including writing and how all the great authors were dead or dying. Hunter later picked up this theme in "Where Are the Writing Talents of Yesteryear?" published in the *Observer* on August 5, 1963.

Hunter rarely talked about his two unpublished novels, but when he did he spoke of them optimistically. To break into the fiction scene, he said, he knew he would have to produce something extraordinary. "Maybe I'll write the next *Ginger Man*," he told Cooke.

Certainly Hunter was living like the Ginger Man. He and McGarr gadded about town constantly, hanging out in bars, chasing women, and discovering the forbidden pleasures of drugs. One night, Hunter came home with a story about the best pot he had ever smoked. He was at an apartment with McGarr and some women when one of McGarr's girlfriends showed up. She had a particular glint in her eye, a kind of stoned look. When she opened her purse he knew why. She was packing a hefty bag of marijuana from some country he had never heard of. "Powerful stuff," said the woman. McGarr and Hunter smoked a bowl and became extremely high. Midway through the second bowl, they found themselves throwing up in the toilet. They spent several more hours with the women smoking dope.

On another night, a party was in full swing in the townhouse after midnight when Cooke suddenly remembered that he was supposed to water the plants in the courtyard. He decided to do it right away, since he hadn't done it for several days and feared they might be too close to death to wait any longer. He excused himself and made his way for the back door. Soon the entire party followed him into the backyard.

Cooke began watering the plants, but Hunter soon took over. Turning the water on as high as it would go, he directed the spray into the open windows of the apartments that surrounded the courtyard. Some of these windows were bedrooms, and the spray hit people asleep in their beds. The revelers laughed as their sleeping neighbors put their heads out and gazed into the sky for signs of clouds.

In one of the windows was a pretty brunette, her hair a sexy tangle and her white pajamas clinging to her shapely form. She looked up at the sky and then ducked back inside. Hunter trained the spray back into her window. Out she came again, this time looking directly into the courtyard.

"Knock it off, you asshole!" she shouted and then ducked back inside.

Hunter put the hose back to work, squirting another stream of water through her window. "Come down and have a drink," he shouted when she popped back through the window. In a few minutes the woman was at the party, sipping a beer and laughing as Hunter continued his water pranks.

In the predawn hours the party started breaking up. Sandy had gone to bed even before the courtyard party began. Cooke recalls Hunter and the woman going off into the night together.

According to many of Hunter's friends, Sandy kept a blind eye turned to many of his actions. Semonin saw her in a mother role with Hunter. "She knew from the start that that would be her lot in life if she were to marry Hunter," said Semonin. "It was her job to take him in and heal him, no matter what."

Cooke found her to be extremely quiet. "She was like a lot of women who are attached to extraordinarily expressive men. You don't really get to know them." In those few times when they did

Hunter's high school yearbook photo.

HUNTER THOMPSON, '55

The Athenaeum Literary Association Christmas Dance, 1954.
Hunter and his date are at far right.

Hunter (at left) and Paul Semonin, in front of Judy Booth's apartment in New York, as they prepare for their fall 1960 cross-country trek.

Paul Semonin with fake "gas can" suitcase, during his road trip with Hunter in 1960.

The beach house in Loiza Aldea (about 17 mi. outside of San Juan), where Hunter,
future wife Sandy, and Paul Semonin lived in mid-1960.
That's Hunter on the tractor.

Hunter at the typewriter in Loiza Aldea.

Hunter's future wife Sandy relaxes on Paul Semonin's sailboat in Puerto Rico.

Hunter makes an appearance at the Attorney General's office in Charlotte Amalie, Virgin Islands.

Gonzo sportsman

Paul Semonin checks out the wild boar that he, Hunter, and Joe Hudson shot in Big Sur (September 1961).

Hunter in scuba gear. Puerto Rico, 1960.

Hunter on the beach in Puerto Rico.

talk in private, Sandy always diverted the conversation to the subject of Hunter. If she didn't talk about something Hunter had said or written, she talked about their life together and how they planned to head for the West Coast very shortly.

After a few weeks, Hunter and Sandy left New York. He told several of his friends that, all things considered, California seemed to be the place to chase his dream of becoming a novelist. Out there he would be subject to a steady stream of good weather, cheap rent, and quiet working conditions, all of which were commodities in poor supply in Manhattan.

The *National Observer* had agreed to make Hunter a roving correspondent. They wanted him to do, in the United States, the kind of thing he had done in South America. The editors were tempted to repeat their offer of a solid job on the staff, but they knew he didn't want that. "We entertained the possibility several times a year," said Ridley, "but Hunter and the cubicles were not made for each other."

Hunter and Sandy rented a house in Glen Ellen, a small town above Sonoma in Northern California. The neighborhood was described as a "rural slum" by Gene McGarr. There were plenty of cows, horses, and chicken in the ample backyards of the other houses, and old shacks with broken down trucks and grass growing around them. Hunter said that all he wanted out of life was "to be a hillbilly."

The small, ranch-style house was an early monument to prefabricated construction. The Thompsons scoured flea markets and secondhand stores for furnishings, which created an "early hippie" decor. One person who was looking for Hunter was directed by a neighbor to "the house where the gypsies live." But the Thompsons weren't gypsies, nor were they hippies. They were just broke.

Even though Hunter was considered a regular contributor to the *Observer*, he wasn't regular enough to make much money. Over the course of the next year and a half, he wrote about thirty pieces. He got $200 per article, but a number of the pieces were book reviews, for which he was paid much less.

T. Floyd Smith, who was living in the Bay Area and dropped in frequently to visit the Thompsons, likened Hunter to Henry Miller. "They both felt that the system did them dirt, and both believed that artists and writers deserve to be supported by their contemporaries. They thought it was not just a right, but a duty for society to support them."

Smith saw other similarities between Hunter and Miller. Both had many friends—male and female—and neither was afraid to call on them any time of the day or night. Neither was afraid to treat their friends like employees or serfs. Smith recalled all-nighters when Hunter, along with whoever was with him, arrived on someone's doorstep and asked for "accommodations" and "country hospitality." Once they got in, they simply took over for a few days. They even spent one night in Henry Miller's tiny cabin on Huntington Ridge while the guru of erotica was out of town.

Another similarity Smith noted between Hunter and Miller was that both men liked subservient women as wives. "Sandy was very much the hausfrau," said Smith. "I wondered when she would get fed up with sharing her husband with all of these people. But for the longest time, she just didn't seem to be bothered."

While Hunter pounded on the keys, Sandy held one job or another to support him. On those frequent nights when he didn't get home until dawn, Sandy walked on eggs all day so he could get his sleep. If any people came to the house before he was up, Sandy met them in the yard to keep them quiet. She knew that Hunter was very cranky and could not work without a full eight or ten hours of sleep, and she went out of her way to see that he got it.

Hunter desperately wanted to publish a novel. Although his two finished novels had failed to find a publisher, he continued to press on. These manuscripts were polished and rewritten, again and again, in hopes they would finally be honed into publishable works. In addition to working on these novels, he wrote some short fiction pieces.

Every couple of weeks, Don Cooke and Judy Booth, now married, got a fat envelope from Hunter. In three or four page "slash and burn" letters, Hunter talked about life in the West, late night drink fests, travails with the *Observer,* and serious bouts with writer's block. "These were guaranteed to be the best thing we would read anywhere that week," said Cooke.

About the fiction pieces that accompanied the letters, Cooke was less complimentary. He found them to be shallow "episodes of one sort or another." Rather than reading like complete short stories with a beginning, middle, and end, they were "extended moments in the lives of various people." Cooke called them "prose snapshots."

"His letters and newspaper stories were filled with such liveliness," said Cooke. "But his fiction was totally flat, it didn't go anywhere. In hindsight, it seemed as though he needed some kind of immediacy to react to. Real life gave him that. What was going on in his mind didn't."

Cooke was blunt with Hunter because he thought that was what his friend wanted. Against his wife's advice, he picked over Hunter's fiction with a copy pencil, writing advice and criticism in the margins. Thanks from Hunter were never forthcoming. Instead, the time between letters became longer and longer, and eventually they no longer contained fiction.

Hunter worked out some of his frustrations about his writing by using the pages of the *Observer* to take pokes at the literary establishment. The most notable of these pieces was "Where Are the Writing Talents of Yesteryear?", which focused on an *Esquire* Magazine article about the American literary "situation" in 1963. Hunter describes it as "depressing." He puts down Truman Capote who, according to *Esquire*, was "'nearly finished with a massive piece of reportage about the murder of a Kansas farm family.'" Ironically, Capote's *In Cold Blood*, eventually published in 1966, broke through tradition by using literary techniques to tell a nonfiction story and established New Journalism, of which Hunter become one of the most famous and controversial practitioners.

Hunter also picks at Nelson Algren and rips Norman Mailer's routine of writing after "a long evening of martinis." It is, he says, "the poor echo of some half-wit myth about Scott Fitzgerald." Hunter later adopted a similar method for himself.

Hunter concludes his grim assessment of the arteriosclerotic decline of the literary establishment with hope that the "hardening . . . signals a coming breakthrough."

In "Donleavy Proves His Lunatic Humor Is Original," Hunter's review of *A Singular Man*, Donleavy's long-awaited follow-up to *The Ginger Man*, Hunter praises Donleavy and attacks, once again, the failing players "in the field of contemporary American fiction."

Many of Hunter's American pieces for the *Observer* were book reviews. His American journalistic pieces lacked the spark of his South American coverage. *Observer* editors, accepting some of the blame for his waning enthusiasm, say they could have come up with better story ideas or been more nurturing in other ways. But Hunter wasn't delivering on his end, either. The train story is a case in point.

In the summer of 1963, Hunter suggested to the editors that he take a train trip across the country, from Maine to San Francisco, to write a story about how the nation's rail system was dying, losing riders to the cheaper and faster airlines. The editors agreed. They sent Hunter to Maine with several hundred dollars in expense money and a cross-country rail ticket. All Hunter had to do was sit on the train and take in the scene, weaving in interviews of passengers and rail employees. "It was the kind of story Hunter did best," said Roscoe Born. "He just had to sit there and the story would come to him."

On the first day of the trip, the editors received a telegram from Hunter requesting more expense money. Something of an unforeseen nature had come up, and he was almost out. The more cynical members of the staff thought Hunter should be left to his own devices; someone opted to wire money to the train's next stop.

One or two days later, another telegram asked for more money. The editors wired more money. In the end, after several telegrams, the editors estimate that advances for that trip totaled almost $2,000, a large sum of money in the midsixties.

Then came a final telegram, this one from Chicago. Hunter announced that he was "emotionally and physically drained" and would not be able to complete the trip or write the story. Instead, he was returning to the West Coast and would contact them later.

The *Observer* editors agreed that the money Hunter was to receive from his articles and book reviews would be deducted from the outstanding expenses. Relations between them and Hunter began to seriously unravel.

Early in 1964, Hunter and Sandy moved to San Francisco. Their first floor apartment at 318 Parnassus in the Haight-Ashbury neighborhood cost them about $100 a month. It was down the hill from the medical center and had, out the big bay window, a panoramic view of Kezar Stadium and Golden Gate Park. A working fireplace provided atmosphere, and the two bedrooms gave the young couple ample space for the child they were now trying to have.

Hunter wrote nostalgically about the changing scene in North Beach, where the beats were no longer center stage. In "When the Beatniks Were Social Lions," an *Observer* article published on April 20, 1964 and reprinted in *The Great Shark Hunt,* he introduces a fabricated character, a free-spirited, heavy-drinking beatnik named Willard whose "one and only encounter with the forces of law and order provided one of the wildest Beat Generation stories of the era." (Willard, described as six foot four inches and 230 pounds, fits the physical description of Gene McGarr.) The story relates how Willard and a friend are arrested and jailed after a sensational drunken painting spree and police chase.

In another *Observer* article, "People Want Bad Taste . . . In Everything" (November 2, 1964), Hunter complains about how the beats' haunts are being replaced by topless bars like the "Condor" and the "Chi Chi." He describes the action in one of these clubs where "the mammary circus was in high gear." The beat scene is dying, he declares, because it "was far too introverted a thing to ever be a real money-maker." People know the names of glitzy strippers like "Exotica" or "Judy Mack," while Ginsberg and Kerouac are forgotten.

Among the other articles Hunter wrote for the *Observer* during this period, "What Lured Hemingway to Ketchum?" printed on May 25, 1964 and anthologized in *The Great Shark Hunt,* was considered by the editors to be one of his finest pieces to date. In it he examines the small Idaho town where Hemingway lived his final years until he committed suicide with a shotgun in July 1961.

The article begins with a quote from one of Hemingway's neighbors establishing the aura of celebrity around the famous writer, even in his dotage. With a few deft phrases, Hunter goes on to portray Ketchum, an outdoorsman's town much like Woody Creek, Colorado, where Hunter would eventually settle. Ketchum was ten minutes away from the celebrity-filled Sun Valley ski resort, yet quite different. It was a proud town populated by solid middle-class people who hunted and fished and drank plenty. Basque sheepherders tended sheep in the mountains.

In the article, Hunter's analysis of a writer's waning powers is prophetic of changes that would happen in Hunter's own life at the peak of his fame.

Today we have Mailer, Jones, and Styron, three potentially great writers bogged down in what seems to be a crisis of convictions brought on, like Hemingway's, by the mean nature of a world that will not stand still long enough for them to see it clear as a whole.

It is not just a writer's crisis, but they are the most obvious victims because the function of art is supposedly to bring order out of chaos, a tall order even when the chaos is static, and a superhuman task in a time when chaos is multiplying.

Hunter goes on to describe how, in Ketchum, Hemingway tried to retreat "from the pressures of a world gone mad," how, like Fitzgerald, he never "understood the vibrations of a world that had shaken them off their thrones," how "the strength of his youth became rigidity as he grew older."

When *Observer* editor Dave Hacker expressed his belief that Hunter's life in many ways mirrored that of the great outdoorsman/writer, Hunter was offended and denied any spiritual or other linkage to Hemingway. Nevertheless, Hunter was very proud of the Hemingway piece, and was shocked and furious to see it imitated in another national magazine a few weeks later.

Hunter's first brush with American politics came in July 1964. Still trying to figure out ways in which he could repay the advance money he owed them from the failed train story, *Observer* editors assigned him to work as a stringer at the 28th Republican National Convention at the Cow Palace, a massive arena near San Francisco.

Barry Goldwater, the ultraconservative senator from Arizona, was considered a shoe-in for the presidential nomination. But there was a groundswell of progressive opposition from supporters of William Scranton, the Pennsylvania governor, who would be more able to sway voters from casting a ballot for Lyndon Johnson, the incumbent Democrat. Although the editors planned to do the writing, they needed a lot of stringers to saturate the convention floor and fish for quotes. Hunter was added at the last minute.

Hunter knew little about politics in those days, After his first day of convention coverage, he showed up for a meeting of the reporters and editors who were spearheading the *Observer* operation. Editor Bill Giles asked for a report from each reporter in turn. Hunter embarrassed himself by talking enthusiastically about "a bright new face" who turned out to be a house leader who'd been around for decades.

Later that night Hunter paid a visit to T. Floyd Smith, who was working as a guard for the Pinkerton Agency, the company providing security for the convention. "I need to get an edge," Hunter told him. "I don't know enough about these people to cover this the usual way."

"Easy," said Smith. "Take my credentials. I can go anywhere I want."

Smith's were the highest level of credentials. Hunter could go places even his press colleagues couldn't go. If anyone asked why he was in caucus rooms with Barry Goldwater, Margaret Chase Smith, or Henry Luce, Hunter showed he was a member of the private police force. The quality of his sources improved substantially, and no one at the *Observer* ever knew why.

Aside from that, Hunter's personal behavior disturbed some members of the *Observer* team, Giles especially. One afternoon, for example, Giles heard Hunter on the telephone brutally swearing at a representative of the phone company. When Giles asked Hunter what was wrong, he was told that the phone company had called Sandy and threatened to turn off his phone for non-payment.

Another time, Hunter angrily blew up at the accounting department for asking for his social-security number. "You people are goddamn slow sending my checks—what the hell are you hired for?" he wrote back. "Stop playing with yourselves."

Tensions between Hunter and the *Observer* editors were building toward a breaking point. "Hunter will always do something to push his employer over the edge," said a friend. "He is like Groucho Marx, who said, 'I don't care to belong to a club that accepts people like me as members.'"

Several editors were becoming more vocal about Hunter's disregard of fact. Roscoe Born declared that some of Hunter's stories had a "fairy-story aura" to them. "He became very unreliable and quite a lot of trouble."

Different editors began to discover different things. Ridley discovered a biblical reference in one of Hunter's pieces. After expending some effort to check the quote, he confronted Hunter with the fact that it wasn't the verse he'd cited. "Well hell," replied Hunter, "one verse or another."

A negative story about Butte, Montana, "Whither the Old Copper Capital Of the West? To Boom or Bust?" (June 1, 1964), put Born in a bind when civic leaders complained about its factual content. Hunter had said horrible things about the town, putting it in the "same sorry league" as "the coal-dust poverty of Weirton, W.Va., or the silent railyards in Jersey Shore, Pa."

Born was able to defend the article to an extent. Hunter had gathered his quotes, all of which were negative, in the course of capturing the citizens' feelings about their town. If nobody liked Butte, it wasn't Hunter's fault.

The people who called to complain didn't accept that explanation. Some claimed to be misquoted. Others said the positive things they said were turned into negative comments. Some high-level citizens charged that some of Hunter's facts about population and the number of employees who worked in a certain plant were completely wrong. By the end of these conversations, Born realized that a mistake had been made. He had one of the editors contact Hunter to answer the complaints. "At that point he said, 'who cares about these kinds of facts?'"

"I began to think that Hunter just wasn't a journalist, at least not in the common definition of the term," said Born. "I now think he knew perfectly well what he was doing. It's just the people who get suckered by him who don't understand."

Other viewpoints differed greatly from Born's. Dave Hacker, the one *Observer* editor who kept in touch with Hunter for years to come, took the long view of Hunter's penchant for mixing fiction and nonfiction. "Tolstoy said: 'Art is a lie that enables us to see the truth,'" commented Hacker. "I believe flatly that there were elements of truth in everything Hunter wrote. Now that element may be the 103rd element in the periodic table and is yet to be discovered, but there was an element of truth.

"I think Hunter was really the best chronicler of the 1960s. Through the bizarreness and exaggerations, the flesh and blood gets added to the bare bones of history."

A seemingly small incident finally split Hunter and the *Observer*. Hunter's laudatory review of Tom Wolfe's first anthology, *The Kandy-Kolored Tangerine-Flake Streamline Baby*, was nixed for containing too much personal opinion. It's impossible to tell now what opinions the review contained, since no copy of it is available.

Hunter was incensed. He gave Ridley a dressing down, although Ridley had fought with the editors above him to publish the piece. Then Hunter mailed a copy of the piece to Wolfe with a note saying it was a copy of the review that the *National Observer* refused to print.

When Ridley heard about this, he wrote Hunter an angry letter. "My position was that, if Hunter had been just an ordinary free-lancer, he could have taken his copy and done any damn thing he wanted with it," said Ridley. "But he had been a quasi staff member for three years and we had supported him in his moments of need, which were many. Because of that, I thought we deserved better treatment and it pissed me off that we didn't get it."

Ridley was saddened by the note that came back. It was short and to the point: You're wrong and goodbye.

Hunter never wrote for the *National Observer* again.

4

HELL'S ANGELS (1964–1966)

Sandy was enormous and about to deliver. The rent was overdue and the Chinese landlord tenaciously reminded Hunter of it at every opportunity. The phone was going to be disconnected and Hunter's beautiful leather billfold was almost as empty as on the day he'd bought it in Bolivia.

Hunter went to the *San Francisco Chronicle* and the *San Francisco Examiner.* Although he had produced impressive work, he did not get hired.

He tried a cab company and a half-dozen grocery stores, in vain. On weekends he stood on Market Street with other men looking for jobs. People cruised by to pick out someone they could hire to do their weekend yard work, but they rarely picked him.

In a letter to Dave Hacker, he wrote that he would be thirty in two years; he thought this might be his last chance. He had heard about a man who had to throw out eight novels before he got the ninth published. "The man must be a lunatic," commented Hunter.

Hunter and Sandy found their neighborhood was rapidly changing. The Haight's forty square blocks of rundown Victorian houses and aging shops, located between Golden Gate Park and a black ghetto known as the Fillmore District, had taken on the nickname

"Hashbury." Hunter described the dramatic evolution of this area in "The 'Hashbury' Is the Capital of the Hippies," a piece that appeared in the *New York Times Magazine* on May 14, 1967 and is anthologized in *The Great Shark Hunt*.

Hunter was already a veteran of many of the drugs coming into vogue. Drugs like benzedrine, methedrine, opium, barbiturates, marijuana, and, of course, alcohol were old hat to Hunter's bloodstream. But there were some new drugs on the black market that he didn't dare try. These, particularly LSD, fit into the category of "mind-expanding" drugs,

Hunter had heard about LSD from Michael Murphy, the owner of the house where he lived in Big Sur. At that time Murphy's wife, Joanne, a research psychiatrist at Stanford University, was conducting experiments with the drug. Although Hunter would have been a willing guinea pig, the Murphys didn't have a good feeling about Hunter and this new drug nicknamed acid. They had seen the way he dealt with the gays in the hot tubs and knew about him chopping up the wild pig and putting its body parts in strategic places. "Some people cannot take LSD," Joanne Murphy told Hunter, "and you're one of them. You are too violent and all that violence might come out."

Although Hunter was avoiding LSD, he took a liberal view of the other stuff being puffed and popped in his neighborhood. With so many people doing it in the open, there was less to worry about from the police, who found it impractical to bust everyone they saw. Because of its sheer number of heads, Haight-Ashbury was becoming a virtual drug fortress where drug use was ignored as long as it was contained within the forty magical blocks.

Hunter noticed another outlaw lifestyle crawling the streets of San Francisco. Its practitioners were the unkempt thugs who rode Harley Davidson motorcycles and liked to travel in packs and wore jackets proclaiming themselves "Hell's Angels." These guys were dirty and dangerous. They seemed to think that all of this peace and love stuff was bullshit. They appeared to be the ultimate social outcasts, but the type that you didn't dare offend. Even the most stoned of the hippies sobered up enough to give them a wide berth.

What little Hunter knew about the Angels he'd read in the newspaper. The stories were taken from police blotters and almost always had to do with fights, forced sex, or some other form of mayhem.

"Who the hell are the Angels, anyway?" he asked Denny Beckler, a *Chronicle* reporter who occasionally drank with him at a folk-music bar called The Drinking Room.

To answer that question, Beckler introduced Hunter to Bernie Jarvis, a *Chronicle* reporter and an ex-Hell's Angel himself.

"We aren't as bad as we seem, but we're pretty bad," said Jarvis. To show what he meant, Jarvis gave the curious reporter a copy of California attorney general Thomas C. Lynch's recent report skewering the Angels. The report, portions of which appear at the beginning of Hunter's *Hell's Angels* book, was entitled "The Hell's Angels Motorcycle Clubs" and might easily have been subtitled "The Best of the Angels." It was a fifteen-page record of brutality and animal behavior, the worst that could be found in the files of California law enforcement.

For example:

On April 2, 1964, a group of eight Hell's Angels invaded the home of an Oakland woman, forcing her male friend out of the house at gunpoint and raping the woman in the presence of her three children. Later that same morning, female companions of the Hell's Angels threatened the victim that if she cooperated with the police, she would be cut on the face with a razor. . . .

Early on the morning of June 2, 1962, it was reported that

three Hell's Angels had seized a 19-year-old woman in a small bar in the northern part of Sacramento and while two of them held her down on the barroom floor, the third removed her outer clothing. The victim was menstruating at the time; her sanitary napkin was removed and the third individual committed cunnilingus upon her. . . .

Public opinion had forced Attorney General Lynch to produce the report when news hit the papers that Angels had raped two girls aged fourteen and fifteen at their 1964 annual Labor Day bash. More than three hundred Angels from clubs all over California had showed up to drink, wrestle, screw, race, pop pills, and smoke dope in the sand dunes near the town of Seaside on the Monterey Peninsula. A couple of teenage girls and their boyfriends wandered into the scene and started drinking. According to the Angels, the girls willfully consented to have sex behind some sand dunes, not realizing that when you agree to have sex with one Angel, you agree to have it with all of them. Both girls panicked at this notion. When they were finally rescued by a sheriff's deputy, one girl was naked and both were practically hysterical. Four Angels were arrested and the rest were run off the beach by a large police contingent. In the end, the charges of rape didn't stick; not only did medical examinations show no signs of forcible rape, but one of the girls refused to testify and the other failed to pass a lie-detector test.

The attorney general's report had all the effect of a well-done publicity campaign. The national media snowballed the story to almost absurd proportions. Everyone wanted to talk to the Angels. Hollywood saw some movie possibilities. Magazines wanted Angels to pose for cover stories and radio talk shows wanted them for call-in programs. Even some of the Berkeley radicals thought it would be a good idea to have Angels at their parties.

Hunter contacted the *Nation,* a liberal magazine in New York, with the idea of writing the "true story" about the Angels. The magazine liked the idea, and he began the research that was to form the substance of his *Nation* piece, "Motorcycle Gangs: Losers and Outsiders," (anthologized in *Violence in the Streets,* compiled by Shalom Endleman), and his book *Hell's Angels.*

In the book, Hunter tells how he was put in touch with an Angel named Frenchy, who agreed to meet him in the DePau Hotel in San Francisco's industrial district. In a room filled with Angels, Frenchy spoke to Hunter at length, divulging a number of colorful tales and trying to squelch some myths about his compadres. For example, Frenchy said that contrary to popular belief, most Angels do not try to smell bad. They bathe as much as most people.

When they write about body order, the Angel suggested, they must be confusing it with our clothes. Frenchy went on to reveal to Hunter an Angels' initiation ritual: pouring a bucket of feces and urine over the jeans and jacket of the new member. The outfit is then coated with oil; however, it can never be washed. When the jeans and jacket start to disintegrate, they are often worn over a new set, as ancient "originals" are a status symbol.

Hunter also asked the Angels for their versions of the Monterey rape controversy. An account of what he heard appears in the *Nation* article.

"One girl was white and pregnant, the other was colored, and they were with five colored studs. . . . The spade went with a few guys and then she wanted to quit, but the pregnant one was really hot to trot; the first four or five guys she was really dragging into her arms, but after that she cooled off, too. By this time, though, one of their boy friends had got scared and gone for the cops—and that's all it was."

Frenchy invited Hunter to attend the Angels' weekly meetings at the DePau. At one meeting, Hunter reported, the Angels kicked out a member who had fallen into disfavor with others in the group. In what sounded like a group therapy session, Angels stood and spoke their minds for and against the disgraced member. "Their conversation is totally frank and open," wrote Hunter. "They speak to and about one another with an honesty that more civilized people couldn't bear."

Hunter often invited several of the Angels over to his apartment. The neighbors in this usually placid area were not accustomed to the throaty sound of Harleys idling up to the curb. Nor did Sandy, at home with their new baby Juan Fitzgerald, expect Hunter to bring outlaws home with him. Terry the Tramp in particular was ominously large.

The Angels would usually arrive at Hunter's around 2:00 A.M. Soon the stereo volume would be jacked up high and the windows opened wide, the music of Bob Dylan and the haze of marijuana smoke mingling in the night air. The Angels would stay at Hunter's apartment until dawn, when they'd kick-start their Harleys and arouse the neighborhood again.

Like all the other Angels stories done in 1965, Hunter's *Nation* piece used the attorney general's report as its news peg. But unlike the others, he ripped holes in the report, exposing it as a one-sided piece of police work that led to numerous examples of lopsided reporting by the media.

[The report hinges on] eighteen incidents in four years, and none except the rape charges are more serious than cases of assault on citizens who, for their own reasons, had become involved with the Hell's Angels prior to the violence. I could find no cases of unwarranted attacks on wholly innocent victims.

Hunter's conclusions about the report should have been obvious to any reporter who properly examined the evidence. But few had. As a result, his was considered a moderate voice in a media circus of shrill overreaction.

The Angels, skeptical of all reporters, now thought of Hunter as being on their side. Not only were they able to drop in on him at any hour and smoke a few joints and listen to Dylan, but he actually liked them in print. Although he also wrote that they were "ignorant," that was nothing next to all the heinous things reporters who had never met them were willing to say. As one Angel put it, "There's not much good you can write about us, but I don't see where that gives people the right to just make up stuff . . . hell, ain't the truth bad enough for 'em?"

Hunter's *Nation* article appeared on May 17, 1965. It caught the attention of Bernard Shir-Cliff, whose job it was to research trends for Bantam Books, then the world's third-largest paperback publisher (now the largest). In the past few months, Shir-Cliff had read articles on the Angels in *Time, Newsweek, Look,* the *Saturday Evening Post,* the *New York Times,* and a host of other newspapers and magazines. None had the insight and analysis of Hunter's piece.

Shir-Cliff wanted to offer Hunter a book contract. With the *Nation* article in hand, he proposed the offer to Bantam president Ian Ballantine, who had founded the publishing company. Ballantine loved the article and the idea of Hunter writing an insider book about the renegades. "Offer him six thousand dollars and see if that's money enough," said Ballantine.

Within a few weeks of the article's publication, Hunter received more than a dozen letters from editors expressing their admiration for his writing talents and asking him to sent them an outline for a book on the Angels. Shir-Cliff's was the only letter that mentioned money and didn't ask for a proposal first. It was irresistible.

Ballantine, who was in the Bay area on other business, dropped by Hunter's apartment to meet his new author and to discuss the terms of the contract.

Ballantine was on the left side of the political spectrum. His uncle was the late Sox Cummings, the first Editor-in-Chief of Random House, where he worked with noted leftists of the day. Ballantine detected a tone of anarchy in Hunter's letters and thought he might hit it off with the renegade. Under different circumstances that may have been true. But Ballantine was approaching Hunter as a member of the business, a position that immediately put them at odds.

Sandy answered the door when Ballantine knocked and quietly led him into the sunny living room where Hunter was reading the paper. Ballantine immediately sensed that the couple had been fighting before his arrival. Although they tried to cover it by making small talk, Ballantine could see by Sandy's reddened eyes that she had been crying. It was an uncomfortable situation for the publisher, who decided to move on to the contract negotiations as quickly as possible so he could leave and let them work out their problems.

Ballantine told Hunter that he was excited about the Hell's Angels book. So much had been written about them that it would be good to finally have an inside account of the club so people could see what it was really like.

"So you think the book will do pretty good, eh?" Hunter asked, pacing nervously around the publisher in his chair.

"I think it will sell very well," he declared.

"Then maybe it's worth more than six thousand dollars," suggested Hunter.

"I don't know about that," said Ballantine, "but if it makes more than that, you'll get royalties."

What happened next is still puzzling to Ballantine. Hunter

stormed out of the living room and into the bedroom, where he started hitting Sandy. Ballantine didn't know what to do.

"I explained to my grandson when he got to be nine that you don't beat up on women, that's one of the rules," Ballantine recalled later. "It looks like Hunter missed a lesson there somewhere."

Ballantine sat uncomfortably until Hunter returned to the living room, acting as though nothing had happened. Hunter then tried to negotiate a higher advance, but Ballantine, shocked by his behavior, wouldn't budge.

At one point, Ballantine remembers, Hunter asked for a motorcycle. Ballantine turned him down.

"The publisher doesn't have a motorcycle; the authors get no motorcycle," declared Ballantine.

Reluctantly Hunter agreed to the advance, and Ballantine promised to have a contract mailed from New York. The two shook hands and parted on good terms. By the time the meeting was over, Ballantine was convinced that Hunter had immersed himself a little too deeply in his research. "I didn't know if he was a Hell's Angel or was just writing a book about them. All in all, he was remarkably bad behaved."

Using the *Nation* story as a passport, Hunter proceeded with his research. He crossed Bay Bridge and introduced himself to Ralph "Sonny" Barger, the Maximum Leader of the Hell's Angels and the man who told a Hollywood agent who wanted to represent the gang, "Before I see anyone use this death's head to make money, I'll kill the motherfucker."

When Hunter explained that he wanted to write a book, Sonny thought long and out loud about stomping Hunter right then and there as an example to all the vermin in the press who kept lying about the Angels. Then he read the *Nation* piece and, convinced that Hunter was on a mission of truth, decided Hunter could stay.

Suddenly Hunter was absorbed by the Angels. He spent three or four days a week hanging out at Angel bars, listening to war stories, admiring bikes, playing pool, and entertaining some of the San Francisco Angels in his apartment. Sometimes, "to get the juice going" (Hunter's phrase), they lined the windowsill with empty beer bottles and shot them off with a .357 Magnum. The glass and bullets flew out the window.

The Angels unnerved Sandy, who felt their eyes followed her more than she liked. In some of her letters to Hunter's mother, she expressed her fear for Hunter and herself.

Hunter was amazed at how chic the Angels were becoming. Radicals and liberals were treating them like Robin Hood's merry men. They were invited to parties and asked their opinion about things they didn't give a damn about. They were contacted by Hollywood agents and actors.

Fame peaked in November 1965, when a *Saturday Evening Post* cover story hit the newsstands. The cover featured Skip Von Bugening, the Angel who Hunter had witnessed being drummed out of the corps at the DePau, and the story contained a number of unnerving photographs of the Angels and their unbound way of life. It may well have been the most degenerate bunch of photographs ever to run in the *Post*.

The article described a house in Fresno in which the Angels had recently staged a party.

I went into the house and stood in the center of what must have once been the living room. It was hard to tell because I had never seen such utter chaos: Every piece of furniture had been smashed; debris littered the floors—broken glass, torn clothing, empty cans, wine and beer bottles, crockery, boxes.

Every door had been ripped off its hinges, and a large hole gaped where an air conditioner had been torn away and carted off. . . . All the walls had been defaced.

There were many other horrors described in the *Post* story. The reporter was harassed at nearly every turn, threatened by Angels and by that fringe group of people who want to become Angels and are therefore often more dangerous than the real thing.

Hunter was placed in the uncomfortable role of unofficial social director for the Angels by people who knew what he was writing. They thought maybe he could bring a couple of Angels to their party. He told Gene McGarr, "I don't think people get it. These guys aren't intellectuals. They just want to ride bikes, party and fuck. That's a bad combination around the intelligentsia." He described his discomfort with this role in *Hell's Angels*. "I was loath to be responsible for their behavior. Their pre-eminence on so many guest lists made it inevitable that a certain amount of looting, assault and rapine would occur if they took the social whirl at full gallop."

The Angels didn't always show up when he gave them the address of a party. In his opinion, Hunter wrote, the only successful connection he made for them was with the novelist Ken Kesey.

While writing *One Flew Over the Cuckoo's Nest* and working at a mental hospital in Palo Alto, California, Kesey had become an experimental subject hired by the federal government to take psychedelic drugs so they could study their effects on the human mind. For $25 a day he sat in a room and took all the mind-expanding drugs the government gave him. He liked the drugs, but had no fondness for the stark white rooms and the white-coated physicians who kept asking him questions and jotting down answers. Finally he stole a batch of acid and brought it out to his friends. Perhaps because of his intense drug use, he decided writing was an archaic form of communication and spent his royalties on film equipment and an old school bus to drive across the country and make a movie. He dubbed the school bus "Furthur" and his followers "the Merry Band of Pranksters."

After swirling the bus with many colors of paint, Kesey and the Pranksters drove to New York for the 1964 World's Fair; they shot twenty-four hours of sixteen-millimeter film, created hundreds of hours of sound, and consumed countless hits of acid. After Kesey got back to his cabin in La Honda, California, near Stanford University, he began staging public LSD parties that he called "acid tests" in various spots around California and Oregon. The tests typically involved drinking Kool-Aid laced with LSD, listening to the Grateful Dead, and watching hours of the out-of-focus film the Pranksters had shot on their bus trip.

Hunter hooked up with Kesey on a talk show on KQED, the public television station in San Francisco. He admired Kesey's writing and had been to an acid test, and went on the talk show partly because Kesey was going to be there. Also, the topic, "What is the Free Speech Movement?," interested Hunter. Eventually he produced an article on the movement, "Nonstudent Left," which appeared in the *Nation* on September 27, 1965 and was anthologized in *The Great Shark Hunt*.

After the show, they went to a local bar. Hunter realized it was getting to be five o'clock and he had to get to the Box Shop (Frenchy's transmission-repair shop, across from the DePau). Kesey wanted to go, too.

The Angels liked Kesey. They all sat around and smoked joints. "I could see that it was a love affair from the start," said Hunter. Kesey wrote down his address and drew a map on a piece of paper, and invited them out to La Honda for an acid test the next weekend, July 22, 1965.

Hunter documents the Angels' visit to La Honda in *Hell's Angels*.

Outside Kesey's gate was a huge red, white, and blue sign that read, THE MERRY PRANKSTERS WELCOME THE HELL'S ANGELS. Across the deep creek that separated Kesey's house from the main road a row of police cars were parked, their gumball lights flashing. From the other side of the creek, the Pranksters were matching the police, light for light. The stereo was blaring Dylan as Harleys pulled in.

"I kept waiting for terrible things to happen," Hunter said later in an interview. "Then I heard that a gang rape was taking place in one of the little studios near the main house."

There were about twenty people in the studio. The woman was drunk and high, not struggling in any way. Hunter turned on his tape recorder and put it up on a shelf. "There were always four or five participating, sort of like a bunch of cats toying with a mouse. And it wasn't always the Angels. There were academics and Pranksters, too. It was just like a party." Eventually she wanted her husband, who was also in the room watching. "She kind of raised up and said, 'kiss me,' and then he fucked her."

Later Hunter loaned the tape of the gang bang to Tom Wolfe, who recreated the incident vividly in *The Electric Kool-Aid Acid Test*, his nonfiction book about Ken Kesey. Hunter keeps the tape handy and sometimes listens to it late at night. "I'll put it on the tape deck and turn it all the way up," he said. "It's as creepy as hell, but it stays with you because it's the kind of stuff you use when you write. Imagine the peer pressure of it that would cause you to drop your pants in the same room with the Hell's Angels and fuck the wife of somebody who is there in the room. Man!"

Kesey had offered Hunter acid earlier in the night and he'd turned it down. After the gang bang, he walked up to Kesey and said, "All right, whatever it is, give it to me." Kesey gave him about 400 micrograms. "I kept waiting for horrible things to happen, but they didn't. And I had a wonderful time. I was highly pleased that I had brought up the bottom of my barrel, and I wasn't violent at all."

The Angels first brush with acid that night at Kesey's was described first-person by Frank Reynolds, the secretary of the Angels, in his autobiography, *Freewheelin' Frank*.

I was attracted to Hunter Thompson's wife. That's the guy who wrote the book *Hell's Angels*—he was there. But it makes a difference how I was attracted to her. I was attracted to the beauty of a woman for the first time . . .

I fell magically in love with the words that were being sung. These strange words that meant so much. It was a new feeling that I'd never felt before or ever thought of feeling . . .

My mind was stripped completely. I felt as though I had been reborn and later I know I was.

After that first night, word of Kesey's bottomless stash of LSD and endless hospitality spread to other chapters of the cycle gang. Soon the winding forest roads of La Honda thundered with bikers heading toward the sign marking Kesey's ranch, the one that read, "No Turn Left Unstoned." There these self-confessed violent persons ate acid and became unusually tranquil.

The Angels loved this forest retreat. It was like a private club, where no cops were allowed. Hunter wrote in *Hell's Angels* a comment he heard from an Angel named Pete: "Man, this is nothing but a goddamn wonderful scene. We didn't know what to expect when we came here, but it turned out just fine. This time it's all ha-ha, not thump-thump."

They loved Kesey too. He displayed a fascination with the underbelly of society. He brushed with the law so much, he was becoming an outlaw in his own right. "If society wants me to be an outlaw, then I'll be an outlaw and a damned good one," he told a reporter. "That's something people need. People at all times need outlaws."

The Angels met a steady stream of the Bay area's luminaries at Kesey's place. LSD guru Richard Alpert made frequent trips up the hill from his Palo Alto residence. Poet Allen Ginsberg came and became an immediate fan of the biker outlaws, immortalizing them in several poems.

LSD became the drug of choice among Angels, and "Acid Angels" could be seen at almost every Angel hangout in Northern California. They were the Angels with the vacant stare that gave the distinct sense nobody was home. Whey they weren't tripping, they spoke almost constantly about LSD, comparing its effects the way connoisseurs compare fine wines and trading addresses of sources outside of La Honda. Some of the more business-minded even started a distribution network.

Hunter became quite an acid-eater himself. He liked to take LSD with the Angels, whom he considered "too ignorant to know what to expect, and too wild to care. They just swallowed the stuff and hung on. . . ."

Gene McGarr, who had come in from New York to work on a film project, remembers a night the two of them went out on the town and found themselves standing at the bar of The Matrix, a hip place where the evening's entertainment was The Jefferson Airplane, on the cusp of making it big. McGarr and Hunter had just ordered drinks when an unkempt man carrying a backpack sat on a stool next to them. The man asked the bartender, "Do you have a place where I can cook?" "Just go in the back," said the bartender, pointing to a door behind the bar.

Shortly thereafter, the man came out with a shot glass full of homemade liquid LSD which the bartender mixed with some fruit juice. Word spread through the bar, and soon everyone was loaded, including the band. People who came in late promptly left because of the odd behavior of the patrons, who were crying and laughing, talking to chairs, or dancing with imaginary partners. Band members forgot where they were in a song, or went off on riffs that made sense only to them. Grace Slick was lying on her back moaning into the microphone.

On another occasion, Hunter, McGarr, and another friend went to watch the Forty-Niners play football at Kezar Stadium. Just before walking through the turnstiles, they each swallowed a capsule of acid. From the moment the game started, they were howling and shrieking. By halftime, after they had polished off a fifth of Jack Daniels and smoked a joint, the seats around them had cleared out, so the people closest to them were at least three rows away. "Fuck 'em if they can't take it," said Hunter. "Tear their eyeballs out!" he shouted at the players. "Maim the fuckers!"

When the game ended, the three weren't ready to call it a day, so Hunter suggested they go to Savage Henry's house. A drug dealer of some note, Henry was a pleasant man who lived in the Castro district with his stunning schoolteacher wife. Their house was a beautifully remodelled Victorian.

At about eight o'clock at night, the stoned trio knocked on Henry's door. Henry was already in his bathrobe, but was glad to see a group that he considered among his best clientele. He took them to the kitchen and heated the griddle on his gas stove. While it was getting good and hot, he took a sharp knife out of the drawer and chopped hashish on a bread board. Then he gave Hunter a metal funnel and told him to stand over the hot griddle and suck in the smoke as he sprinkled hash on the surface. Hunter took a few hits and passed the funnel to McGarr. "It was like a heroin suppository," remembers McGarr. "We were now high on LSD, Jack Daniels, marijuana and hash."

Henry produced some opium balls, which they swallowed like

chocolate bonbons. Then he mixed a few drinks "to help with the digestion." When he noticed they were about to crash, he chopped a few lines of cocaine for them to snort. McGarr started to go crazy. He told Henry that he was the biggest piece of shit that ever lived, and tried to take away Henry's wife. Hunter and their other friend couldn't coax McGarr out the door. Finally they abandoned McGarr.

After leaving Henry's, Hunter began to experience heart palpitations. He had the horrible feeling that he was going to die. With painstaking slowness, because the two were too loaded to drive fast, they made it to the emergency room of the medical center. In an examining room, Hunter gave a complete rundown of the night's festivities. "You look okay," said the doctor. "And you're heart's strong."

"Yeah, but I feel like shit," declared Hunter. "Give me a shot. Any shot."

The doctor shrugged and soon a nurse came back into the room with a loaded syringe. "Who gets it?" she asked.

Suddenly the friend jumped up and dropped his pants. "It's for me! It's for me!"

Hunter was writing at a fast clip. Shir-Cliff remembers the manuscript arriving thirty to sixty pages at a time, typed on paper that looked yellow, like it had been around for a couple of years.

"It had a lot of juice," said Shir-Cliff. "I would read it immediately and send back a letter, usually of praise. The stuff that was coming in was a little disorganized, but I could see what was going on, and I liked what I saw."

Random House had agreed to publish a hardcover version of the book before Bantam's paperback. Random House editor Jim Silberman paid Bantam $3,000, half of which was sent to Hunter, who used it to buy a BSA 650 motorcycle.

As Hunter recounts in *Hell's Angels,* within three weeks of owning the cycle, he was arrested three times and was threatened with the loss of his California driver's license. Hunter found his sudden bad driving record puzzling. He considered himself a good driver, and had received only two moving violations in twelve years. "Are the cops around here blind?" he asked McGarr. "Can't they tell a BSA from a Harley?"

Hunter's Angel friends had a laugh about that one. "Of course they can tell the difference," said Tiny. "They're just fucking with you because you have a bike. If you really want to get them all over you, wear some colors. They'll stick to you like fuckin' fly paper."

Although all cyclists were equal in the eyes of the law, not all cycles were equal in the eyes of the Angels. Hunter was scorned and ridiculed for buying a BSA. The Angels considered it just one step up from a Honda, and Hondas were a step below garbage. When he parked his cycle by the Box Shop or in front of the El Adobe Bar in Oakland, he got bad comments from the Angels.

Still, the cycle was an integral part of his writing. He liked to ride it late at night when he had a head full of acid and needed to get some adrenaline going. He told a reporter years later, "Those nights were like looking out the window and suddenly realizing that you could walk on air. It was a very high feeling."

Along with the cycle, benzedrine was an integral part of Hunter's writing routine. The deadline for the book was approaching, and he was in constant fear of missing it. "Speed became his savior," said McGarr, "a real necessity. To get his ass off the ground, he would take some speed."

During one of his rides, speeding down a backstreet with actor John Tibeau on the back, he hit some railroad tracks at an angle and flipped the bike. When he came to, Tibeau was at the side of the road clutching a broken leg. Hunter had a stream of blood running down his face and a good portion of his scalp was torn away from his skull. The BSA was badly damaged.

Hunter spent several days in the hospital, a stay made more miserable by threats from Tibeau that he was going to sue for damages. In a panic for money, Hunter had Sandy write to Ballantine and ask for an advance. The publisher politely declined, offering his sympathy and hopes for a rapid recovery.

A few weeks later, Ballantine was in San Francisco and stopped by to visit Hunter. This time the scene was entirely different. Despite the refusal of more funds, Hunter was gracious. Joe Hudson was there, visiting for the day from Big Sur. Soon the three were drinking and telling stories. As the afternoon wore on, Ballantine became more and more sympathetic to the plight of his spirited writer. Before closing time in New York he called his treasurer and had him wire $3,000 to Hunter.

"We'll never get a book from you, Thompson," said Ballantine. "But I had a wonderful time."

One thing that Kesey, Ginsberg, and all the hopeful radicals seemed to forget was that the Hell's Angels were anti-Communist. Although they weren't opposed to dropping acid with hippies and frolicking in the forest with their long-haired women, opposition to war was out of the question for most of them.

Hunter knew how the Angels felt about Vietnam. No matter what you called them, and there were many things they could be called, the Angels were not unpatriotic. Like the Congress of the United States or the Mafia, they believed in the superiority of the American system over all others because it allowed them to live free and wild with few restraints.

On October 16, 1965, when 15,000 protesters marched from the Berkeley campus toward the Oakland Army Terminal, where men and war goods were shipped to Southeast Asia, Hunter predicted the Angels would strut their patriotism and make the demonstration violent. "I guarantee there's going to be some head cracking," he said. With Paul Semonin, he approached the scene from the Oakland side. A sea of protesters walked towards hundreds of Oakland police, whose helmets, riot sticks, and stern demeanor made it clear that the march was going to stop right there. As the marchers closed the gap, a small group of Angels pushed through the crowd and past the policemen. The renegades punched protesters, tore up signs, and broke a policeman's leg before they were finally subdued by the police.

The leftists were shocked and tried to dismiss the well-planned attack as a mistake. But Hunter knew the Angels better than any outsider and, as far as he was concerned, it was the leftists, not the Angels, who just didn't get it. "These guys are thugs," he told Semonin. "They think all of these protesters are just gutless, fucking cowards."

Another march on the Oakland Army Terminal was planned for November 20, and frantic efforts were made to get the Angels to switch sides. Members of the Vietnam Day Committee, a radical union united to protest the war, met with the Angels a number of times. Barger loved the attention, but when it came time to vote, he was thumbs down on supporting the protesters.

Then Ken Kesey and Allen Ginsberg met at Barger's house. Kesey argued eloquently on behalf of the New Left and Ginsberg had the entire group chanting the Buddhist Prajnaparamita Sutra. Joan Baez and Bob Dylan records were played and acid was dropped.

"The day before the march," recounted Hunter in *Hell's Angels*, "the Angels called a press conference to announce they would not man the barricades." Sonny Barger further shocked the assembled press by distributing a telegram that was being sent to President Lyndon B. Johnson:

> On behalf of myself and my associates I volunteer a group of loyal Americans for behind the lines duty in Viet Nam. We feel that a crack group of trained gorrillas (sic) would demoralize the Viet Cong and advance the cause of freedom. We are available for training and duty immediately.

The President declined Barger's offer and continued to fight the war without the Angel volunteers.

Some of the Angels resented Hunter's presence. During one meeting at the DePau, Frank Reynolds, the club's secretary, got drunk and became surly with Hunter. "Goddamnit," he said angrily, "I should have written a book, not you."

"I agree," said Hunter, taken aback by the anger in Frank's voice. "Shit, you've been here for ten years, you should have written it." (Frank's autobiography, *Freewheelin' Frank: Secretary of the Angels*, came out after Hunter's book.)

When Hunter first started hanging out with the gang, the issue was not money, only truth. "We don't ask for nothing but the truth," Barger told him. After Hunter had hung out with them for a year, the tune had changed.

Hunter realized that the end was near when one of the Angels cornered him at an Angel hangout and threatened to "turnout" Sandy if money wasn't paid. "You have a tasty little mama," he threatened. "We've all noticed her so I wouldn't piss us off if I was you."

After that threat Hunter knew his travels with the Angels were about to end. He just didn't know when or how.

The stomping of Hunter S. Thompson, described at the end of

Hell's Angels, was not, to the Angels, a significant event at the 1966 Labor Day bash at Russian River. In Frank's detailed account of that weekend, there is no mention of the episode, just a stream-of-consciousness rap about sex orgies with Angel mamas and civilians, swilling wine, belching, smoking dope, dropping acid, and pissing on society for not understanding the Angel way of life.

Frank's account does relate a story that reveals the Angel mindset toward outsiders. The names and other details are different, but this story is very much about Hunter and those like him who think they can fit in with the Angels for any period of time.

At the Luau Bar in Oakland one time three men of Spanish tongue were talking to Frip, also Spanish and a member. He disagreed with something they said and threw a right cross, which started an avalanche of angry Angels coming to his aid and kicking the shit out of the three men. Right or wrong we are right. . . . If ever they turn into another bar of ours, they'll be a lot wiser or else they'll leave quickly.

Hunter's situation was very much like the one in Frank's story. He had driven his car to the bash with the intention of taking some pictures for the book. He got stoned and drunk, and fell into an argument about which bike was faster, the Harley or the BSA. He recalled, "All of a sudden this little weasel hit me in the face. I didn't want to fight, so I grabbed him and pinned his arms to his own body. He started to scream like some fucking banshee and I turned to this other Angel and started laughing. Real funny. That was another rule I violated. If you fight one Angel, you fight them all.

"The next thing I knew there were a bunch of Angels standing in a circle around me just stomping me with their boots. I looked up and there was one with a big rock, ready to bring it down on my head.

"That was when Tiny stopped everyone. God bless him. He grabbed the rock and said, 'He's had enough.'

"I didn't even thank Tiny. I just stumbled into my car and started driving to the nearest emergency room, about fifty miles away. In the rear-view mirror I could see that my face was a mess and my rib hurt like hell, but . . . as stompings go, it wasn't much worse than falling down the stairs."

Hunter says he never got medical help, but his broken nose hurt so bad that he pulled off the road and decided to set it himself. He drank a beer to kill the pain and then turned on the dome light. Using the rearview mirror, he popped the bones back into place.

As he told *Playboy* in a 1974 interview, "I couldn't breathe for about a year, and people thought I was a coke freak before I actually was, but I think I did a pretty good job."

Although Hunter had been writing for the last six months, he was only about two-thirds of the way through. This was his first book and he actually believed that he had to make the deadline, which was only a few weeks away. As he said in the 1974 *Playboy* interview, "There's no avoiding it—not even when you have a fine full-bore story like the Angels that's still running . . . so one day you just don't appear at the El Adobe bar anymore: you shut the door, paint the windows black, rent an electric typewriter and become the monster you always were—the writer."

Besides the deadline, other problems added to Hunter's mood of panic. Juan was just a baby, and no amount of motherly attention could keep him quiet all the time. The rent was two months overdue, and the Chinese landlord badgered them constantly with the news that, unless the rent was paid, they would be evicted.

Other interruptions included Frenchy, Terry the Tramp, or other Angels who dropped by with speed, stolen cases of beer, and girls to read pages of the book. It made Hunter nervous when they did that. Many of the things he had to say weren't very complimentary, and he kept expecting his harsh words to settle into their thick skulls and a rain of violence to come down on his. But no matter how much they read of the manuscript, and they read a lot, they never seemed to get it. "They didn't really believe I was actually writing a book," said Hunter. "They were always strangely detached." The only objection he got was from Terry, who asked him to remove the word "sodomy" from the text because it would offend his mother.

Finally Hunter could tolerate no more interruptions. He packed up his electric typewriter, four quarts of Wild Turkey, and a load of speed and drove up the coast highway in his English Ford until he found a motel that seemed peaceful. Then he burrowed in for four straight days of work, coming out only for an infrequent McDonald's hamburger. After a hundred hours of work, the first draft was finally done.

The book was a big hit with the New York editors. Bernard Shir-Cliff and Jim Silberman thought it would be a minor classic, if not a bestseller. Silberman saw in Hunter's manuscript a sense of outrage at society that few could yet articulate so well. With help from Shir-Cliff, he convinced Hunter to come to New York City to work out the kinks in the book and think of a sequel.

Hunter arrived in New York in the Spring of 1967. Silberman had him booked in the Delmonico, an Upper East Side residential hotel. From there, they said, he could walk or catch a cab to Random House and work on the manuscript. There was no problem with the writing, they assured him. The only thing they wanted to do was reorganize some sections of the book to make it more comprehensible. "We have a winner here," Shir-Cliff said.

"We just want to polish it up and give it the high gloss it deserves."

The two editors met Hunter at Pete's Tavern in Gramercy Park. Pete's is a dark, wood-paneled place with the literary distinction of being the bar in which O'Henry drank himself to death.

When the editors walked into the bar at five o'clock, the place was jammed. Neither had ever seen Hunter. They began scanning the room for someone who looked like a Hell's Angel or a San Francisco hippie. Shir-Cliff's eyes settled on a lean man wearing sunglasses, quite young, but already going bald. The man was wearing a waist-length zipper jacket and had what looked to be a lumberjack shirt underneath it. In front of him was a double Wild Turkey, the glass filled to the brim with ice. With two fingers he held a cigarette holder to his lips, drawing smoke slowly and deliberately into his mouth. He looked like a spring wound tightly.

"There's our man," Shir-Cliff said, rounding the bar. He was right.

The three took a booth and began drinking. It was dinnertime, so Shir-Cliff and Silberman ordered food from the menu. Hunter refused. As the editors ate heartily, Hunter ordered more Wild Turkey, drinking at a rapid clip.

Shir-Cliff doesn't remember much of the conversation that night. He remembers being intrigued at the image Hunter projected. Although this was Hunter's first shot at the big time after years of being a journeyman journalist, he did not seem impressed to be holding court with top New York editors. When they talked about their enthusiasm for the book, he simply shrugged. "He was very cool," said Shir-Cliff. "We kept saying that this was going to be a big break for him, but for him it was no big deal. 'We'll see,' he said in that low and staccato way of talking. 'We'll see.'"

After about four hours of talk, the editors decided to call it a night. Shir-Cliff picked up the tab and was shocked that Hunter's bar tab was nearly seventy dollars. At about three dollars a drink, that totaled more than twenty drinks.

Amazing, thought Shir-Cliff as he watched Hunter walk into the night. Twenty double Wild Turkeys in four hours and he can still walk a straight line.

Over the next week, the three met several times in Silberman's office. They dealt with some of the structural problems of *Hell's Angels*, but those were easy and were handled mainly by one of Silberman's assistants. What the editors really wanted to figure out was an encore.

Many possible options were considered. The hippie movement came and went quickly as a topic that lacked the necessary drama in Hunter's eyes. The idea of sending him to Vietnam for some front-lines reporting got an almost immediate thumbs down. The same was true for sending him to Africa to join mercenary forces fighting a third-world government. "Too dangerous," he said. Writing about politics came up. "Not interesting enough," he said.

"We would have these three hour meetings where we would knock around ideas that would then just sort of fade away," said Shir-Cliff.

The one idea that didn't fade away was the one where Hunter would write about the death of the American dream. Exactly what this meant was unclear. Instead of a "one subject" book like *Hell's Angels*, Hunter said, this would be a "theme" book in which a number of different subjects related to popular culture would be dissected by his outrage. The editors were willing to take a chance and sign him to a contract. But in the end he decided to wait until a more solid idea came along.

"He could never really get a handle on the idea," said Shir-Cliff. "I don't think he wanted to try another big book like *Hell's Angels*. When he started that book he didn't know where it was going to go and I think that scared him." A theme like the death of the

American dream could go in a million different directions or it could shatter in as many different pieces. "Plus," said Shir-Cliff, "he demonstrated such a special palette in *Hell's Angels* for handling these wild and outrageous characters. What do you do for an encore?"

After a few days of editorial go-rounds, Shir-Cliff noticed that their star writer was getting edgy. He didn't like some of the changes suggested for the book and objected in an uncivil fashion. He didn't like the editorial idea meetings. "He didn't want to be hassled," said Shir-Cliff. "He just wanted to go home."

Hunter had arrived at the hotel with two duffle bags, one containing clothing, pharmaceuticals, and a .357 Magnum pistol (these were the days before airport X-ray machines), while in the other was an eight-foot snake. He was snake-sitting for a friend and Sandy didn't want to take care of the snake while he was gone, so he took it with him.

One afternoon he returned to his hotel room to find the lobby in chaos. A frightened maid was clutching her breasts and talking to police, who kept glancing over her shoulder at something on the ground. Other people were standing around, so Hunter had to push through to see what the attraction was.

There, stretched out on the floor and lying on a bedsheet, was Hunter's snake. Blood marked the spot where a bellhop had beaten it to death with a vacuum-cleaner tube.

Hunter blew up. The maid had no business reporting the snake and the hotel had no business killing it, he yelled. They had destroyed personal property and he was going to sue for damages.

The hotel said they catered to an upscale clientele and were not in the habit of letting reptiles stay in their facilities.

With that, Hunter moved out of the hotel. The next day he flew back to California.

Hell's Angels: A Strange and Terrible Saga was published in

March 1967 to generally rave reviews. *Newsweek* magazine gave the book two pages, calling Hunter "a serious social scanner who is not afraid to swing." The *New Yorker,* in its typically understated fashion, said: "His book, for all its uninhibited tone and its sardonic humor, is a thoughtful piece of work."

New Republic enthused, "Thompson's fascinating invocation to, evocation *of,* and reportage *about* the Hell's Angels . . . is certainly the most informative, thorough, and vividly written account of this phenomenon yet to appear." The reviewer says the book has "the cranky peevishness" of some of George Orwell's work, as well as a "Rimbaud delirium of spirit." All of which leads to the conclusion that "Hunter S. Thompson is a writer whose career is worth watching."

United Press International called him "an honest reporter" whose book's "violent episodes . . . have an impact reminiscent of the old master, Hemingway."

The *New York Times Book Review* did not review the book, but they did include it on their "New and Recommended" list, next to a brief story about Hunter, who was in town for a press tour. "I've a lot in common with the Angels, the main difference being I've got a gimmick," they quoted him as saying about his writing. The article's writer went on to give his impression of the author:

A tall man of 26, he was wearing corduroy pants, normal, but also was wearing a tie in deference to New York's quaint restaurant customs. Like the Angels, he likes fast motorcycles; like them, he gives the impression of enjoying a certain amount of violence. When here, he was a young man beset. . . . When he was here for the usual TV and radio appearances, Random House had sold out the first printing and there weren't to be more books for a week or so, leaving an angry young man to discuss an unavailable product.

Perhaps the least complimentary review was published in a new freak magazine from San Francisco, *Rolling Stone*. The reviewer, John Grissim, Jr., was less than enthusiastic about Hunter's writing and reporting abilities:

> On the whole Thompson does ample justice to his subject, despite his failure to really get inside the character of the Angels. While his descriptions of their behavior are profuse, they nevertheless have a superficial quality to them, making it difficult to draw any firm conclusions.

Hell's Angels sold about forty thousand copies in hardcover, making it a minor bestseller in 1967. The paperback was published in 1968 and, as of September 1988, had gone through twenty-nine printings, selling approximately two million copies.

When asked by a UPI reporter what he planned to write next, Hunter said, "I'd like to do a book on people who play polo and give me a lot of free booze. I got tired of living in that Hell's Angels' world . . . and fooling around in a lot of crummy bars. . . ."

5

THE DEATH OF THE AMERICAN DREAM (1967-1972)

Hunter was ready to leave San Francisco. Haight-Ashbury had lost its neighborhood feel. An influx of hippies from around the world had descended on the area, and the summer of 1967, called "The Summer of Love," promised mayhem. The Diggers, one of many groups espousing alternative lifestyles, estimated that between 50,000 and 200,000 newcomers would flow into San Francisco to find out what the hip life was all about. The Diggers wanted to set up a tentmakers' assemblage so many of these people could be housed in a tent city on Mount Tamalpais "or anywhere." Hunter thought that "anywhere" might be on his doorstep.

Hunter later described this scene in "The Battle of Aspen," published in *Rolling Stone* on October 1, 1970, and anthologized as "Freak Power in the Rockies" in *The Great Shark Hunt.*

I lived a block above Haight Street for two years but by the end of '66 the whole neighborhood had become a cop-magnet and a bad sideshow. Between the narcs and the psychedelic hustlers, there was not much room to live.

What happened in the Haight echoed earlier scenes in North Beach and the Village . . . and it proved, once again, the basic futility of seizing turf you can't control. The pattern never varies; a low-rent area suddenly blooms new and loose and human—and then fashionable . . . expense-account tastes drive local rents and street prices out of reach of the original settlers . . . who are forced, once again, to move on.

Hunter's English Ford had finally fallen apart, the cracking of a cylinder head signaling its inevitable demise. He bought a new Saab and tried to sell the Ford. When he received no offers, he decided on a more theatrical method of auto disposal. With Sandy and Juan following in the Saab, he drove the Ford to Big Sur.

"I took it down to a cliff in Big Sur and soaked the whole interior with ten gallons of gasoline, then executed the fucker with six shots from a .44 magnum in the engine block at point-blank range," he told a *Playboy* reporter. "After that we rolled it off the cliff—the radio going, lights on, everything going—and at the last minute, we threw a burning towel in. The explosion was ungodly; it almost blew us into the ocean. I had no idea what ten gallons of gas in an English Ford could do."

With the car a mass of twisted, burning metal on the lip of the Pacific Ocean, Hunter was ready to get out of California. They returned to the Haight-Ashbury apartment. After loading boxes into a trailer attached to the back of the Saab, they set out for New York. There, said Hunter, he planned to "whoop it up like Fitzgerald, be a famous writer."

They stopped when they hit Aspen. Like the Haight of a few years before, Aspen was in one of those periods of transition, a golden moment if you were looking for "freaks, heads, fun-hogs and weird night-people of every description." There they found people like themselves who were dissatisfied with the "hip" scenes around the country and were heading an exodus to rural communities.

Silver mining had spurred the boom that built the town in 1879. In the early sixties, Billy Janss began a new boom when a planned a ski area called Snowmass-at-Aspen, later changed to Snowmass Resort.

Aspen had always lured ski bums. During World War II, skiers from the army's Tenth Mountain Division were trained in nearby Leadville. Many of them returned after the war to live in Aspen as the town's first ski bums. A ski lift was built in 1946, and many more skiers came in the fifties, when Aspen had the reputation of being the place to live if you wanted to be a ski racer or just dress like one.

The ski scene Janss and his brothers envisioned was different. It included condos, smoothed-down ski slopes and efficient lifts as well as golf courses, tennis courts, restaurants, and bars. The Janss family sold most of their interest in Snowmass and went on to develop the Sun Valley ski resort in Idaho. But the Aspen ski village was built and so were others. Soon tourism was the main source of revenue for the tiny town.

Ted Kennedy and his family hung out there, as did other celebrities, bringing national attention to the beauty of the Rockies and the manicured ski slopes of Aspen. But land values had not yet shot up to the point where only stars and moguls could afford to buy acreage. And nobody was buying land or houses in Woody Creek, about five miles northwest of Aspen.

Hunter bought his house and 110 acres for a little more than $75,000. The arrangement was a lease with an option to buy, so he didn't have to part with a down payment. The man who sold it was a former public relations man for the San Francisco police department. He liked Hunter and understood why he was fleeing San Francisco. Almost everyone around Aspen was a refugee from someplace. "Nothing began in Aspen," wrote one long-time resident, Peggy Clifford, in her book *To Aspen and Back*. "It begins someplace else and migrates here."

Hunter had first heard about Aspen from Paul Semonin, who had gone there after their cross-country trip, when Hunter was in Big Sur. Semonin's letters had described a mountain paradise filled with great bars and young people living cheaply outside the mainstream. Semonin bought a miner's cabin off the main slope for $500. He was working as a waiter while he wrote his memoirs, *The Collected Thoughts of a Tramp Thinker*, which to date has not been published.

Semonin had been particularly intrigued by a peculiar enterprise known as the Aspen Institute for Humanistic Studies, a mountain think tank founded by Walter Paepcke as a place for nurturing "the whole of man," his intellectual and physical being. Paepcke convinced intellectuals like Albert Schweitzer and Thornton Wilder to come, and soon others followed.

Hunter first visited Aspen in the fall of 1961. He was delivering a car to its owner, an interior decorator. The car roof was loaded with bamboo bird cages; in the backseat, Hunter's Doberman Agar squirmed inside the huge dog carrier Hunter was going to use to transport the dog back with him by train to San Francisco; in the front seat were a few more bird cages that didn't fit on the roof and a large jug of red wine to keep Hunter company.

Semonin was out of town, so Hunter looked up Semonin's friend Peggy Clifford, who owned a bookstore. Clifford took in the exhausted Hunter and his nervous pet and fed them both. Then she and Hunter drove the car to its owner.

The designer invited the two in and gave them drinks. But instead of paying Hunter his $50 so they could be on their way, she went back to playing cards with her bridge club. Hunter and Clifford waited impatiently as the woman ignored them. "Jesus," said Hunter. "Semonin's dream looks like the Louisville Country Club."

In the morning, Clifford drove Hunter out to see Semonin's cabin. He liked the cabin and its rustic setting, but didn't seem overwhelmed. That afternoon Clifford drove him to the train station in Glenwood Springs, and he went back to San Francisco.

Two years later, in 1963, when he was traveling west after his stint in South America, he and Sandy moved into temporary quarters in Woody Creek while he wrote three pieces on the Aspen scene for the *Observer*. One story dealt with a union dispute in which the ski patrol was striking for a salary raise that would pay them $2.30 an hour, up from $1.75. Another concerned deer-hunting season and was datelined Woody Creek. The third was about the Aspen Institute, specifically their executive program, where "the unwashed American businessman" got together with the likes of Robert Kennedy, Dr. Jonas Salk, and Eric Sevareid to discuss topics like the relevance of Good and Evil to modern man and mankind's possible spiritual links to Socrates.

This time Hunter found an Aspen that was more to his liking. He went to a jazz party at the Jerome Hotel, an Aspen landmark built by the president of Macy's department store in the 1890s. A man named Dick Gibson had rented the dining room and charged several hundred people $25 each for a weekend of jazz. The hall was jammed with a cross section of Aspen. Dinner jackets, minks, and evening gowns mixed with tweeds, leather jackets, and blue jeans. The audience egged the musicians on with shouts and applause.

Hunter, Semonin, and Peggy Clifford stayed until closing at two in the morning, and then came back for the breakfast show, drinking Bloody Marys. An elegant piano player named Ralph Sutton led Clifford to later write that "he contained orchestras in his hand, more chords and notes than ever existed before."

Late in the afternoon, when the jazz show was over, the three left the Jerome, drunk and spent. It was a beautiful day outside, crisp and rejuvenating to the spirit. "Man, it doesn't get much better than this," approved Hunter.

That had been over four years ago. Now Hunter was back. He could walk naked on the porch of his mountain house, take a leak on the porch in a blue toilet bowl with a palm tree growing out of it, and squeeze off a few .44 slugs at some gongs mounted on the hillside. He could chew mescaline and turn up the stereo to one hundred decibels without pissing off the neighbors or having a billy club rapped on his door. This was the hillbilly life he had always wanted.

Offers to write were coming to him from everywhere. He got letters from *Playboy, Esquire, Harpers, Pageant,* the *Saturday Evening Post,* all anxious for more of the electricity they saw in *Hell's Angels.*

The problem was that his style wasn't right for everybody. For example, *Playboy* assigned him a piece on Jean-Claude Killy, an Olympic skier turned Chevy pitchman. *Playboy* rejected the article; an editor fumed in a memo, "Thompson's ugly, stupid arrogance is an insult to everything we stand for." The piece eventually ran as "The Temptations of Jean-Claude Killy," in March 1970 in *Scanlan's Monthly,* a magazine coedited by Warren Hinckle.

Hinckle had first met Hunter in San Francisco in 1967. At that time he was editing *Ramparts,* a leftist magazine similar to *Scanlan's.* In the course of its five-year history, *Ramparts* took on the CIA, hippies, rock music, the FBI, corporations, Black Panthers, and Richard Nixon. After reading the galleys of *Hell's Angels,* Hinckle saw in Hunter a kindred spirit. He invited Hunter to the office for a visit.

Hunter arrived carrying a knapsack. He tossed the sack onto

Hinckle's couch and the two went out drinking. The office monkey, named "Henry Luce," escaped from his cage and got into the bottles of pills in Hunter's sack. Hunter and Hinckle returned to find the monkey screeching at the top of his lungs and leaping all over the office. Hunter flew into a drunken rage and chased the monkey around, but couldn't catch him. After a few days the monkey turned back into the good old conservative Henry Luce everyone knew and loved.

Another magazine that liked Hunter's style was *Pageant*. The editors there assigned him a piece on the 1968 political rebirth of Richard Nixon. Hunter was supposed to meet the Nixon entourage in New Hampshire and spend a few days researching a profile. The idea intrigued Hunter, who thought of Nixon as "just another sad old geek limping back into politics for another beating." "Presenting: The Richard Nixon Doll," the story of Hunter's encounter with Nixon, appeared in the July 1968 *Pageant*.

Hunter wrote how he had to beg hard for an interview with Nixon. Only after George Romney bailed out the night before the election, leaving Nixon a virtual shoe-in, did Ray Price pluck Hunter out of the press corps and offer to let him make the hour-and-a-half trip to the airport where Nixon's private jet was waiting. Nixon wanted to relax, said Price, he didn't want to talk of Vietnam or campus riots; he wanted to talk about football, and Hunter was the only person in the press corps who seemed to know anything about football. "If you mention anything else," warned Price, "you'll be hitchhiking back to Manchester."

Hunter agreed and kept his word. They talked only about football all the way to the airport, where they drove onto the runway and next to the Lear jet that was taking the future president to his Key Biscayne home. Like old friends, the two shook hands. "Nice to talk to you," said Nixon.

"You too," said Hunter.

As Nixon walked toward the plane, Hunter reached into his pocket for a cigarette. He was in the midst of lighting it when he was tackled from the side, his cigarette lighter ripped from his hands.

"I thought they had mistaken me for an assassin and they mistook the lighter for some kind of weapon," said Hunter. "But the Secret Service agent who tackled me helped me up and began apologizing very quickly. It turned out they were fueling the plane and I was standing just a few feet from the gas tank. I could have blown the fucker up and saved this nation a lot of trouble."

Nixon had witnessed the whole episode from the door of the plane. When he saw Hunter get up, he waved and stepped inside.

Hunter's brush with presidential politics intrigued him. On June 5, 1968, he and a friend were watching the coverage of the California primaries at Peggy Clifford's house. Late that night, Bobby Kennedy was assassinated. Although Hunter had been away from the screen at the moment when it happened, he felt he had witnessed the death of the American dream on television. In hopes of witnessing the death of the American dream firsthand, Hunter decided to attend the Democratic National Convention in Chicago in August.

The political left, with its large contingent of draft-aged students, had vowed to take a stand against the Vietnam war at the convention. Mayor Richard Daley swore that the protesters would not be allowed to use his city for their demonstrations. Hunter asked Paul Semonin to go with him, but Semonin declined. Then he tried to get Gene McGarr, who was busy with his job. He went to see the death of the American dream alone. For weeks afterward, he couldn't talk about what happened in Chicago without crying.

He was waiting with other members of the press to get into the convention hall when he observed a crowd of demonstrators advancing against a line of policemen at the corner of Michigan and

Balboa. Suddenly the police attacked with billy clubs. He found himself surrounded by frantic demonstrators, desperate to flee from a police force run amok. Although his press credentials were prominently displayed on his chest, they seemed not to protect him but to mark him for a special beating. He was hit in the stomach by one of the long riot clubs and could have suffered a serious head injury had he not been wearing a motorcycle helmet that he decided to take with him at the last minute. Finally, he was pushed through a plate glass window. That saved him further beating as the police continued to sweep the streets.

What happened in Chicago made him see the futility in national politics, and also the need to protect his own turf. "First, you change a small town," he concluded.

When he returned to Aspen, he saw the town through newly political eyes. He wrote, "I went to the Democratic Convention as a journalist, and returned a raving beast." He said the convention had "permanently altered my brain chemistry."

Developers were planning to replace Aspen's quaint old houses and country roads with a four-lane highway and condominiums. They wanted to create a tourist haven for the rich, and seemingly didn't care what the locals thought. Hunter proposed a new political party called Freak Power. Its aim, as reviewed by Hunter in "The Battle of Aspen" in the October 1, 1970 *Rolling Stone*, was to "create a town where people could live like human beings, instead of slaves to some bogus sense of Progress that is driving us all mad."

A candidate chosen by the "powermongers" was running unopposed for mayor. Hunter got together with a couple of other locals and began looking for someone to run against him. After a brief search, they found a "weird enough" possibility in Joe Edwards, a local attorney. A year earlier, Edwards had sued the city on behalf of two longhairs who claimed the city had discriminated against them with an arrest for vagrancy. "Vagrancy" and "blocking the sidewalk" were common charges against hippies; the developers urged the police to make arrests, and each charge carried a ninety-day jail sentence and a $200 fine. Edwards won the suit and now hippies roamed unmolested.

Hunter and two other members of the party got together with Edwards to drink beer in the lobby of the Jerome Hotel. Hunter saw right away that Edwards could lure the female vote. He was slim and handsome, with well-coifed hair and a Clark Gable mustache. He was pleasant yet skeptical as he listened to Hunter ramble on about the need for a new candidate. "Jesus, Joe," pleaded Hunter, "hundreds of people in this town don't agree with the way this place is being run. But the greedheads are acting like they own this place."

The other two party members, screenwriter Jim Salter (*Downhill Racer*) and housepainter Michael Solheim, were silent through most of the meeting. As they later confessed to Hunter, they felt out of their league trying to convince someone to run for office when they had no idea how to run a campaign. But Hunter had no problem at all. He went on discussing the appeal Edwards would have as a candidate who came out in favor of the old-timers and ranchers and against developers who wanted to chew up the ranches and feed them to tourists. Finally Edwards said, "Fuck it, why not?" and the campaign was launched.

No one in the Freak Power Party knew what they were doing, but they ran a respectable campaign nonetheless. Their platform included a call to replace the streets of Aspen with sod, turn the downtown into grassy malls where only pedestrians were allowed to roam, and turn the policemen into garbage collectors. The main opposition was Eve Homeyer, a Republican who ran on the platform that progress and development were good for the local economy. She was backed by bestselling author Leon Uris and fellow conservatives, including the Elks Club, a group of chauvinistic businessmen who decided they would even back a woman rather than the hippie candidate.

Although Homeyer won in the end, the race was extremely close. Hunter and his staff arranged excellent publicity. Radio ads used Herbie Mann's mournful rendition of "The Battle Hymn of the Republic" as a background to a voice-over about "land rapers" and "greedheads." Peggy Clifford, now a columnist at the *Aspen Times,* wrote stories with pro-freak headlines like "Aspen— 1984" and "When Will Aspen Become the Place You Left?" Newspaper ads took a step toward the surreal, with retouched photos of Aspen covered with tract homes and laced with freeways. Underneath this vision of doom was written: "There is still time. Vote for Joe Edwards for mayor."

A voter registration drive focused on the disenfranchised who had moved to Aspen to get away from things like politics and who didn't vote in elections of any kind. As Hunter pointed out, most of these people "would prefer jail . . . to the horror of actually registering to vote." But a "fireball" pitch was made that signed up 486 new registrations, most of them for Edwards. In a town that had only 1,623 registered voters, that was a significant enough number to make the greedheads sweat.

The Freak Power Party dealings were done out in the open at their "campaign headquarters," a table in the bar of the Jerome Hotel, where supporters could find Hunter and other campaign officials whenever they were looking for him.

Despite every legal campaign trick possible, including last minute calls to Edwards supporters who had not yet voted, the Freak Power candidate fell six votes short of winning the mayoral seat. The freaks had lost out to progress. But Hunter didn't consider the lost election a complete defeat. He was impressed by the show of force his fledgling party had mustered, and in any case he wasn't sure what they really would have done had Joe Edwards won.

Hunter had become addicted to grassroots politics. The electoral system, he was surprised to find, was open to someone without a law degree or traditional party affiliation, even to someone who talked about eating mescaline and doing acid. "Hunter never wanted to be anything but a part of the system," said an Aspen friend. "He doesn't want to destroy the system, he just wants to evolve it to his liking."

Politics also indulged Hunter's theatrical streak. In the political forum, the public actually could vote on whether or not they liked the act.

At the end of this long tale of populist politics, Hunter declared his candidacy for the upcoming sheriff's race. He announced a tentative platform: the streets of Aspen were to be ripped up and replaced with sod; the name was to be changed to "Fat City," which would prevent "greedheads, land-rapers and other human jackals from capitalizing on the name 'Aspen'"; drug sales were to be controlled by the sheriff's department to keep dealers honest, and drug dealing was to be as legal as selling used cars; hunting and fishing were to be banned for all nonresidents; weapons were not to be worn in public by the sheriff or his deputies.

The most frightening portion of Hunter's platform, at least to the "greedheads," was the final paragraph which called for the sheriff's office to "savagely harass all those who engage in any form of land-rape." It provided for the possibility of a writ of seizure or assumption for any "greedhead who has managed to get around our antiquated laws."

"The die is already cast in my race," wrote Hunter. "And the only remaining question is how many Freaks, heads, criminals, anarchists, beatniks, poachers, Wobblies, bikers, and Persons of Weird Persuasion will come out of their holes and vote for me."

· · ·

Hunter had originally promised the "Battle of Aspen" article to Warren Hinckle at *Scanlan's*. But he wasn't sure if it would reach the right crowd in such a publication. In fact, he didn't think of this piece as an article at all, but an advertisement for himself. Then he got an opportunity to publish it in *Rolling Stone*, a magazine that was even less establishment than *Scanlan's*.

In the past he had called *Rolling Stone* "a magazine for pansies." His dislike for the magazine might have been due to conversations he had had with Hinckle. *Rolling Stone's* founder, Jann Wenner, had worked for Hinckle as the entertainment editor of *Sunday Ramparts*, a newspaper version of the mother magazine. In his autobiography Hinckle calls Wenner a "fat and pudgy kid" who was "considerably frustrated by my oafish refusal to print his dope and rock stories in the magazine, as I considered rock reporting as a state of the journalistic art on a level with Ben Gay ads."

Wenner left when *Sunday Ramparts* folded in May 1966. He worked as a postman while he pursued his dream of starting a magazine dedicated to rock music. He was soon joined in this effort by Ralph Gleason, a *Chronicle* columnist and *Ramparts* editor who left *Ramparts* in a fit of pique over an article Hinckle commissioned on hippies. As Hinckle recalls, "I dumped on his flower children without giving him a chance to defend the little fascists."

Wenner and Gleason developed a magazine that would reach the Love Generation through its rock music. Gleason suggested the magazine be named "Rolling Stone" after the title of a Muddy Waters song that was taken from a proverb. That was fine with Wenner, who wasn't wedded to the best name he could come up with, "The Electric Newspaper."

The magazine ran music reviews, profiles, and interviews with rock legends, the longest interviews anyone in publishing had ever seen. The prestigious *Columbia Journalism Review* reported that the magazine has "spoken for—and to—an entire generation of young Americans." *Parade* called Wenner "the young publishing genius," and *Time* praised him as the man "in charge of a unique and valuable medium."

Then, in 1969, a number of incidents gave the counterculture a bad name—student demonstrations ending in violence in Chicago and Berkeley, the murder at the Rolling Stones' concert at Altamont (which Hinckle called "the Pearl Harbor of the Woodstock Generation"), the Manson murders. Wenner did not see a good future for his magazine. Rock musicians were becoming more faceless, the creators of Muzak for a new generation.

Some of Wenner's top editors wanted to "detrivialize" the magazine by paying more attention to world politics. Wenner insisted they were "just a little rock magazine" and would stay that way. John Burks, the highly respected managing editor, quit. Jon Carroll was fired. Greil Marcus was fired after he trashed Bob Dylan's *Self-Portrait* album in a review that never ran. Other editors were fired or resigned after they failed to comply with Wenner's vision of the magazine.

What was that vision? That was the question asked by the three remaining staffers, Charles Perry, Ben Fong-Torres, and John Lombardi. The answer, thought Lombardi, might be Hunter S. Thompson. Lombardi had read Hunter's work in the *National Observer* when he edited the *Distant Drummer*, a freak newspaper in Philadelphia.

As Hunter recalls, Lombardi called him and told him that "things were really fucked up and that Wenner was a control freak. He [Wenner] had fired most of the staff and was looking for something to jazz up the magazine. I might be it, said Lombardi, but I would have to impress Wenner first. I decided to take the unconventional approach." Lombardi invited Hunter to Wenner's office.

Hunter, tall and gaunt, wearing black leather gloves, tennis shoes, white chinos, a Mexican shirt and a wig, arrived holding a six-pack of beer, a manuscript, and a box filled with hats and sipping a beer. "What have you brought us?" Wenner, grinning uncomfortably, asked Lombardi.

Hunter launched into his life's story, giving special emphasis to the political conversion brought about by his beating at the Chicago Democratic Convention. He explained his attempt to get Joe Edwards elected mayor and how he was going to run for sheriff on the Freak Power ticket, and he described the Freak platform. The monologue lasted about an hour. All the while Hunter paced the room, drank beer, and tried on different hats. When he stopped and went down the hall to use the facilities, Wenner straightened up in his chair and took a deep breath. "I know I am supposed to be the spokesman for the counterculture and all that," he said, "but what the fuck is *this?*"

At the time Wenner didn't know that it was writing's equivalent of a rock and roll star. Hunter came back into the room carrying a syringe full of gin and wearing a demented grin. He shoved the syringe through his shirt and into his stomach and slowly injected the alcohol. When the syringe was empty, Hunter burped. It was a parlor trick; the gin is injected into a hollow ball concealed beneath the belt. Hunter repeated it often to the same reaction of shock and disbelief that he got this time.

When Hunter finally lurched out of the office and onto the elevator, Wenner agreed with Lombardi to give him a chance, starting with the piece about Freak Power in Aspen.

Hinckle was angry when he lost the Aspen piece to Wenner. Hunter swore he would make it up to Hinckle, which he did within a few weeks.

Hunter and Sandy were having dinner at the home of Jim Salter and his wife. When it came up in conversation that Hunter was from Kentucky, Salter asked if Hunter was going to go to the Kentucky Derby. Although the Derby had never interested him before, it suddenly flashed on him as an excellent story idea. With the sheriff's election seven months away and the Aspen story not slated to run for a few more months, he had time to check it out. He called Hinckle in San Francisco at about 3:30 A.M.

Even at this ungodly hour, Hinckle could see the idea was brilliant. The Derby was a sacred event to horse racing enthusiasts. What better way to bash it than to send an iconoclast like Hunter to write about it?

Hinckle wanted to send a photographer, but Hunter hated photographers for the reality they imparted and because they always got in the way. He suggested editorial cartoonist Pat Oliphant. Hinckle liked the choice, but when Hunter called Oliphant at the *Denver Post,* he found Oliphant was under a tight contract and unavailable for assignments.

Hinckle had seen the work of Ralph Steadman, an English illustrator, in a collection of the artist's works called *Still Life With Raspberries.* Steadman's style was garish and full of extremes. He had illustrated an edition of *Alice in Wonderland* with contemporary characters, and he crucified politicians for *Private Eye* magazine. He had a way of making a situation look more twisted than it really was.

Hinckle called Steadman in England and found that he was already in the States looking for illustrator work. J.C. Suares, a *Scanlan's* editor, tracked him down on Long Island, where he was staying with a friend. Suarez asked if he was up for a trip to Kentucky to cover the Derby, and Steadman agreed without hesitation.

At the age of thirty-four, Steadman had worked at a number of jobs before he'd found his career. "When I discovered the truth about cartoons," he said, "was when I learned they are a wonderful shorthand language to say what I have to say quickly." After ten years of drawing caricatures for the *Times, Daily Mail,* and *Telegraph*, he wanted to make a statement with his work. Now that his marriage was breaking up, he had decided to come to America, where journalism was more open.

Steadman's instructions were to meet Hunter at the Derby press room. Hunter informed him right off that they were not there to look at horses. "It's my old hometown. I have hideous recollections of awful faces and I've come back to look for a most hideous face. In fact, I'm a little worried because I was told that you're from England and you live a sedate lifestyle. That's what I hear about English people. Whether you can handle this, I'm not sure. Maybe you should have a drink. Do you drink?"

"I'll have a beer," Steadman said coolly.

"Okay, let's go have a beer," said Hunter, pulling the Englishman toward the bar. "Do you bet?"

"I bet once in 1962 on the English Grand National," said Steadman proudly. "I bet on Early Miss and I won."

"Oh, lucky streak," fired Hunter. "Did it pay off? I'll tell you what, let's not bet money, let's just pick a horse for the next race and see if we can win on a dry run."

They sidled up to the bar and ordered a beer. A race was starting on the TV screen so Ralph chose a horse. A minute or so later it crossed the finish line a winner.

"Oh shit," said Hunter. "You should do this more often."

Ralph tried again, but this horse lost. "So much for beginner's luck," barked Hunter.

They settled down to their beers. Although, according to Steadman, they were as different as "chalk and cheese," they had the shared experience of being mavericks who wanted to produce weirder material than most publishers were willing to buy. They drank and talked for quite a while. Steadman descended into an alcoholic haze. "It was the jet lag and the drinking," he said, "and the fact that Hunter never seemed to sleep. He just paced around and muttered all the time. I had been a Boy Scout in England so I kept thinking of the Boy Scout motto: 'Be prepared.' That kept bouncing around in my mind this whole week. 'Be prepared.' But I never was. I was always off balance."

Hunter took Steadman with him everywhere. He seemed to be using this foreigner, with his unusual and naive perceptions, as a fresh pair of eyes. As Hunter pointed out later, "You look through a glass darkly, Ralph, and see things that I had forgotten all about."

The two staggered around the clubhouses and grandstands, gawking at everybody and everything. Sometimes Ralph stopped to sketch a scene in his notebook or snap a picture that he would use later as a reference for an illustration. As he sketched, he talked about what he was seeing, and Hunter jotted notes on a large yellow pad. Steadman noticed that the notes were scrawled about two or three lines at a time, written in the same way Hunter talked. Before long, Hunter had amassed a tremendous number of pages, much of it observation from Steadman.

"It kept occurring to me that I was going to become part of the story," said Ralph. "I could tell from his notes that he was looking at things through my eyes, which made sense. This was the first time I had ever seen anything like this, so therefore I asked a lot of naive questions. To him, I must have looked like a new toy."

Hunter, Steadman, and Hunter's brother Davidson met at a restaurant. After drinks were served, Steadman pulled out his sketch pad and began to work up a caricature of Davidson. It was a habit he had from when he'd worked pubs in England, drawing people in exchange for drinks. Davidson's honor at being sketched turned to distress as he saw the image take shape.

"It's like you're insulting him," said Hunter when Davidson excused himself to use the rest room. "I wish you would stop that filthy habit. It's like you're smashing him in the face. Don't keep doing that."

But Steadman did keep doing it. That night he and Hunter went to a pool hall where somebody's wife at another table took a liking to the artist. She was a beautiful woman with long hair and a willowy figure. She invite Ralph to a game of pool. In the course of playing, she discovered Ralph was an artist. "Draw me," she demanded in a Southern drawl.

Ralph sketched the beauty before him, making her look deformed, demented, and ugly. "That ain't pretty!" cried the woman when Ralph handed her the rendering. The woman and her husband glared at the artist. "I'm pretty, aren't I? That ain't pretty!" Ralph apologized, but the woman wouldn't drop it at that. "Can I draw you?" she asked defensively. He handed her the paper, and she began scribbling hard and mean all over it. "There, that's you!" she screamed.

When the couple left, Hunter ambled close to his new friend. "Quit that," he advised seriously. "People are really getting upset. Don't keep doing that."

At the end of Derby week, *Scanlan's* brought Hunter and Steadman to New York to put together the story. Steadman had a sketchbook full of caricatures and the worst hangover he'd ever had. Having lost his colors and drawing pencils, he borrowed lipstick and eye shadow from the wife of the managing editor and, using them, completed seven drawings in two days.

The editors put Hunter up in the Royalton Hotel and told him to produce, but nothing happened. Copyboys and secretaries made frequent trips to the room to gather pages, but they left emptyhanded. Managing editor Don Goddard came to the room and had a heart-to-heart talk with Hunter. "We need something, now don't we?" he said, his English calm hiding his desperation. "We can't publish empty pages, can we?"

For two days nothing came out. As Hunter later described it, this was "a terminal writer's block." On the third day, he soaked in a hot bathtub and took counsel from a quart of White Horse Scotch that he drank straight out of the bottle. He thought about the idle presses and his friend Hinckle waiting in San Francisco for something to slap on those twelve empty pages in the front of the magazine. Finally, he ripped a few pages out of his notebook and handed them to a copyboy who was waiting to deliver copy to the New York office. Then he turned on the TV and waited for an editor to call and scream a torrent of abuse. Instead the copyboy came back and said they wanted more.

Hunter read his notes and tore out more pages. A little while later, Hinckle called from San Francisco. He had received the telecopied pages from New York and he loved them. Send more.

Hunter edited his notes and handed them to the copyboy, who ran them to Goddard, who reshuffled the order of some of the material and sent it to San Francisco.

"I was full of grief and shame," Hunter told a reporter from *High Times* magazine. "This time I made it, but in what I considered to be the foulest and cheapest way. . . . I slunk back to Colorado and said oh fuck, when it comes out I'm going to take a tremendous beating from a lot of people."

The piece, "The Kentucky Derby Is Decadent and Depraved," was published in June 1970. Immediately Hunter started getting letters and phone calls of congratulation on a piece well done. One of those letters came from Bill Cardoza, editor of the *Boston Globe Sunday Magazine*, who considered the piece a breakthrough in journalism. "Forget all this shit you've been writing, this is it; this is pure Gonzo. If this is a start, keep rolling."

This was the first time the word "Gonzo" was used in reference to Hunter's work. By 1979, Webster's New Twentieth Century Dictionary would include the word "Gonzo," defining it as: "adjective (origin unknown): bizarre, unrestrained, specifically designating a style of personal journalism so characterized."

Hunter didn't know exactly what it was he had done. The piece had been an instinctual one, a coherent batch of notes taken by a pro who had been reporting for ten years. Hunter has tried to describe Gonzo many times, but his most succinct answer to the question "what is Gonzo?" is, "Gonzo is what I do."

Back in Aspen, the race was on. There were now three candidates for sheriff: Hunter, the incumbent Carroll Whitmire, and Glenn Ricks, a former deputy.

Whitmire and Ricks were cops from the same mold. Slim and hard, they spoke in direct phrases about "professional lawmen" and the need for "solid law and order." During a series of debates attended by the three candidates, Hunter, in shorts and white sneakers, sat between them and smoked endlessly as he sipped from a can of beer. Perhaps most startling was his shaved head, an accident of haircutting committed by a barber who accidentally shaved a portion of Hunter's head bald and had to go ahead and finish the job.

Hunter rattled his fellow candidates with rambling diatribes about land developers and personal freedom. He threatened to do things like eat mescaline on slow nights around the sheriff's office and harass real-estate developers with a crack team of "freak" deputies.

His campaign ads cried for Jeffersonian democracy to stop "Chicago style traffic," "Oakland style drug busts," and "New York stockbrokers and art hustlers" selling real estate. With artist Tom Benton, he founded a newspaper, the *Aspen Wallposter*, to overcome negative publicity from the local paper. A typical banner headline was "Aspen, Summer of Hate, 1970 . . . Will the Sheriff be Killed?" while a typical story lead was:

> No doubt the Reds are Evil and the Young are Crazy but it's hard to imagine how anybody—whatever their age or politics—could destroy this valley more efficiently than it's being destroyed by all the Right and Respectable People.

Even drug dealers weren't immune from the *Wallposter*'s moralistic editor. Hunter threatened to expose them in print if they "attempt to make money in Aspen by means of dishonest drug dealing." He made good his threat by writing about "Edson T. Harris III . . . a seller of extremely rotten 'mescaline'. . . . Probably a combination of nutmeg and rat poison. . . . Avoid any dealings with this person; he sells bad product & refuses to talk about refunds."

Unlike Joe Edwards, who truly wanted to be mayor, Hunter was not committed to the office of sheriff. He told people his race was one of outrage designed to "zap the greedheads."

"This was really done out of self defense," he said. "People were treating Aspen like it was theirs to develop and sell and they didn't care about the rest of us. The best way I could think of to get their attention was by presenting the possibility that someone like me might have enough support to be sheriff. That would scare the fuck out of them."

The support his platform mustered scared everyone, including Hunter, who began to fear that he might be forced into public office by a groundswell of populist support. He started to backpedal, promising to function as an ombudsman if he won and turn his salary of $10,000 a year over to a qualified sheriff under his control. This proposal seemed to swell his support and increase the paranoia that he might win.

Paranoia reached a peak when a man in Hell's Angels colors walked ominously into an Aspen bar and ordered a drink. When the drink arrived, he stirred it with a switchblade for a long time to make sure everyone saw.

"Where does Hunter Thompson live?" he demanded of the bartender.

A while later he rode up to Hunter's house and gruffly introduced himself as a representative of Sonny Barger, the maximum leader of the Angels. He had been sent, he said, with a message: "Your fucking house will be blown up and you'll be fucking killed if you win the election."

Hunter didn't buy it. The guy looked like a fraud to him. Although the Angel's colors were right, the cycle wasn't a Harley and there was no way an Angel would be seen on anything but a Harley. He decided the man was a narc or a bad actor. "The problem is," he told an Aspen friend, "I don't know which theatre company he acts for."

Several days later, the biker showed up at Hunter's headquarters with good news. He had talked to Sonny Barger and now the Angels were behind Hunter's election 100 per cent. He had been instructed to work for Hunter in every way he could. His first suggestion was to blow up a few bridges and beat up some people.

Hunter told his supporters that the man was probably "just some crazy" who should be avoided or ignored. But an Aspen policeman gave him the truth about the biker's identity. He was an undercover agent brought by Sheriff Whitmire to stir up trouble.

Hunter and his supporters confronted Whitmire with this evidence, and Whitmire admitted to bringing in a federal agent from Englewood to investigate reports that a secret contingent of

Weathermen was holed up in Aspen, planning terrorist attacks. Whitmire held a press conference to discuss the presence of this undercover cop. He had never instructed the man to infiltrate the Thompson campaign. But his search for the Weathermen led him to Hunter and his followers, the most obvious radical elements in town.

The federal agent left town after the press conference, but the controversy didn't go away. An issue of the *Wallposter* devoted a full page to "Whitmire's paranoid frenizes," which included a "Death List," written by radicals and containing his name along with other city officials.

The unsigned story read:

> The plot, according to Whitmire, was for a full-scale invasion of the town: Several thousand drug-crazed motorcycle thugs, led by the Hell's Angels, would make a twin-pincer frontal assault on the Courthouse and City Hall. . . while, at the same moment, the town would be blasted and terrorized by a series of dynamite explosions set off by well-trained demo-teams of Black Panthers and Weathermen. Then, while the police were fighting for their lives in a fog of smoke and burning rubble, assassins would roam through the town and search out their victims—killing them one by one.

Hunter was clearly zapping the "greedheads," and they in turn were doing everything they could to defame him. It was a political war, complete with dirty tricks and enemy lists. A piece mailed anonymously called Hunter "a Hell's Angel reject from Oakland" who wrote about his subversive campaign in "his *Mein Kampf*" (the underground *Rolling Stone*). Few had seen anything like this before in Aspen.

In September, in the midst of all this, Hunter was called away on assignment. Hinckle wanted the Gonzo team to tarnish the America's Cup yacht race in Rhode Island. Like the Derby, the race was an international sporting spectacle that many held dear. Specially designed sailboats from all over the world chase each other around a course of buoys, the winners progressing until they finally wash out or become the victor. A boat with crew costs millions of dollars to race and is usually funded by corporations.

"Weird people are there, half-million-dollar yachts, gin-and-tonic types—your sort of people, Ralph," Hunter told Steadman.

Steadman liked working with Hunter, but he confessed that Hunter's use of drugs at the Derby made him nervous. Hunter said he respected Ralph's point of view. "I never advocate the use of drugs for everyone," he reassured Ralph, "but they have always worked for me."

Hunter and Steadman were lodged on a two-masted, forty-foot sailboat with some members of a rock-and-roll band. By day the boat followed the contestants over the racing course. Hunter lay on deck, notebook in hand, and jotted down notes. Ralph found he couldn't be creative because he had to concentrate on not throwing up by standing bolt upright, facing into the wind. He found himself envious of Hunter, who was perfectly comfortable.

After they docked on the third evening, Steadman asked, "What are those pills you keep taking?"

"Oh, just pills," said Hunter. "You know, some sort of drug that makes me feel good."

"Could I take one?" asked Ralph, thinking it might cure the seasickness.

"Well, it's up to you," said Hunter, holding one in his open hand. "I don't want to push these things."

Ralph took the pill and swallowed it. Then they crawled into their boat's dinghy and rowed to shore to have a few drinks in one of the waterfront pubs. Ralph was taking a sip of beer when he suddenly felt funny, like he was being jolted with a slight electric current. He looked out the door and saw red dogs fighting in the middle of the street. It was a vicious tangle, but there was no sound. Also, no one else seemed to see them.

"Look at those dogs," he exclaimed to Hunter.

"There are no dogs, Ralph," said Hunter.

Ralph noticed that the other people sitting at the bar seemed to be very angry, their mouths curled and snarling. Ralph tried to hear what they were saying, but they were growling more than talking.

"Why is everyone in here so mad?" he asked.

"They aren't," Hunter reassured him. "They're laughing. Let's take a walk."

They drained their beers and hit the street. A few shops down, Hunter saw a jackknife in the window and went in and bought it. He came back out with its razor-sharp blade extended.

"This is a good knife, a great knife, perfect, useful," said Hunter. "This is going to be useful for all of our plans."

Hunter's plans were diabolical. He had started talking about them as soon as they arrived. He wanted to row silently, in the middle of the night, to the Australian boat *Gretel* and have Ralph paint "Fuck the Pope" just above her waterline.

"It would be the ultimate prank!" declared Hunter. "Just imagine! The *Gretel* gets out on the course and begins to pick up speed. Then it heels over, blooming with full sail and there it is, exposed on the side of the hull, FUCK THE POPE! The officials race to the *Gretel* in their speedboats and wave frantically. They point to the side of the boat, but no one on deck can figure out just what the hell is going on. 'We can't be damaged, we're going too fast,' they think. One of the deck hands runs to the side and hangs over. 'Eeee-Gawds,' he yells, but by then it's too late. TV cameras have seen it, newsmen have seen it, and suddenly this sailboat race becomes an international incident!"

Ralph never thought "their plan" would be carried out. He especially didn't think it would be carried out on this night, after the drugs had taken hold and the ugliness of the scene was exposed for Ralph to see. All the way to the dinghy, Ralph was frightened by what he saw. Everyone and everything seemed angry and hateful. Even the buildings had a scowl that made his heart race and sweat dampen his shirt.

The two crawled into the dinghy and Hunter began rowing. But instead of steering a course for their boat, he turned toward the Australian and American entries—the *Gretel* and *Intrepid*—and rowed next to them. Then he cut back across the harbor and headed for their own boat.

Ralph couldn't go down below. "It's too cramped down there," he said. "The walls close in and they won't let me breathe."

"Yes, yes," said Hunter, writing down everything Ralph was saying in his thick notebook.

"I want to escape," said Ralph. "But I'll drown or get wet. My hair feels so slick and greasy. God, I feel evil! I feel like Hitler!"

"Yes, yes," said Hunter, still scrawling like a psychiatrist.

"And the moon! Look at it! It's red! It's dripping like a blood fruit!"

"Yes, yes. . ."

So it went until late that night when Hunter decided to launch The Plan. He got two cans of spray paint from Ralph's room and then helped his friend into the dinghy. Ralph needed all the help he could get. He was sweating and shaking and expressing great concern for his heart, which was pounding fast and hard.

"You're the artist, you know," said Hunter, rowing expertly for the *Gretel*. "You came all the way here from England. Now is your chance to make a statement. You must write 'Fuck the Pope' on the side of this sailboat! You must!"

It made perfect sense to Ralph. "Let's do it!" he agreed, completely without fear.

Hunter pulled in the oars and let the dinghy drift against the *Gretel*'s massive hull. Ralph picked up one of the spray-paint cans and shook it, rattling the tiny ball inside.

"Who's down there!" yelled someone on deck. A head popped over the railing.

"It's just us!" shouted Ralph, panic in his voice. "We are here. We are from England. We just wanted to see one of these big things up close!"

Crew members arose from wherever they were sleeping and raced to the railing. "Let's have some light!" someone yelled. A man on the dock reached inside a jeep and flipped on its lights. Someone on the boat turned on a powerful flashlight. The Gonzo pirates were trapped in a horrifying circle of daylight.

"We must flee, Ralph, we must flee!" Hunter reached for the oars but missed them and fell backwards into the boat. "We must flee! We must flee! There will be pigs everywhere in a minute! They have guns! We could be shot in the water!"

Hunter found the oars and began rowing for their boat. In a few minutes they were back on board. Ralph's heart was beating so fast he could hardly stand up. The moon was still red. To add to that hallucination, the harbor water had the look of breathing, pulsing protoplasm.

"We have failed," sighed Hunter. He was standing there with what looked like a cap-and-ball pistol from the early days of the English navy. "But it's a better story . . . it's a better story. What I must do now is alert everyone in the harbor that we have failed." He got out a gun and rescue flares.

Ralph's physical state would not allow him to utter "no." It probably wouldn't have mattered anyway. Hunter shot a green flare into the air and then a red one. The flares bathed the harbor in their light and arched into a slow descent. One landed on the deck of a nearby boat.

"Jesus God!" shouted Hunter. "We must flee!"

"We" was right. As he watched the fire grow on the deck of the boat across the harbor, Ralph realized he was an accessory to criminal madness. The sirens of fireboats wailed. The Gonzo team activated itself and rowed desperately to shore where, at the crack of dawn, they escaped into a coffee shop. While Ralph drank a cup of coffee to steady his paranoia, Hunter went to a pay phone in the back. When he came back, he slapped a dollar on the counter and grabbed Ralph by the arm. "We're out of here," he explained. "I just called Aspen and things are heating up in the sheriff's race. I have to go home. They'll kill us here if we stick around much longer anyway."

The fire was almost out and already police were asking the people who had gathered on the dock if they had seen the per-petrators. It was only a matter of time before they would be singled out and linked to the crime.

Ralph looked at himself in a window. His eyes were dark pools of suffering, troubled by the world they had seen during the last sixteen hours and horrified at what they saw now. He had no shoes, his pants were wet and rumpled, his shirt sagged outside his belt, and his hair looked like a tossed heap of black straw. He felt his back pocket. There was his passport. He felt his side pocket. There was a small wad of bills. That would have to do. There was no going back to the boat. They barely had time to get to the airport ahead of the police.

"Come on Ralph!" cried Hunter. "I just hired a Cessna to fly us back to Boston. We'll get you back to New York from there."

The Cessna flight was a horror of air pockets and sharp turns.

More than once Ralph thought he was going to black out. When they landed at Logan Airport, Ralph felt sicker and weirder than when they took off.

"I have to catch my plane to Aspen," said Hunter, running for the gate. "Your ticket to New York is in your pocket. You leave in a half hour."

Afraid police were looking for him, Ralph ran toward his gate from pillar to pillar, always peeking out to see if the coast was clear before running to the next one. He reached his flight just before the plane left. He refused to sit down because, as he told the stewardess, "If I sit down I'll die. If I close my eyes, all I can see is purple flesh."

In New York, Ralph found he had almost no money. He threw himself on the mercy of Anne Beneduce, an old friend from England. She got him a doctor, who gave him an injection of Librium, and he slept for twenty-four hours. When he woke up, he set up a studio in Anne's living room and began drawing images of what happened in Rhode Island. The first image that came to paper was a boat that looked like a jackknife with "Fuck the Pope" written across it in red.

Neither Ralph nor Hunter ever published their work from the America's Cup race. After a controversial eight issues, *Scanlan's* died. Hunter's "Fuck the Pope" prank was a routine story treatment for Hinckle and his co-editor Sidney Zion. *Scanlan's* had ruined the multi-million dollar advertising campaign of Lufthansa Airlines, which was trying to lure tourists with the slogan, "Next year, think twice about Germany," by running the slogan over a picture of a man in Nazi costume whipping a naked woman. What finally did *Scanlan's* in was an issue on how to wage guerilla war in America. Printers in the U.S. refused to print it because of its "seditious" content. Canadian printers finally did the job, but the issue was stopped at the border. After a protracted legal battle, the magazine went broke.

Hunter, returned to Aspen, came within five hundred votes of putting a badge on his chest. He was "stomped brutally" in two of the precincts that mattered most and beaten by a three to one margin—not bad for a campaign that began as a warning to "greedheads" and "a joke," as *The New York Times* called it.

In the *Aspen Wallposter*, he ran a picture of himself wearing all black and talking on the telephone. His head is shaved so clean and smooth and the rims of his round sunglasses are so shiny that he resembles an alien. The caption reads:

> In his final, election night speech for the national press and TV, the candidate lost control of himself and had to be restrained: "This is my last press conference!" he shouted. "You won't have Hunter Thompson to kick around anymore, you pigfuckers!" He then rushed out of the room to confer with his personal Swami, who later told reporters that Dr. Thompson had decided to "depart this country in the spring" and take up permanent residence at a luxurious Ashram on the Bay of Bengal.

Hunter took refuge in his writing, not on the Bay of Bengal. Hooked on radical politics, he proposed to *Rolling Stone* an article idea about alleged police brutality and repression of citizens in the Chicano ghetto of East Los Angeles. The editors had liked his Aspen story and wanted to expand their magazine's political coverage. The East L.A. piece, "Strange Rumblings in Aztlan," came out on April 29, 1971 and is anthologized in *The Great Shark Hunt*.

The news peg was the shooting death of Ruben Salazar, a radio producer for a Hispanic station and weekly columnist for the *Los Angeles Times*. Salazar and a radio reporter were covering a large protest march that turned into a riot in East L.A. The two had stopped for a beer in the Silver Dollar Cafe on Whittier Boulevard when sheriff's deputies sealed off the door. An anonymous caller had warned them that a man with a gun was in the bar. The deputies shouted for the man to come out. When no one did, they tried to flush him out with tear gas. A tear gas shell fired through the door struck Salazar in the head and killed him. Later the man with the gun was captured but not arrested.

The sheriff's office denied that any of its officers had killed Salazar; first they blamed street snipers, then "errant gunfire" from the riot. Finally, when witnesses began stepping forward, the police admitted they had fired the fatal gas shell. By then a coroner's report had confirmed that the projectile caused the death.

The outcry in the Chicano community was immediate. "Remember Ruben Salazar" became a battle cry of young Chicanos, and Salazar was the personification of their repression. East Los Angeles was heated to a full boil.

Hunter heard about the ghetto rumblings from Oscar Zeta Acosta, a former Legal Aid lawyer who now primarily represented East Los Angeles Chicanos. The two had met by chance in a bar shortly after Hunter had moved to Aspen. At the time, Acosta had been drifting around the country, having had a mental breakdown after his secretary at his Legal Aid job in Oakland died. Fat, plagued by ulcers and searching for the meaning of life, Acosta had had only one legal client, John Tibeau, the actor who had broken his leg in a motorcycle accident with Hunter. Tibeau convinced Acosta to go to Aspen in search of a fellow with a cure for ulcers.

Tibeau then was still in a full leg cast from the crash. He was angry at Hunter for his reckless driving and wrote long letters to him in Aspen about the pain of the healing process, his loss of employment opportunities, and the possibility of a lawsuit. Acosta knew none of this when he met Hunter by chance in Aspen's Daisy Duck bar. When Hunter heard Acosta was a friend of Turk's, he became immediately defensive. Acosta describes this first meeting in his *Autobiography of a Brown Buffalo*.

'Say tell me,' I said, 'do the Hell's Angels really carry chains and bullwhips?'

'When they're out on a rumble they do,' he said.

'Is that what you and Turk [Tibeau] were doing when he busted his leg?'

King [Hunter] gave me a thin-lipped smile and looked me straight in the eye. 'No . . . we were out looking for greasers.'

'I take it you didn't find any.'

Miller said, 'Hell, they wouldn't know what to do with them if they did find any. King [Hunter] would probably just interview them while they cut his balls off.'

'Yeh,' he nodded, 'I probably would, if I had an interpreter.'

Acosta asked Hunter if he was really a professional writer. "I guess I'm about as much a writer as you are a lawyer," Hunter replied.

Acosta had an interesting history. Born in El Paso and raised in Riverbank, California, he studied at San Francisco Law School, "the oldest night law school in the state," and passed his bar examination on the second try. In his autobiography, he views himself as someone trying to overcome an inferiority complex and chides himself for being overweight; he tells of his childhood resentment when his white classmates called him "jigaboo" for his dark brown skin, and his humiliation when his brothers poked fun at his "tiny penis."

Pictures of Acosta don't betray his massive insecurities. They show a large man, dark and Aztec-looking, with an angry scowl that most people wouldn't miss if they saw him on the street, though they wouldn't want to stare too long for fear of retribution. Yet his voice was extremely soft and his demeanor disarmingly pleasant.

"He was a real sweetheart," said Harriet Fier, who worked on the *Rolling Stone* switchboard in those days but rose to the position of managing editor in 1978. "He had a very soft, whispery voice and he had a very feminine side. He loved women and his kids. When he got filled up with a bunch of stuff he acted very tough. But he always came back to being very gentle."

Acosta became Hunter's Chicano liaison in East L.A. From the start, Hunter had difficulties with the Salazar story. Hunter was staying in the Hotel Ashmun, which he described as being, at the time, a hovel inhabited by many alcoholics and junkies. People banged on his door all night. They either wanted to use his bathroom or wanted him to turn down his tape player, on which he played the Stones' *Let It Bleed* album almost constantly.

Acosta and his friends would gather in the room. A bunch of them, carrying blocks of ice and bottles of rum, showed up when Hunter first checked in. They sat around all night making rum drinks and eating speed, which became a daily ritual after that. Any time after about noon, Acosta or his buddies might show up. These were tough guys, ex-cons, alleged fire bombers and "veteran acid eaters." Even though they shared with Hunter a paranoid world view and love of booze and speed, they viewed him as a "gabacho." They made Hunter feel that they didn't like a "hillbilly" (Acosta's word) hanging out in their neighborhood. At one meeting someone shouted angrily, "What the hell is this goddamn gabacho pig writer doing here?"

Acosta was preoccupied with the upcoming defense of the "Biltmore Six" (six Chicanos accused of trying to burn down the Biltmore Hotel while Governor Ronald Reagan delivered a speech in the ballroom). When Hunter tried to talk to Acosta about life in the barrio, their conversations were frequently interrupted by people dropping by.

One night Hunter tried to lighten it up by kidnapping Acosta and taking him over to pick up Gene McGarr, who was working at a nearby advertising agency. They started the evening cruising drugstores and buying boxes of amyl nitrate capsules, which they spent the rest of the night using.

The next day it was business as usual, with Hunter in the background as Acosta planned radical politics. "He was the only Mexican lawyer around who specialized in 'Chicano law,'" explained Hunter. "Everyone who was pissed at the cops or a landlord wanted to talk to Oscar."

Frustrated by the Chicano culture in East L.A., Hunter had the idea of doing a piece about the American dream in Las Vegas, a follow-up to the Kentucky Derby piece. He called Ralph Steadman and asked him if he'd like to go to Vegas and cover a police convention; Steadman passed. Then an editor friend at *Sports Illustrated* asked Hunter if he was interested in covering the Las Vegas Mint 400 motorcycle race.

Hunter got Acosta into his rental car and drove across town to the Beverly Hills Hotel. Over drinks at the Polo Lounge, Acosta apologized for his lack of attention. "As a militant leader," he said, "it makes it impossible for me to be too friendly with a gabacho. It's like spending too much time with the enemy."

Hunter replied that he needed to spend some time with Acosta to "sort out the evil realities" of the Salazar story. "How about an all-expenses-paid trip to Las Vegas," Hunter asked. Acosta liked the idea. Hunter waved a waiter over, ordered a telephone sent to the table, and called *Sports Illustrated*.

Hunter knew that if he got Acosta to Las Vegas "we would both go crazy and try to outdo one another. And that's exactly what we did. We fucking stomped the ground in Vegas. We took enough speed to keep Hitler awake in the bunker for fifty days and enough acid to make him think he was in the Austrian Alps. We ran up such a massive hotel bill that it was frightening. And the most frightening thing of all was that Oscar flew back to Los Angeles after the weekend and left me there to cope with everything."

Sports Illustrated wanted the facts in a few hundred words so they could write captions for the pictures their photographer was taking. Hunter and Acosta "freaked out their photographer . . . in the condition we were in." Then Hunter produced a piece of over 2,000 words, and *Sports Illustrated* rejected it.

According to Hunter's account, published in *The Great Shark Hunt* as "Jacket Copy for Fear & Loathing in Las Vegas: A Savage Journey to the Heart of the American Dream," he spent the next thirty-six hours in his room at the Mint Hotel furiously writing notes, trying to remember everything he could about the previous forty-eight hours. This frenzy of note taking was not what he had originally planned. His hope had been to record everything "as it happened." In that method, he wrote, "the eye & mind would be functioning as a camera. The writing would be selective & necessarily interpretive—but once the image was written the words would be final; in the same way that a Cartier-Bresson photograph is always (he says) the full-frame negative. No alterations in the darkroom, no cutting or cropping, no spotting . . . no editing."

On the other hand, Cartier-Bresson didn't work loaded on

psychedelics. Neither did Hunter, usually. He had tried to write once while tripping on mescaline in a Los Angeles hotel and the result was a three-day diary filled with paranoid scratchings and surreal images, which eventually was excerpted in *Songs of the Doomed* under the title "First Visit with Mescalito." It included such entries as "Stay away from the phone, watch the red arrow . . . this typewriter is keeping me on my rails, without it I'd be completely adrift and weird." and "I feel like both me and the typewriter have become weightless. . . . I could step off the balcony right now and float gently down to the sidewalk."

His drugs of choice while writing were speed and alcohol, a combination that helped him stay alert and organized. But the Gonzo style of journalism called for him to be "as personally involved as possible" in the story, "right in the middle of whatever I am writing about." Since Hunter and Acosta were taking a sixties "trip" into the seventies, being in the middle of the story meant, to Hunter, taking copious amounts of psychedelic drugs. This meant losing the photographic clarity he had originally intended.

Shortly after Acosta left, Hunter realized he hadn't been as attentive to his notebook as he would have been had he not been "higher than a stack of trapeze artists." He began to jot down short teletype bursts of hallucinatory Vegas memories packed with paranoia: "Pterodactyls lumbering around the corridors in pools of fresh blood. . . . The Circus-Circus is what the whole hep world would be doing on Saturday night if the Nazis had won the war. . . . Right smack above your head is a half-naked fourteen-year-old girl being chased through air by snarling wolverines. . . ."

With his notebook full of such scribbles and, according to his accounts, an unpaid bill for his room, Hunter fled Vegas.

With serious work to do on two stories, Hunter moved his base of operations from the Hotel Ashmun to a Ramada Inn near the Santa

Anita racetrack in Pasadena. It was a clean, well-lighted place. David Felton, the *Rolling Stone* editor assigned to handle the Salazar piece, lived in Pasadena.

Hunter lay in a good supply of beer, dug out his usual stash of speed and grass, cracked open a fresh bottle of whiskey, put on the Stones' *Let It Bleed* tape, and went to work. During the daytime he wrote the Salazar piece, which eventually topped out at 19,000 words. At night he wrote for fun, weaving the madness of the Las Vegas weekend into a metaphor for the seventies. Writing had never been so much fun for him; he had agreed with Hinckle's belief that writing was the flip-side of sex because "it's only good when it's over." This was different. He later wrote, "it's a rare goddamn trip for a locked-in, rent-paying writer to get into a gig that, even in retrospect, was a kinghell, highlife fuckaround from start to finish. . . ."

Hunter had amplified his ideas of letting the notes do the talking and the writer as photographer. "True Gonzo reporting needs the talents of a master journalist, the eye of an artist/photographer and the heavy balls of an actor," he wrote later in the article published in *The Great Shark Hunt*. "Because the writer *must* be a participant in the scene. . . ."

After a week at the Ramada Inn, Hunter took nineteen pages to Felton. Although Felton had never met Hunter, he had heard about Hunter's legendary first meeting with Wenner and he expected at his door a madman drunk, out-of-control, and with a syringe full of booze.

The skinny, nervous man who arrived looked far straighter than most of the people Felton saw around Los Angeles. He opened the door and was greeted by a pile of pages instead of a handshake. "Sit down and read this," said Hunter. "This isn't the Salazar piece, this is my own idea."

As Hunter paced the room, Felton read:

We were somewhere around Barstow on the edge of the desert when the drugs began to take hold. I remember saying something like "I feel a bit lightheaded; maybe you should drive. . . ." And suddenly there was a terrible roar all around us and the sky was full of what looked like huge bats, all swooping and screeching and diving around the car, which was going around a hundred miles an hour with the top down to Las Vegas. And a voice was screaming: "Holy Jesus! What are these goddamn animals?"

Felton was no stranger to psychedelic drugs. He howled with laughter at the images Hunter had concocted on the page. The thing read like a movie.

"This stuff is great," said Felton, handing the pages back. "I think you are really onto something. Keep it up."

Felton described Hunter's innovation later as "a personalized form of journalism, happening at the moment of the action, not later. But it was different from journalism because it was provoked. Most of these events were real, they just wouldn't have happened in many cases if the writer had not provoked them." He equated it to creating a novel.

Hunter flew up to San Francisco to hand deliver his work to *Rolling Stone*'s Paul Scanlon, soon to become the magazine's new managing editor. Hunter came into the office in shorts, T-shirt, and a "weird" jacket and dumped the contents of his rucksack onto Scanlon's desk. From a pile of junk that included a pistol and a bottle of Wild Turkey, Hunter pulled a copy of the pages Felton had read.

"With a little smirk he handed me the pages," said Scanlon. "I read them and was immediately in hysterics. This thing was so fucking funny I couldn't believe it. It was like nothing I had ever seen before."

The same pages were given to Wenner, who took them to his office and emerged gleeful about half an hour later. "Keep it up," he said.

Hunter stayed in San Francisco to finish the Salazar piece and continue working on his new creation. He was put in the record library, a room Charles Perry, the chief copy editor, kept under lock and key to prevent theft.

Perry was a Princeton graduate with no formal journalism training but a working knowledge of roughly twenty languages, including French, Italian, German, Greek (modern and ancient), Sanskrit, Gaelic, and some Urdu. He was a stickler for detail and very serious about deadlines. Planning to study Arabic at the University of California and then either become an academic or work for an oil company, he had moved to Berkeley in 1963. The following year he had introduced LSD to a new tenant in his apartment house, Augustus Owsley Stanley III, who decided to try making the stuff. A few million capsules later, Owsley Acid was the standard for all psychedelic drugs in the Bay area, and Owsley was known in the newspapers as "Mr. LSD." Psychedelics caused a career crisis for Perry. In February 1968 he offered his eccentric talents to *Rolling Stone*.

Perry was a gentle soul, but he had his angry moments. One of those came when David Felton experienced "deadline-itis" and couldn't finish a piece. Furious, Perry held Felton out a window and threatened to let go if he didn't finish the story. "Of all the people you should watch out for," Felton told Hunter, who was known to have deadline problems, "Perry is number one."

One day while Hunter was working on the Salazar piece, Perry walked into the room. "How you doing?" he asked Hunter casually. Hunter jumped like a man struck by lightning. "Jesus, it's great," he said, striking a few typewriter keys. "I've really got a lot of momentum there. It's like a train on greased wheels. I've just got to keep the momentum up!"

Two days later, Perry stuck his head into the room and asked the same question.

"Jesus Christ, I lost the momentum. I'm trying to keep it up. I've taken methedrine, I haven't changed my clothes in two days and I think my feet are rotten."

Later, Perry ran into Hunter in the men's room. He was taking a leak and drinking a beer. He looked exhausted.

"How you doing?" asked Perry.

Hunter took a gulp of beer. "I'm feeling redundant."

When Hunter finally got the Salazar piece out of the way, he moved into Wenner's apartment to get away from the pressures of the office and devote himself full-time to the Vegas piece. Soon his all-night pacing and frenetic mumblings drove Jann and his wife, Jane, to distraction. "They liked Hunter, but they also liked to sleep at night," said one staffer. "The way he's up all night almost drove them over the edge."

One night Scanlon and Grover Lewis, a new writer who joined the magazine from the *Houston Chronicle,* visited the apartment with a mutual woman friend. Wenner opened the door and Hunter was standing behind him with a smirk plastered on his face. He was wearing a tie-dyed shirt with a purplish bull's-eye around his navel area, and was drawing the contents of a bottle of 150-proof rum into a huge horse syringe. With a gleam in his eye he plunged the needle into his navel and moaned in agony. Then he injected the contents slowly and withdrew the needle. "Shoot it right into your navel," he said, then burped. "Goes directly into the blood-stream, you know." The woman with Scanlon and Lewis turned pale and had to sit down.

As Hunter was wrapping up the first half of *Fear and Loathing in*

Las Vegas, Felton heard about a narcotics convention, the National District Attorneys Association's Third Annual Institute on Narcotics and Dangerous Drugs, being held in Vegas. He told Hunter, who saw this as a way of expanding the story into a book-length piece. "We weren't trying to get him to write a novel," said Felton. "It just came together naturally."

Hunter called Acosta and the two returned to Vegas. Acosta was in the middle of the Biltmore Six case. He had taken some outrageous tacks to defend his clients. In one defense, according to Hunter's article "Strange Rumblings in Aztlan," published in *Rolling Stone* on April 29, 1971 and anthologized in *The Great Shark Hunt*, Acosta had subpoenaed every superior court judge in Los Angeles, 109 in all, and cross-examined them about racism in the court system to prove that no Chicano could possibly get a fair trial. In *The Revolt of the Cockroach People*, a record of his legal dealings in the barrio, Acosta tells of spending several days in jail for contempt of court for arguing with the judge. One night Felton received a phone call from Hunter in Vegas. There was screaming and what sounded like the crashing of dishes in the background, and Hunter seemed beside himself with fear. "I can't control him! Oscar's out of countrol!" shouted Hunter. "You gotta send money!" Felton realized later that this was part of a game, but at the time he insisted that the bookkeeping department wire $500 to Vegas. Wenner deducted the money from Hunter's story fee. No matter how angrily Hunter pleaded his case when he discovered this, Wenner refused to reimburse the money as expenses.

After Hunter and Acosta got back to San Francisco, they were doing the town with Felton one night and stopped by Wenner's apartment. Hunter, who knew no one was home, let himself in with a key he had and came out with one of Wenner's stereo amplifiers under his arm. "Now it's settled," he said.

About six months after the second Vegas trip, *Fear and Loath-*

ing in Las Vegas arrived at *Rolling Stone*. Unlike Hunter's earlier work, the manuscript came in one package, completely polished and cleanly typed. It was a running narrative of a weekend in which the journalist "Raoul Duke" and Dr. Gonzo, his "300-pound Samoan attorney," live up to the statement that opens the book: "'He who makes a beast of himself gets rid of the pain of being a man.'—Dr. Johnson."

This is the book's description of the drugs that were stashed in their trunk and consumed on the trip: "two bags of grass, seventy-five pellets of mescaline, five sheets of high-powered blotter acid, a salt shaker half full of cocaine, and a whole galaxy of multi-colored uppers, downers, screamers, laughers . . . and also a quart of tequila, a quart of rum, a case of Budweiser, a pint of raw ether and two dozen amyls."

Later, when I was interviewing Hunter for *Running* magazine, I asked, "Did you guys really have that many drugs?"

"Maybe."

"Did you really take as many drugs as you said you did in the book?"

Hunter wouldn't give a straight answer, but said, "'Fiction is the truest form of journalism.' Faulkner said something like that. You figure it out."

I consulted an independent medical counsel, who calculated that the total drug consumption written about in the book approximated the amount in the trunk, and that such a staggering amount consumed in a forty-eight-hour period would be fatal "in normal men."

However many substances they in fact did ingest, Raoul Duke and Dr. Gonzo greet the "law and order" seventies with a final blast from the sixties. No one in Vegas is safe from their comic terror. Hitchhikers are threatened, chambermaids are molested, tourists harassed. Raoul Duke and Dr. Gonzo steal hundreds of bars of

Neutrogena soap from the hotel, order musical instruments and pistols from room service, damage rental cars, and try to drive into a laundromat at the Landmark Hotel. However, they manage to stay out of jail because they are in Vegas, the capital city of excess.

"It was a kind of a weird celebration for an era that I figured was ending," Hunter recalled. "I kind of assumed that this was sort of a last fling; that Nixon and Mitchell and all those people would make it very soon impossible for anybody to behave that way and get away with it. It wouldn't be a matter of a small fine. Your head would be cut off."

The manuscript was passed around the office, with each editor being given a day to read it. Perry, who was among the first readers, said, "There had always been a suppressed craziness in his writing. There were scenes in the Salazar piece where this almost came out. But with *Fear and Loathing* he hit his stride as a Gonzo maniac. I felt an extreme literary exhilaration. He had found his tone and was riding the dragon."

At Hunter's insistence, the manuscript was sent to Ralph Steadman for illustration. Ralph saw that Hunter "was lucky to have Oscar, because he was crazier than me. . . . I get a warm glow just thinking how devilishly funny that book is. It transcends journalism to become a piece of literature. This is as close to writing a novel as Hunter has ever gotten."

Paul Scanlon said the day Ralph's art came in was "one of the best days of my life." It arrived in big tubes that art director Bob Kingsbury brought in and opened at Scanlon's desk. Everyone crowded around as the drawings were unrolled: lizard people biting one another on the shoulder, blood dripping onto the carpet; Oscar hugging a commode and heaving his guts out; fat, garish tourists aghast at the demented behavior of Hunter and Oscar in the car next to them; a frightened young hitchhiker, in the backseat of a speeding car in the desert, convinced that this is his last ride.

Fear and Loathing in Las Vegas came out in November 1971. It was a tremendous success. Letters poured in from people who loved Hunter's writing and wanted to live just like him. They sent drugs and pictures and even asked if they could accompany him on his next voyage to Vegas.

One person who wasn't happy with the book was Oscar Zeta Acosta. He came up to San Francisco and hung around the offices of *Rolling Stone* and drank with the staffers at Jerry's Inn. "Doctor Gonzo isn't any 300-pound Samoan," he told them. "He was me, a 250-pound Chicano attorney."

Hunter had not intended to incur Acosta's wrath by changing his identity. He thought an attorney who was constantly at war with the L.A. judicial system did not need a *Rolling Stone* article about him running wild all over Vegas.

Acosta was well on his way to disbarment anyway. After a hard day in court, he and two of his assistants were speeding back to East L.A., doing sixty-five in a fifty MPH zone, when they were pulled over and searched by police. Acosta was found to be in possession of about thirty amphetamine tablets. At first he denied they were his, claiming that the police planted the drugs to damage the Brown Power Movement. The more staid barrio politicians, who had always thought Acosta too radical, used the bust as an opportunity to discredit him. Before long, he was out of business.

Acosta wanted to assume his rightful place as the star of the book that Tom Wolfe called "a scorching, epochal sensation." Having dumped the legal profession, he decided to become a writer like Hunter. "He was very confused at this point in his life," said Felton. "He lived in the shadow of Hunter and really thought that he had it made."

Eventually he became embittered by Hunter's success. For years, even after he left San Francisco for Mazatlan, Mexico, with his teenage son Marco, he considered suing his friend for half of the proceeds from the book and a co-author credit on the cover. The idea for the story had been concocted in advance, he declared, which meant he had helped Hunter plot the story and had even contributed a good portion of the dialogue. "In a way it made sense," said one of the editors. "If Gonzo means making the story up in advance, then he was more than the subject of the piece, he was a part of the creative process."

Acosta left his sign, the name "ZETA" carved with a knife in the wooden frame of the men's-room mirror of the *Rolling Stone* office. Sometime after 1974 he disappeared without a trace. His son Marco had last seen him boarding a small sailboat bound for the United States.

"I think he got involved in some kind of drug smuggling deal and got shot and thrown overboard," surmised Hunter. "The last time I saw him was in '74, when he wanted me to loan him some money for some shady deal that I didn't think he should get involved in. I think that was the deal that did him in. . . . That was the last time I saw him, 1974 in San Francisco."

There have been a dozen or so "Oscar sightings" since he supposedly disappeared beneath the waves. Some claim that he is nursing his ulcer and living quietly in Mexico or Europe. Others have sworn they've saw him running drugs up the coast of Mexico or up from Cuba. Some say they have seen him in border towns like Juarez or even on the streets of Los Angeles. Like a Chicano Elvis, he continues to pop up.

After *Rolling Stone* moved to New York City in 1977, hospital bills with "Oscar Zeta Acosta" on them started showing up in their accounting department. One was for a broken arm. Harriet Fier tried to track the bills, but to no avail.

6

THE CAMPAIGN TRAIL
(1972–1973)

Hunter told a reporter, "*Rolling Stone* was the first place I had been where I could write exactly what I felt. It was terrific."

"There is no other magazine that would have hired Hunter, let alone hire him to do what he did at *Rolling Stone*," said Paul Scanlon. "He was too much of a nonconformist and a misfit for any magazine besides us and *Scanlan's*, and they were out of business."

In *Rolling Stone*, stories typically ran five to ten thousand words long, and longer pieces were frequent and encouraged by the editors. "This was the beginning of the literary era of *Rolling Stone*," said Scanlon. "The place became a magnet for writers who couldn't do this sort of thing any place else."

The masthead became a rogue's gallery of the underground literati of American journalism. Along with Hunter, there were Tim Cahill, Tim Crouse, David Felton, Grover Lewis, Joe Eszterhas, Ben Fong-Torres, Timothy Ferris, Jerry Hopkins, Jon Landau, Charles Perry, and Paul Scanlon.

Grover Lewis' piece on the making of the movie "The Last Picture Show" was 14,000 words, a piece by Joe Eszterhas on motorcycle daredevil Evel Knievel ran 20,000 words, and a two-parter by David Felton on the Mel Lyman death cult was 40,000 words. "Over the years I still chafe when I hear editors at other magazines say we weren't edited," said Scanlon. "We were edited. We just let the stories run. We were overindulgent, but we edited."

They broke not only the length barrier, but also the language barrier. Fuck, shit, pigfucker, bastard, and all the slang and swear words of the English language laced the stories. The style barrier was broken too. Overzealous editors did not homogenize writers' copy. "Hunter taught me an important lesson as an editor," said Felton. "He taught me that different writers have different styles and that we shouldn't make them fit some mold that isn't theirs. He was very strict about not having words changed. His scream about copy changes was quite famous. And it wasn't a joke, it was a real scream of anguish."

Other staff writers were the same if not worse. Hunter had the peculiarity that he refused to read his galleys. Some editors braved changes after he passed on the edited copy. His refusal upset the people in the production department, who used his picture as a dart board.

As a celebration of the new literary era of his magazine, Wenner called *Rolling Stone's* first editorial conference, to be held at the Esalen Institute in Big Sur. In addition to the San Francisco editors, Wenner brought Hunter from Woody Creek, Jerry Hopkins from Los Angeles, Timothy Ferris from New York, Andrew Bailey from England, Robert Greenfield from Boston, Jon Landau, and Timothy Crouse, a new writer whose main contributions consisted of the shorter pieces in the front of the magazine. The only women present were Wenner's wife, Jane, and Annie Leibovitz, the staff photographer. To keep everyone focused, Wenner held the paychecks and would not pass them out until the last day of the conference.

The purpose of the meeting was to map out strategy for the coming year. "Jann wanted to become more group minded," said

Perry. "He wanted England to know what San Francisco was thinking."

Several meetings were scheduled each day at a conference room in a nearby hotel. According to Scanlon, they ran "eight or nine excruciating and painful hours. There was a lot of confusion about our goals and nothing seemed to be going on, but it still took a long time. In a very short period we all wanted out of there, fast."

They had to stay in Esalen's rustic cabins, dine at Esalen's organic meal hall, and socialize with Esalen human-potential students on the picturesque grounds. Everyone complained about the lice and bedbugs. There was no hot water for showers. The food was inedible. They served chard and potatoes at every meal. "Jesus, it was awful," said Perry. "They also served things like underdone beets, which were similar to chewing on shoe leather."

Hunter slept most of the day. He parked his car against the door of his cabin to indicate that he didn't want to be disturbed. When he finally showed up for Wenner's marathon planning sessions, he wore a hospital smock and carried a six-pack of Budweiser. When the meetings got dull, he pulled a police gumball light from his big leather bag, put it on the table, and turned it on. "It's for authority," he told Wenner when the publisher asked him to put it away.

One night Hunter led the staffers on a sentimental tour of the Esalen grounds. When they got to the hot tubs, they stripped and climbed in. Hunter brought a six-pack out of his bag and passed the cans around. Before long a beefy Hell's Angels type named Jocko, one of the Esalen caretakers, informed them that no alcohol could be consumed in the hot tubs. "You can smoke dope," he said, "but no beer allowed."

"Fuck you," said Hunter, reminding Jocko that grass, not beer, was illegal.

"Yeah, fuck you," said the other staffers, inspired by Hunter's surliness.

"Pretty soon the guy just left," said Felton. "After that the people at Esalen treated us with something close to pure hostility. We were as compatible as water and oil."

On the second or third night, Hunter led Felton and Leibovitz on a search for a hamburger stand. Hunter was seriously high on mescaline and Wild Turkey. They made it to Big Sur, but couldn't find a burger stand. On their way back to Esalen, they were pulled over by the highway patrol. "It was like that scene out of *Fear and Loathing* where Hunter is stopped by the police while drinking a can of Budweiser," said Felton. "There was a bottle of Wild Turkey on the seat next to him when the police came to the window and asked us to step outside."

Hunter tried to convince the troopers that he was sober. But the liquor on his breath and the gone look in his eyes, plus the fact that he couldn't perform any of the other simple tasks of a sobriety test like walking a straight line, made him an almost certain candidate for arrest. "Look, I'm not drunk," he insisted. "I can hold my liquor. Would you say I am in good enough shape to drive if I can flip my sunglasses over my head and catch them midair?"

The cops grinned at one another and agreed to the challenge.

As Leibovitz took pictures, Hunter flipped his glasses off the top of his head and caught them in midair. The police, impressed with the performance, let Hunter drive back to Esalen.

"In a way he did have their number," said Felton. "He said that the cops had contempt for people who just give in. 'Hell, they're sporting guys,' he said. 'They like a challenge.'"

Instead of stopping at Esalen, they drove down to Carmel where they found a bar that served food. They ate and drank beers while watching a movie on television. Just before the movie was over, the bartender turned the set off.

"Hey, why'd you do that?" shouted Hunter.

"I'm tired of the TV," said the bartender.

"Well that's cruel," shouted Hunter. "I've never seen such a cruel thing."

Hunter roused the other patrons in the bar and soon everyone was shouting at the bartender, who became visibly angry.

"Finally the bartender told Hunter to stop it or he would throw him out," said Felton. "And that was it, Hunter stopped. Back in those days he knew just how far to push it."

On the fifth day of the conference, Wenner began to discuss the notion that a political campaign was much like a rock-and-roll tour and could be covered as such. The notion aroused little interest among the staffers, who judged this conference to be the most boring week they had ever spent in their lives. "We figured, 'who the fuck really cares about politics?'" said one staffer.

Wenner insisted there was a populist movement in American politics because of the youth movement, the civil-rights movement, and the Vietnam war. A change was coming, he said, and this was a chance to be involved in a groundswell. He announced his plan for Hunter, as newly-appointed national affairs editor, to cover the 1972 presidential campaign. Traveling with Hunter as his "leg man" would be Timothy Crouse.

"There were howls of laughter in the room," said Scanlon. "Nobody knew what this meant. We thought it was one of the worst ideas we'd ever heard." The only people in the room not laughing were Wenner, Hunter, and Timothy Crouse.

Shortly after the Esalen conference, *National Observer* editor Dave Hacker, in Maryland, got a late-night telephone call from Hunter in Woody Creek. "I'm in hot water," Hunter said; his staccato voice sounded worried. "I'm coming to Washington and I need some help. *Rolling Stone* wants me to cover the election and I don't know shit about politics. Do you have any suggestions about people I should talk to, some insiders maybe . . .?"

Hacker thought a moment. The only one he could really think of was Robert Novak, the conservative writer who, along with Rowland Evans, had just started writing a syndicated newspaper column. Hacker knew Novak from when they used to work for the *Wall Street Journal*. "I'll call Novak for you," he offered. "He's a little more conservative than you are but he knows all the players and he's a good place to start."

The next day he called Novak, who had never heard of *Rolling Stone*, Hunter S. Thompson, or the Hell's Angels. As a favor, however, he agreed to talk to Hunter when he got to Washington.

Hunter, Sandy, and Juan arrived in Maryland early on a Friday morning, just ahead of rush-hour traffic. Towing an orange U-Haul trailer behind their new six-cylinder Volvo, they rented a house on the "black side" of Rock Creek Park in a "marginal" neighborhood, one that Hunter considered a two-Doberman part of town. He brought one of his Dobermans with him from Colorado. The 2,000-mile car trip practically made the dog insane and caused it to have intestinal problems for several days after the trip was over. Hunter called home to have another dog shipped out.

Sandy was pregnant again. She had considered staying in Woody Creek, where Hunter had intended to file many of his dispatches when he was on the road anyway, but she wanted to stay close to him for the first several months. She's had at least one miscarriage since Juan was born and, according to friends, thought Maryland had superior medical care that could help her carry this child to term. However, she miscarried within a few weeks after their arrival.

Hunter, a perennially stoned Colorado anarchist, was not particularly welcomed by Washington insiders. He kept muttering things about "the swine in charge" and "those pigfuckers on the hill," and calling the Washington press corps "a sycophantic bunch" who sat around waiting for handouts from politicians. Someone who met him shortly after he arrived said, "He was here to clean up Dodge. He kept talking about his search for honesty in politics as though he had been sent on some mission from God. It put everyone off. No one likes to be called dishonest or have their community called it, least of all by someone who doesn't even know the town."

Wenner didn't want to spend the money it would take waiting for Hunter to develop sources; rather, he wanted a running commentary of Hunter's travails in Washington. For almost three months, from December to March, Hunter filed mostly pedestrian rewrites of the *Washington Post* and other dailies. Many of the editors thought his dispatches were so lame they should be relegated to the back of the magazine, with no reference on the cover. Wenner insisted that Hunter's work be put in the front of the magazine and that it always get a sizzling cover line.

Twenty-five million voters, the Youth Vote, had reached voting age and were approaching their new right with more skepticism than any generation before. Unlike Teddy White or Stewart Alsop or any of the dozens of other establishment correspondents, Hunter was an outsider. When the youth voters read him, Wenner predicted, they read one of their own.

In the ring for the 1972 Democratic primary were a dozen candidates, including former Johnson vice president Hubert Humphrey, 1968 peace candidate Eugene McCarthy, former New York City mayor John Lindsay, Maine senator Edmund Muskie, Southern conservative George Wallace, and black congresswoman Shirley Chisholm. South Dakota senator George McGovern was Hunter's favorite because he was publicly opposed to the Vietnam War and in favor of amnesty for draft dodgers. Ted Kennedy had not yet declared himself a candidate, but people thought he would.

Like the other reporters and writers covering the campaign, Hunter had to unravel this mess of politicians. But he had to do it with little background knowledge or inside information, few contacts, and no real help from the home office. Where most of the entrenched journalists had a large staff and the power of an organization behind them, he had only Timothy Crouse.

"When I went to Washington," Hunter later said in a *Playboy* interview, "I went with the same attitude I take anywhere as a journalist: hammer and tongs—and God's mercy on anybody who gets in the way. Nothing is off the record. . . . But if you're an indiscreet blabbermouth and a fool, nobody is going to talk to you—not even your friends."

At first the longest conversations he had were with hitchhikers. A talk with a Kennedy staffer ended on a bad note when Hunter made an oblique reference to "smack" being a way of getting over the liberal pain of Nixon's conservative appointees to the Supreme Court.

"He wanted to go as someone who didn't plan to be a political correspondent," said Charles Perry. "He didn't want to owe anybody any favors. He was just going to call the shots as he saw them."

Hunter's Gonzo attitude finally clicked while he was covering the Muskie campaign in Florida. As Hunter recounts in *Fear and Loathing: On the Campaign Trail '72,* Muskie was riding "The Sunshine Special," a train outfitted to make a whistle-stop tour in the days leading up to the Florida primary. At each stop, football player Roosevelt Grier came out of the caboose. With the help of a band, he led the crowd through a few stanzas of "Let the Sun Shine In." After a certain amount of time, Muskie waved his way onto the platform and delivered a short speech.

Hunter was soon to derail the Sunshine Special. According to Hunter's account, he was intrigued by a man named Peter Sheridan, who was desperate to get to Miami, where the Sunshine Special was headed, but had no money. Hunter, figuring he could get on the train without his credentials, gave his press pass to Sheridan.

In the morning, however, when the train left the station, Hunter was still asleep in the Ramada Inn. As the train picked up steam, Sheridan was tearing it up in the bar car, becoming exceedingly drunk and offensive. The rumor swept the train that Hunter S. Thompson from *Rolling Stone* had dropped acid and was rapidly turning into Mr. Hyde.

When the train pulled into Miami, Sheridan got off and took a position right below Muskie on the platform. This was to be the crowning speech of Muskie's Sunshine tour. But as the candidate spoke, Sheridan reached up and grabbed Muskie's ankle, causing the senator to stumble backwards. A student reporter, quoted in Hunter's book, said that Sheridan was "waving an empty martini glass" at the senator and shouting, "'Get your lying ass back inside and make me another drink, you worthless old fart!'"

The *Miami Herald,* the *Washington Star,* and even *Women's Wear Daily* carried stories about the "yahoo" on Muskie's train. Individual journalists thought it was a travesty that Hunter had surrendered his credentials willingly to anyone, let alone an obvious looney like Sheridan. The Muskie camp pulled Hunter's credentials and banned him from the campaign.

Hunter took his outlaw status to the McGovern campaign. After one of his stories on the Wisconsin primary, McGovern told Hunter that the piece was "brilliant." With that one remark, spoken in a group of reporters, almost everyone covering the campaign began reading *Rolling Stone.* Some even had their home office telefax the stories as soon as issues came off the press.

One enthusiastic television reporter in Los Angeles cornered Crouse and told him that "we will all write like Hunter after the revolution." *Washington Post* columnist Nicholas Von Hoffman said, "Thompson's is the best stuff on the campaign I've read anywhere. In fact, it's the only stuff on this campaign I can bear to read." Stewart Alsop of *Newsweek* gave Hunter an angry lecture about his caustic comments, but then went on to quote him in a column about Hubert Humphrey, "a treacherous, gutless old ward-heeler who should be put in a goddamn bottle and sent out with the Japanese current."

Another section of *Newsweek* published a brief profile of Hunter with more of his sparky comments on the presidential contenders:

NIXON: "Getting assigned to cover Nixon [is] like being sentenced to six months in a Holiday Inn."

HUMPHREY: "He looks like he died in 1959 and has been frozen ever since."

MCGOVERN: "To be President, McGovern would need at least one dark kinky streak of Mick Jagger in his soul."

MUSKIE (campaigning in Wisconsin): "He talked like a farmer with terminal cancer trying to borrow money on next year's crop."

WALLACE (campaigning in Florida): "The air was electric even before he started talking, and by the time he was five or six minutes into his spiel I had a sense that the bastard had somehow levitated himself and was hovering over us. It reminded me of a Janis Joplin concert."

Hunter gave brutal assessments of old-line politicians who thought they were above personal attacks like these. He was tough on all the candidates, even McGovern at times, but he spewed his most potent vitriol on Muskie, whom he called a "mushmouth, middle-of-the-road compromiser" with a staff so fat that most them required help getting out of cars and elevators. "If I were running a

Hunter gets ready to tackle his latest medium—"shotgun art"

The Doctor of Gonzo during some of his tamer moments

*Hunter talks to reporters during
the trial.*

Hunter's partner-in-crime, Ralph Steadman.

Hunter flashes the victory sign during his trial at Aspen's Pitkin County Courthouse. The charges of sexual assault and possession of controlled substances and incendiary devices were dismissed.

The house at Woody Creek.

Hunter at Woody Creek.

Hunter and Laila Nabulshi relaxing on Hunter's porch at Woody Creek.

A reunion of the old Louisville gang. Left to right—Davidson Thompson (Hunter's brother), Gerald Tyrrell, Duke Rice, Jay Stewart, and Hunter.

Hunter S. Thompson.

campaign against Muskie," he noted, "I would arrange for some anonymous creep to buy time on national TV and announce that twenty-two years ago he and Ed spent a summer working as male whores at a Peg House somewhere in the North Woods."

This was all just name-calling. Then Hunter engaged in his first full-scale act of Gonzo political journalism, recounted in detail in *Fear and Loathing: On the Campaign Trail '72*. He claimed that Muskie was rumored to be campaigning under the influence of a rare African drug called Ibogaine, which was responsible for much of Muskie's erratic behavior.

These were all rumors, Hunter wrote. He could not check them out because he had been banned from the Muskie campaign.

The media immediately began asking the Muskie camp puzzling questions about the candidate's drug use, which Muskie denied. Then Hunter denied that he had said Muskie was using Ibogaine. "I said it was a rumor to that effect," wrote Hunter later. "I made up the rumor."

"We laughed our asses off in the office about the Ibogaine affair," said Scanlon. "It was in many ways the kind of material we expected from Hunter. When the action slowed down, he was supposed to do something to pick it up."

"Politics was treated with too much reverence back then, as it is today," said Felton. "Journalists were spoon-fed propaganda and they in turn spoon-fed it to the public. This was Hunter's way of feeding some of the propaganda back to them."

Hunter's inventive and irreverent style horrified some members of the press corps, many of whom decided to ostracize him. However, some of the journalists bought his approach, even admired it. J. Anthony Lucas wrote a profile in *More*, the national journalism review, that called Hunter "the Prince of Gonzo" and "the quintessential Outlaw Journalist."

During the Ohio primary, Hunter began to resort to the original story-filing method—telefaxing raw notes—from which Gonzo was born. This piece, unlike the Derby article, actually looked like he filed his notes. Several columns of type are taken up with short sentences, ellipsis and exclamation points, all of which combine to make it read like a Walter Winchell column. No hard nuggets of news are distilled from the chaos and disorder.

Although done out of desperation, filing notes had the effect of reproducing just how exciting, banal, boring, and exhausting covering a political campaign actually is. The notes present a minute-by-minute account of a night in which Hunter watched a Jimmy Stewart movie on TV, talked to Warren Beatty, listened to Frank Mankiewicz talk to organizers on the telephone, ate hamburgers, watched returns on the networks, listened to organizers cancel a McGovern appearance on the Today Show, and so forth. All this blends together with the strategizing, power plays, and legal wrangling that make American politics the great sport that it is.

For readers of *Rolling Stone*, it was the perfect approach. "For them," noted Renata Adler in the *New Yorker*, "the reporter's basic question—what is the story and what is the point—was resolved autobiographically: story and point were whatever happened to impinge on the author's sensibilities."

Even with the expedient of filing his notes, Hunter was consistently late with his copy. His editors could count on only one thing, a biweekly bummer as they sat up all night waiting for the "mojo wire" (telefax) to wheeze into action, its drum spinning, the finished pages spewing out at the pathetically slow rate of one every six minutes.

The pages didn't have numbers. Hunter labeled them "Insert XX" or "Insert X to follow Sub-Y." It was a mosaic of sections and seemingly disconnected parts. "I don't know to this day if he had a great master plan worked out in his mind," said Scanlon. "I think he sent this stuff to us like this because he didn't want anybody fucking with his copy. To keep that from happening, he turned it ass backwards and gave it to us that way."

The editors tried to make sense of it. As sections came in on the wire, they were immediately photocopied, since no one liked to handle the sticky thermofax paper. A copy was given to Charles Perry, who did what he could at that point to copy edit the sections. David Felton, who was in charge of content editing, put a copy on the floor; as new pages came in, he moved them around like pieces of a jigsaw puzzle. "It was like catching something being thrown at you when you were blindfolded," said Scanlon. "You never knew when it was going to come and were never real sure about what it would be when it got there."

Front-line editor Felton broke down in tears more than once over Hunter's deep inability to write any sooner than the last minute. "Typically, I would call him about once an hour as the deadline neared just to try and get him to send something," said Felton. "And then the next hour I would get him to send more, hoping that it had something to do with the previous hour's material. This would go on for about thirty-six hours straight and then he would crash and I would sit up all night trying to put together everything he had sent. Then he would get up and it would start all over again, only now Hunter was much more disagreeable. Finally I would just start thinking, 'Why am I doing this? I don't need this!' I would be cranky, tired, and alone and sometimes I would just start to cry."

The production department had to keep a dozen or so people on overtime while everyone waited for the sacred telefax wire to start spinning and spewing. Finally the most angry staffers put pressure on Wenner to insist that Hunter comply with the deadlines. Wenner wrote Hunter a memo stating, "We can no longer go through this deadline scene as we have now with every one of your reports." The memo was telefaxed to Hunter and posted around the office, but it did no good. Hunter continued to file late, some-times forcing the magazine to be sent to the printer with five or six empty pages holding up the presses.

Wenner tried calling Hunter and yelling at him. If he couldn't get through, he yelled at Timothy Crouse. Wenner wasn't fond of Crouse anyway. Crouse stuttered, so he was no verbal match for Wenner, who, switched into full automatic, could talk as fast as a machine gun. Wenner saw Crouse as Hunter's gofer, the guy who took care of Hunter's every need and saw to it that he made his deadlines. Hunter saw Crouse in a different light. He was a good reporter with a sharp eye and better than average writing abilities. To Hunter, Crouse was almost an equal and anything but a gofer. He sent Crouse to do interviews with campaign staffers and to gather information from other reporters, a task he handled excep-tionally well because he was in the process of writing a book about how the press covered the campaign (*The Boys on the Bus*, pub-lished in 1973).

The Crouse issue came to a head in Wisconsin, where Crouse had been covering the second place McGovern while Hunter was still dogging the front runner, Muskie. On election night, the unexpected happened. McGovern won.

Hunter called Wenner and told him that Crouse should write the main story. Wenner vociferously disagreed. He wanted Hunter to write the piece. If Crouse attempted to do it, he would pull him off the campaign.

Hunter took the publisher's threat as a challenge to his authority. He convinced Crouse to write the article and paced the room, egging him on, as the young Bostonian banged out page after page.

Wenner was furious when the article arrived and immediately ordered Crouse to come home. But before he could leave, a *New York Times* piece came out praising Crouse's work. Grudgingly, Wenner reassigned Crouse to the campaign. Gradually more and more of his work appeared. He wrote the story on the most dramatic event of the entire campaign, the attempted assassination of Alabama Governor George Wallace, who was shot in a shopping center parking lot in Silver Springs, Maryland, not ten minutes away from where Hunter was staying in Rock Creek.

Hunter writes that he was in the New York office of *Rolling Stone* trying to borrow money for cab fare when he heard about the shooting of the segregationist governor on the radio. Looking out the window at rush hour traffic, he began to work the phones, calling contacts in Washington to get the details on the shooting. Because of the heavy traffic, Hunter didn't think he could reach the airport in less than two hours. Then Crouse called. He was close to Logan Airport in Boston and planned to catch the shuttle down to D.C. immediately. He would be in Washington before Hunter could even get out of Manhattan. He would go to Holy Cross Hospital in Silver Springs and pull the story together.

Crouse produced an excellent story and freed Hunter to head for California, where the primary was shifting into high gear.

Chris Lydon, the *New York Times* reporter who had been following the campaign with Hunter and Crouse, was in the waiting room in the Silver Springs hospital with Crouse. While they sat waiting for information, Lydon casually said that "Hunter Thompson should be here to record this for history."

The comment was an indication of how things were starting to go for Hunter. More and more, in Wisconsin, Ohio, California, and New York, people approached Hunter at press conferences and asked for his autograph. This typically happened to TV journalists like Dan Rather and John Chancellor, but print journalists, read and not seen, were a different story. Few people knew what Stewart Alsop or James Reston looked like. Hunter had a cult following, and he was becoming a star. "It can be like travelling with a rock star," Crouse told some of the editors.

By Hunter's own admission, not all of his campaign coverage was true. His premise was that a cloud of bullshit surrounds political campaigns and taints all the information that comes out.

There was also Hunter's Gonzo use of overt fiction, like the Ibogaine rumor. Because of the furor that rumor aroused, he changed his procedure when dispensing Gonzo fictions. At the end of each falsification, he wrote, "My God, why do I write crazy stuff like this?" Still, that wasn't always good enough, and reporters still called to see if Frank Mankiewicz, McGovern's campaign manager, had really jumped Hunter from behind a bush, or if he'd really spotted Humphrey stalking the halls of a hotel drooling and raving to himself. People believed the written word and they wouldn't put any of this stuff past the candidates.

Hunter was not concerned that his fictions might be taken seriously enough to maybe skew the election. "Fuck 'em if they can't take a joke," he said. "The people who mattered, McGovern, Mankiewicz and even some of the guys in the Nixon White House like Pat Buchanan liked my coverage. And almost everyone who read it understood what was Gonzo and what wasn't. What the fuck. I can't be held responsible for the rest."

At the Democratic Convention in Miami, Hunter was joined by Wenner, who was convinced more than ever that politics was the rock and roll of the seventies. There was excitement that built to a crescendo, staging and back-room action, groupies galore, and drugs.

Wenner was sympathetic to Hunter's deadline plights. He understood Hunter needed various substances and the adrenalin that fear of failure caused. On the surface he may have rebuked Hunter for being consistently late with his copy, but below it all they both believed that inspiration sometimes needed to be jolted from its hiding place.

Wenner brought in Ralph Steadman to cover the convention and go on the road with Hunter for the duration of the campaign. He wanted Steadman's naive presence to inspire new heights in Gonzo antics.

Steadman drank too much on the flight over and became terribly dehydrated. He was barely able to sit up in the back seat of the cab that took him to the Doral Hotel. He found Hunter sitting on a couch in his suite, telephone pressed to his ear, surrounded by newspapers, half-eaten meals on room service trays, ashtrays filled with cigarette butts, and bottles of booze. Hunter let Steadman in and kept babbling on the telephone, rattling on like a bookie as he talked about the odds of various candidates winning.

Hunter took Steadman to the convention hall. The place was a roiling caldron. State delegates screamed their support of individual candidates, and special interest groups screamed their support of causes. "Hunter was enthralled with the scene but it just made me sick," said Steadman. "The convention was the worst example of what I have always called the screaming lifestyle of America. It totally broke my spirit." The signs, the buttons, the jockeying for position, whatever the position might be, were all grotesque to Steadman. He couldn't get into it.

"Get into it anyway," advised Hunter.

It struck Steadman as a giant white rat experiment in which the rats, replaced by people, were rewarded for carrying large cardboard signs and shouting like fools. He couldn't tell what the reward was.

Outside the convention hall, crippled Vietnam vets in wheelchairs rolled around shouting "No more war! and waving banners. Around them swirled hippies, yippies, SDSers, women's righters, blacks, Native Americans, and a host of special-interest groups clamoring for media attention. Hunter agreed with Steadman's disgust at the protest scene. When these same people showed up a few weeks later for the Republican Convention, he savaged them. "With the lone exception of the Vietnam Veterans Against the War, the demonstrators in Miami were a useless mob of ignorant, chicken-shit ego-junkies whose only accomplishment was to embarrass the whole tradition of public protest . . . about half of them were so wasted on grass, wine, and downers that they couldn't say for sure whether they were raising hell in Miami or San Diego."

For relief, Hunter took Steadman to the beach, where Steadman got sunburned. "I'm sick," he told Hunter, and went back to the hotel. He began packing his bags. When Hunter came into the room, Steadman said, "I'm going home. I can't stand this scene."

"What do you mean, 'going home'? You can't go home. Jann has spent a shitload of money to bring us here and you want to go home? Jann will go crazy!"

Steadman was sweating profusely now and was quite certain that he had caught a flu bug. Hunter followed him down to the lobby. "You can't leave," he insisted. "We have plans."

"Forget the plans, Hunter. I'll still do the drawings for your articles. I've been here three days, I have enough material. The rest of it I'll get from television back in England."

Hunter continued to argue all the way through the lobby and out the front door. As Steadman loaded his luggage into a cab, a tiny bird hopped across the covered entrance to the Doral, pecking at crumbs as it dodged cars and cabs.

"See that bird?" asked Ralph. "Well, that's how vulnerable I feel. This atmosphere is very oppressive. I feel like a desperately hungry little bird stuck beneath heavy traffic."

The analogy left Hunter speechless.

By the time Steadman reached the airport, he felt much better.

On his way to the gate he saw a vending machine that said, "Make Your Own Alligator, 25 Cents." He fished a quarter out of his pocket and dropped it in the slot. A blob of hot plastic dropped into an injection mold and a hiss of hot air shaped it into an alligator. The reptile fell down a chute and into Ralph's hand.

"The thing that came out was filthy and ugly," said Ralph. "It represented all that I needed. That was it. There I had my symbol of the American political experience." The airport alligator appeared, in one of Steadman's drawings, as Richard Nixon, with members of the media walking stupidly down his nose and straight into his mouth to be chewed up and swallowed.

Hunter and Wenner thought they had, in McGovern, a rock-and-roll candidate complete with a rock-and-roll staff and the right message for the youth culture: no more Vietnam and amnesty for all draft dodgers. Shortly after winning the nomination, however, McGovern took what he later described as an "emotional and physical beating," and his campaign began to crumble. He was forced to make a hasty decision on a vice presidential running mate. His people, concerned that the "old party hacks" would try to throw in somebody like Humphrey or Mayor Daley of Chicago, chose Missouri senator Thomas Eagleton without first giving him an adequate background check. Had they done so, they would have found that Eagleton had a history of mental illness and electric shock treatments.

The news and the irreparable damage it did to the McGovern campaign was far too serious for Gonzo, at least from Hunter's perspective.

McGovern clustered with his staff to decide how to handle the debacle. After first promising to stick with Eagleton, McGovern finally had to give in to negative popular sentiment. He chose Sargent Shriver to fill the now tainted position. One good thing about Shriver, intoned Hunter, was that he was a Kennedy by marriage and a good friend of both Humphrey and Daley; another good thing was that he beat out the real "bums and hacks" on the list of possible candidates, including the little-known Georgia governor Jimmy Carter. "Given the nature and the mood of the people . . .," noted Hunter, "McGovern might have found himself running with Evel Knievel."

By the end of September, it was obvious to Hunter that he was not on the winning team. The youth vote was not lining up to support McGovern, whose mistakes—along with his willingness to discuss them in public—made him look like the wrong man for the job.

With the polls indicating a decisive loss for McGovern, Hunter got drunk in *Rolling Stone*'s national affairs suite at the Washington Hilton and wrote a stirring eulogy to the '72 campaign.

> The tragedy of all this is that George McGovern, for all his mistakes and all his imprecise talk about "new politics" and "honesty in government," is one of the few men who've run for President of the United States in this century who really understands what a fantastic monument to all the best instincts of the human race this country might have been, if we could have kept it out of the hands of greedy little hustlers like Richard Nixon.

"After that, Hunter just hit the skids," said Scanlon. "By October, Hunter was burned out on the campaign."

With the fate of the McGovern candidacy painfully obvious in the polls, Hunter just wanted to go home and rest. He was blocked, exhausted, and filled with depression about the American political system. But there were still pages to fill and issues to get out.

. . .

The editors resorted to desperate measures. They interviewed Hunter and ran the rambling question-and-answer session in place of a story. His fans wanted his highly charged boozed-up, stoned-out, exhausted take on politics.

"At this point Hunter was being rewarded for being at his worst," said Felton. "And of course he loved it. Why should he work hard and try to write better when he makes a perfectly good living and doesn't do any work at all?" Some of the editors joked that, if the magazine's readers were the only ones voting for president, Hunter would win as a write-in candidate.

Hunter briefly considered moving to Washington and doing nothing but political writing. "I got treated like a king in that place," he recalled later. "Even the Republicans tolerated me. The ones who understood me actually came to like me."

At one point Wenner planned to start a magazine called *Politics*, but pulled the plug on it when the editor, a former JFK staffer named Richard Goodwin, opted to leave the project because he wasn't hitting it off with Wenner. The opportunity to stay in Washington had been presented to Hunter at that time, but he decided to go back to his mountain hideaway.

He later explained why he had decided against cashing in on his sudden Washington fame. "If I stuck around the capitol and kept doing political coverage, I'd get in a rut. Pretty soon people would just look at me as another Teddy White and treat me like I couldn't do anything else. I'd be in a rut, and I didn't want that."

He also felt he would miss the freedoms he enjoyed in Woody Creek. "In Washington I couldn't sit on my porch naked and take a piss off the deck like I can on the farm." He told a reporter from *The Washington Post* that, in Woody Creek, "I can get loaded on mescaline and fire my .44 magnum out into the dark . . . that long blue flame. . . ."

In Washington, said Hunter in an interview, "there is no such

thing as paranoia. The truth is, your worst fears always come
true. . . . You only have to come to the east to understand why
everyone picked up and headed west."

While editing *Fear and Loathing: On the Campaign Trail, '72*,
Hunter stayed in San Francisco at the Seal Rock Inn, at the ocean
end of Geary Street. One afternoon David Felton took Harriet Fier
there to meet the legend. At that time Fier was an associate editor
at *Rolling Stone.*

Hunter answered the door with the intense look of someone
hard at work. When he saw Felton and Fier, he broke into a cordial
grin and waved them into the room. He was wearing his usual:
Hawaiian-print shirt, Bermuda shorts, and canvas sneakers; a
cigarette was smoldering in its plastic holder.

"The place was totally torn up," said Fier. "The mattresses were
turned over on the floor and laundry was strewn all over the room.
Lamps were upside down, beer cans and joints were all over the
floor, and pieces of his book were thrown around like confetti—
literally. He was going through his pieces in *Rolling Stone* and
cutting and pasting them for the book and scissored pieces were
tossed all around."

Despite the mess in the room and the obvious frenzy that Hunter
was in to make the publisher's deadline, Fier found him to be very
much a "Southern gentleman."

"There is a gentlemanly aspect of Hunter that comes through
when he is trying to be nice or maybe when he is trying not to be
macho. I don't know which it is, but he was very much a gentleman
that day. He made coffee for us and we went out on this terrace,
which had a view of the Pacific Ocean, and talked."

The book came out in 1973. Random House sent a copy to
Frank Mankiewicz, who Hunter said commented that the book was

"the least accurate yet most truthful" account of the campaign yet published. Dozens of reviews unleashed an avalanche of commentary about Hunter and the nature of Gonzo journalism. Much of it was good, some bad or puzzling.

Kurt Vonnegut, Jr.'s review, in *Harper's* Magazine July 1973, focuses on Hunter's physician's declaration that he has never seen anyone with a worse case of anxiety, and that Hunter is "on the verge of a complete mental, physical and emotional collapse."

"Why would [Hunter] tell us this?" asks Vonnegut. "What could this be but a cry for help? And what can we do to help him? It isn't as though he doesn't try to help himself . . . If he is to be believed, (he) has sampled the entire rainbow of legal and illegal drugs in heroic efforts to feel better than he does."

Vonnegut declares that Hunter is suffering from "Hunter Thompson's disease," a malady that afflicts " all those who feel that Americans can be as easily led to beauty as to ugliness, to truth as to public relations, to joy as to bitterness. . . ."

The *Columbia Journalism Review* was less complimentary. Wayne Booth, a former dean of the University of Chicago College of English, calls Hunter's writing style "tough-guy gush" and says that Hunter has produced coverage full of "libelous epithets, the hot-rodding, the drinking, the speed, the smack, all in a rush to tell us that this 'new' journalist is—despite his balding pate—still the hottest thing coming down the pike."

Booth also lambasts Hunter for being "so hostile to politicians that he just cannot bother to understand them." He criticizes Hunter's use of a serious campaign as a backdrop for Gonzo antics, and concludes with a harsh swipe: "If Thompson enters future histories, it will be as an example of intellectual decline and fall."

When a reporter mentioned this review to Hunter, he angrily swept it aside. "Fuck *Columbia Journalism Review*. They don't pay the rent."

Perhaps the most puzzling response was not a review of the book, but a review of its author's drug use. Entitled "Dr. Hunter S. Thompson and a New Psychiatry," it was written by Dr. Arnold Mandell, then cochairman of the psychiatry department of the University of California at San Diego. In it he expresses his opinion that Hunter's drug use is necessary to his writing, and suggests that he could continue to function as an interesting writer and "build good character" if he used more exact doses of less dangerous drugs.

Mescaline, Mandell points out, opens up the hemisphere of the right brain and lets it play, while amphetamines tighten up loose thinking and help a person get organized. Thus speed helps Hunter create "explosive, rapid, repetitious, paranoid, complicated and endless" prose, while the mescaline provides "richness." Booze "shoves a grandiose but nervous mind into a trench of this world and fills it with impatience about the future."

Mandell's professional analysis comes very close to Hunter's own assessment of the effects of his drug intake as they combine to hit that "moment of perfect clarity."

7

PRISONER OF GONZO
(1973–1980)

On the campaign trail, Hunter filed more than 100,000 words under heavy deadline pressure. Knowing the entire staff was deep into overtime led him to write sentences like:

Sitting in front of my blank page at 2:30 a.m., with the paper due tomorrow, I am desperate. But suddenly I have an idea. I'll write about how it feels to be sitting in front of my blank page . . .

or,

This is about the thirteenth lead I've written for this goddamn mess, and they are getting progressively worse . . . which hardly matters now, because we are down to the deadline again . . . and those thugs out in San Francisco will be screaming for Copy. Words! Wisdom! Gibberish! Anything! The presses roll at noon . . . This room reeks of failure once again . . .

These lines may have worked as a way of making readers feel the first-hand anxiety of a deadline crunch. But the pressure was real.

Some of the editors in the *Rolling Stone* office felt that Hunter was exhausted from the campaign and the need to please his audience by acting like a Gonzo madman at every opportunity. He had started out at such a high level of craziness that there seemed to be nowhere left to go. Joe Eszterhas and Grover Lewis had warned him, when *Fear and Loathing in Las Vegas* was published, and Eszterhas had said, "Don't paint yourself into a corner. You might be sorry for it in the end." Scanlon thought it was time for Hunter to follow the basic tenet of survival as explained by Charles Darwin, "Evolve or die."

In January 1973, when Hunter was almost finished editing the *Fear and Loathing: On the Campaign Trail '72*, Scanlon had a talk with him at Jerry's Inn in San Francisco. "I think you should take a year off and relax," the managing editor suggested while Hunter sipped Wild Turkey. "Then maybe come back doing something else besides Gonzo. To write that stuff means you have to keep acting crazier and crazier and I don't know how you can keep doing it. Maybe you could start writing some traditional nonfiction and leave Gonzo behind for a while."

Hunter said nothing, just stared. He reached for his billfold and pulled out a tab of Mr. Natural acid. Smirking at Scanlon, he popped it into his mouth and pursed his lips as the chemical dissolved. Then he got up and left. Scanlon later said it was the biggest put-down of his life.

Hunter's output after the campaign showed that Scanlon's worries had more than a note of truth to them. Indeed they had an entire orchestra of truth. Hunter's failed attempts to write for *Rolling Stone* proved quite expensive and extremely frustrating for the editors. His erratic behavior and spotty output led to the most often asked question at the magazine: Whatever happened to Hunter S. Thompson?

Hunter was in the Watergate Hotel, he later wrote, from about 8:00 P.M. until 1:00 A.M. on June 17, 1972, the night a group of White House operatives burglarized the Democratic National Headquarters. He swam laps in the pool for two hours and then drank tequila in the Watergate Bar with Tom Quinn, a sports columnist at the *Washington Daily News*. As they were ordering their last rounds, G. Gordon Liddy and E. Howard Hunt were "monitoring the break-in by walkie-talkie," in a room just above the bar.

"All this was happening less than 100 yards from where we were sitting in the bar," Hunter wrote, "sucking limes and salt with our Sauza Gold and muttering darkly about the fate of Duane Thomas and the pigs who run the National Football League."

On August 2, 1973, in a strange and somewhat incoherent story entitled "Memo from the Sports Desk & Rude Notes from a Decompression Chamber in Miami," Hunter announced his intention to cover the Watergate hearings. The piece, later anthologized in *The Great Shark Hunt*, includes an "Editor's Note" about Hunter nearly drowning while scuba diving for black coral in the Yucatan at a depth of 300 feet. Because he was forced to rise quickly to the surface, he was hospitalized with a near fatal case of the bends and put in a decompression chamber for almost three weeks. There, with great difficulty, he watched the Watergate hearings and communicated with Raoul Duke via a loudspeaker tube and handwritten notes.

The diving accident, of course, never happened. But it set the piece up for a memo from Duke, Hunter's alter ego and source of invented quotes, who explained Hunter's real problem was that the hearings were more Gonzo than anything he could make up:

Whether or not he will write anything coherent is a moot point, I think, because *whatever* he writes—if anything—will necessarily be long out of date by the time it appears in print. Not even the *Washington Post* and the *New York Times*, which arrive daily (but three days late) out here in Woody Creek, can compete with the spontaneous, brain-boggling horrors belching constantly out of the TV set.

Hunter set up the national affairs desk at the Watergate and began digging for news, color, Gonzo, anything the national press didn't already have under its thumb. He found nothing. He had an interview with Pat Buchanan, but the information gleaned was unspectacular and the reportage uninspired.

He invented a Gonzo scene in which he and other co-conspirators planned to kidnap Charles Colson, one of Nixon's top command, and drag him behind a car down Pennsylvania Avenue. It never came off, but the plan occupied a considerable amount of space in the article.

He even tried name dropping, saying that either Warren Beatty or pollster Pat Caddell had caused damage to his rental car that forced him to spend a considerable amount of time filling out a damage report for Avis. As one editor who worked on the story said, "How could he forget whether Beatty or Caddell caused the damage? This was just his way of getting both names into the story."

Finally Hunter closed down the national affairs desk and went home to Woody Creek where he sat naked on his deck and watched the hearings on TV. "Fear and Loathing at the Watergate: Mr. Nixon Has Cashed His Check," the story which came out in September 1973, went on long after it had anything more to say. "Hunter always threw everything into his stories, including the kitchen sink," said one staffer. "It was just that this time the kitchen sink was from K-Mart."

Several publications, including *Time* magazine, singled out Hunter's piece as a dull spot in what should have been a shining moment for a veteran Nixon hater. The *Rolling Stone* coverage included numerous Steadman illustrations, but still the article didn't sizzle.

"After the '72 campaign everything became more problematic," said Felton. "His stuff was not as coherent as it used to be. There are some brilliant flashes in it, but it really became weak." Scanlon took the analysis a step further: "[His work] became screed without substance."

When it was clear by the end of July 1974 that Nixon was going to be impeached or forced to resign, Felton came up with the idea that Hunter should write an article entitled "The Quitter." Wenner latched onto the idea.

Scanlon had been replaced as managing editor by John Walsh, a legally blind sports editor from *Newsday* on Long Island whom Wenner hired over the telephone. Some of the staff did not like Walsh and took pleasure in his discomfort when Wenner told him that a special issue would be produced on Nixon and Hunter would write the main piece. Walsh argued that Hunter was becoming more difficult to work with and that writing such a piece under deadline might be impossible.

"Just do it," Wenner instructed Walsh.

Hunter went to Washington for the two weeks leading up to Nixon's resignation on August 9 and subsequent departure from the White House. He was there on the White House lawn when Nixon and his family walked to the big green helicopter that would carry them to the waiting Air Force One. He saw the stiff-armed wave and noticed that Nixon bumped into the door and almost lost his balance as he ducked into the helicopter.

Walsh recruited Scanlon, the man he had replaced, to pull the article from Hunter. Scanlon was a veteran of "ragged edge" deadline work with Hunter. To get Hunter in the mood to write, Scanlon brought him to San Francisco where he could work in the office and have his every need filled. Scanlon honestly thought Hunter would produce.

All day Hunter sat before his typewriter with the title "The Quitter" typed at the top of the page. Afternoon turned to evening and night fell. The page remained blank, except for the title.

"Finally I said 'Goodnight, Hunter' and I left," said Scanlon. "When I came back the next morning it looked like he hadn't moved. He still had the title on the page and that was it."

Hunter couldn't find the words. He was blocked, frozen. Panic ensued. Scanlon contacted another writer. Meanwhile the photo staff culled through the Watergate-related photos of Annie Leibovitz, pulling out some excellent work that otherwise might not have appeared. Her photos were run with a collage of Hunter's writing on Watergate, Nixon and "all the President's men" clipped from previous issues by the editors, who did their work in the conference room with scissors and paste.

It was a low point for Hunter, who was always on the tightrope when it came to deadlines but had never fallen off. It was also a low point for John Walsh, who was fired from his managing editor position after less than a year for his failure to get Hunter to perform.

"After that there was always the chance that Hunter wouldn't file," said Felton, who also had a reputation as a blocked writer. "I certainly understand what it means not to file a piece. You certainly can't feel much lower. It's a horrible thing to sit there under pressure and the words just don't come. It was clearly a failure and something I'm sure he couldn't help. But it was not something I wanted to talk to him about."

Ironically, Hunter's failure brought Annie Leibovitz into the limelight. The massive exposure of her work made the young photographer a superstar.

Hunter eventually filed a story on Nixon's final days. "Fear and Loathing in Limbo: The Scum Also Rises" appeared on October 10, 1974, two months after Nixon left office, and was later anthologized in *The Great Shark Hunt*. A large portion of the article deals with the effects of history on Hunter—how the chain of events happened so rapidly and publicly that it left him exhausted and "wasted beyond the help of anything but the most extreme kind of chemo-therapy."

> It takes about a month to recover physically from a collapse of that magnitude, and at least a year to shake the memory. The only thing I can think of that compares to it is that long, long moment of indescribably intense sadness that comes just before drowning at sea, those last few seconds on the cusp when the body is still struggling but the mind has given up . . . a sense of absolute failure and a very clear understanding of it that makes the last few seconds before the blackout seem almost peaceful.

To get a take on Nixon's mentality, Hunter relates in the article a story in which he and two friends, when they were in their twenties, moved to Lexington, Kentucky for a weekend with the express purpose of robbing a gas station. On three consecutive nights, Hunter and his partners broke into the gas station across the street from their apartment and took all the cash they could find. After the third robbery of the gas station, undercover cops dressed as attendants manned the facility with the express purpose of nailing the perpetrators. Hunter realized he and his friends were pushing their luck and decided to end his life of crime.

"The original point, I think," he wrote, "had to do with the street-punk mentality that caused Nixon to push his luck so far that it was finally almost impossible *not* to get himself busted."

Hunter had been assigned to cover the 1974 Superbowl in Houston, but the resulting article, "Fear and Loathing at the Superbowl: No Rest for the Wretched," later anthologized in *The Great Shark Hunt*, was almost a self-parody. It read like the Kentucky Derby piece without Ralph, or *Fear and Loathing in Las Vegas* without Oscar. At the Superbowl, Hunter had no one who could react to his madness.

Some of the editors speculated that Gonzo was like an Abbott and Costello routine, and Hunter needed a straight man. This piece of criticism got back to him and made him furious.

Other editors calculated that Gonzo was made for straight all-American events like the Superbowl; Hunter's failure to produce a good piece led them to speculate that something was dreadfully wrong with him.

David Felton thought that cocaine had gone to Hunter's head. Up until now, Hunter had used cocaine only sparingly and had often expressed his belief that coke was "a drug for fruits." Now he appeared to be into using coke at every opportunity.

Felton remembered how Hunter first discovered coke. Hunter had been given an assignment to review Sigmund Freud's *The Cocaine Papers*, a reissued book of essays and case studies of cocaine use. Felton got a call one night from Hunter, who was sitting in front of the fireplace in his "chemotherapy chair," where he sat to take drugs at home. "This is such a bullshit drug," he said to Felton. "Describe how you feel when you are high on cocaine."

Felton thought a moment. "It's like speed. It's exhilarating."

Hunter laughed, "See, you can't describe it any better than anyone else. It's just ritual and all that. It's a middle class rip-off. But as long as we're talking, I might as well finish off this envelope."

"From that moment on, he had to have cocaine," said Felton. "And I remember, he would be on deadline in the office, and trying to write, and he couldn't because his mind would be frozen and it really panicked him. Frozen for that moment because of the coke."

It was cocaine that ruined him, thought Felton.

Other editors couldn't deny that cocaine was having a bad effect on Hunter. They could see it in the surly way he was dealing with the people in the office, especially Wenner. Hunter and Wenner had always had an adversarial relationship, "a *mano a mano* togetherness," as one editor put it. Now the relationship was becoming increasingly explosive. They argued constantly, Hunter about the lack of money from Wenner and Wenner about the lack of material from his star writer. Hunter kept trying to write off cocaine as an expense, which the bookkeeping department refused to do. "What the fuck," protested Hunter. "It's a legitimate business expense. I need it to write."

The bad effect of cocaine could not be denied, but neither could the stardom that Hunter was experiencing. Celebrity had landed on Hunter like a chronic disease. More and more people sought him out for autographs or wanted to hang out with him and "get nuts."

An enterprising individual in the *Rolling Stone* business department started a speaker's bureau, making the editors and writers available to the rapidly growing college speaking circuit. The only one who really got bookings was Hunter. Student activity coordinators paid thousands of dollars to watch Hunter amble around on stage like a drunken bear, swigging Wild Turkey and answering questions hollered from the audience.

"He made a lot of money on the lecture circuit," said Scanlon, "and all he had to do was go out and act crazy."

"Being a celebrity is easier than being a writer," said Felton. "One thing Hunter does not enjoy is writing. He hates it and he fears it. He would rather do anything than write, even be a celebrity."

In fall 1974, for example, Hunter had an engagement to speak at Duke University. From the moment he arrived on campus, Hunter started smoking hash. He wiled away the afternoon drinking beer and watching TV and then, right before the scheduled stage time, he opened a bottle of Wild Turkey. He appeared on stage forty-five minutes late, muttering and belligerent, carrying a glass of Wild Turkey filled with ice cubes.

"I'm very happy to be here at the alma mater of Richard Nixon," he said, starting the evening on a humorous vein. As usual he had no prepared speech. He just stood there and fielded questions. Most of these focused on his Gonzo lifestyle: Did he really live on the jagged edge of madness and deadlines that he always wrote about? Is LSD or speed a better drug for writing? How much dope did he consume on an average day?

Then somebody asked if Terry Sanford was going to run for the presidency in 1976. Hunter's reaction was almost knee-jerk. "He was part of the stop-McGovern movement so I think he was a worthless pigfucker."

Sanford was then president of Duke. When Hunter was informed of this fact, he threw his Wild Turkey high into the air, staining the velvet curtain behind him. A student from the lecture committee approached Hunter and asked him to leave. He walked off to a chorus of boos, some directed at him.

"It was painful to see him becoming a prisoner of his image," wrote student journalist Steve Cummings in the campus newspaper. "All we can do, though, is wish him well as he battles the

Great American Success Machine, an enemy as corrupt as the Hell's Angels, as elusive as an LSD vision."

Scenes like this happened on campuses all over America. Like stars in any field, Hunter was rewarded most by his fans for what he had done in the past. "They always wanted him loaded and nuts," said one editor. "They liked Gonzo and they wanted to see the same thing, over and over again."

Sometimes the audience wanted more than he was willing to deliver. "It was interesting that a guy who built his reputation and vision on excess would get outstripped by his audience," said Fier. "But the culture that read him caught up with him. They became excessive because of his example. And then the demand was for him to become more excessive and more excessive. He may have gotten closeted. But one thing is certain, finally he was just too far gone to write."

Another problem was the sense of repetition he was feeling in his work. As Steadman noted, "This idea of everything having to be Gonzo. I know it was working, but it's an irksome thing doing the same kind of nonstory . . . the coke, the women, the fame all contributed to something going greatly wrong."

"He couldn't orchestrate," said Harriet Fier. "If you believe that Gonzo was a play and he was writing himself into it, then the more well known he became, the more impossible it became for him to control those situations. Because the more everybody else was jumping all over him, then the less he could write himself in when he wanted to and leave himself out when he wanted. He was being inserted into the story whether he wanted to be or not. It was changing the nature of the experience."

Wenner had become as close to Hunter as he could possibly be with any member of his staff. The two spent a lot of time on the phone and wrote frequent letters to one another about music, drugs, and politics. When he went skiing in Aspen, Wenner visited

Hunter, and Hunter sometimes stayed with Wenner when he was in San Francisco. Wenner loved it when Hunter came to town because it gave him the opportunity to live the Gonzo lifestyle. "When Hunter was around, Jann could just be one of the boys and go out and get crazy," remembered Felton. Wenner even promised Hunter a job in his cabinet when he was elected president of the United States.

"The richer Jann got, the harder it was for Hunter to deal with him," said Fier. "It seemed he could not cope with the fact that Jann was rich but he wasn't."

Hunter was paid only $1,000 a month to cover the campaign. His expenses, totaling more than $30,000, were being deducted from his campaign book royalties.

Hunter pressed all of Wenner's buttons, calling him "cheap" and a "slave driver" and even resorting to more personal attacks like calling him fat. Wenner begged, threatened, relied on their friendship, did everything he could to get Hunter into the writing groove.

"Money seemed to be the only stick that Jann had over Hunter," said Fier. "He couldn't appeal to his pride or to his better sense of judgment or anything else. Finally he could only threaten to cut him off. It was like a child arguing over food. The whole thing escalated badly."

Hunter's celebrity status took an unexpected turn in 1975. He was walking down the steps of the Supreme Court when people started pointing at him, laughing and muttering, "There he is, Uncle Duke." He asked someone what was going on and was directed to the morning's newspaper. He had become the dope-eating uncle of Zonker Harris in *Doonesbury*, the popular newspaper comic strip by Garry Trudeau.

At first Hunter was flattered. Then, as time went on, he told friends he would "rip Trudeau's lungs out" if he ever saw him. When NBC wanted to do a profile of Hunter, he said he would comply only if they sent Jane Pauley, Trudeau's wife, to do the interview. The producer said she would check, but she never called back.

Despite the comic strip's sometimes harsh portrayal, Hunter's friends at *Rolling Stone* doubted that he was really put off by his image in *Doonesbury*. "It helped perpetuate the myth better than anything we could do," said Scanlon. The myth meant money.

In the fall of 1974, Bob Arum, a former *Scanlan's* lawyer turned fight promoter, convinced Hunter that the Ali-Foreman heavyweight-championship fight in Kinshasa, capital of Zaire, Africa, was the place to be. Everyone who is anyone will be there, declared Arum—Norman Mailer for *Playboy*, George Plimpton for *Sports Illustrated*, and dozens of other writers from around the world. Hunter called Steadman.

"Gonzo, Gonzo, Gonzo," sighed Steadman. "How long do you think we can keep doing this kind of Gonzo thing?"

There was a moment of thoughtful silence on the line. "I guess we can keep doing this kind of thing until one of us dies," Hunter replied.

"Okay," responded Steadman, reluctantly. "Let's do it again."

Arriving in Zaire at dawn, Steadman was conveyed from the Kinshasa airport to the Intercontinental Hotel in a Russian-built cab he felt had no shock absorbers. As Steadman recalls, the buildings of the city were low and made of slate gray cement matching the color of the sky. Skinny animals picked through the garbage and a few tired people made their way around the cracked sidewalks. The cabdriver talked about the great progress Zaire had made, but the only visible progress was that a few potholes the size of bomb craters had been filled up to keep cabs from disappearing beneath the dirty water.

Steadman had a letter confirming his reservation at the Intercontinental Hotel. The hotel management insisted he was never registered there and that they had never heard of Hunter S. Thompson or *Rolling Stone* magazine. Steadman's cool British veneer was about to crack when Hunter, a glass of whiskey in one hand and a beer in the other, came running across the lobby. "Ralph, where have you been?" Behind him was Bill Cardoza of *New Times* magazine, who had been there six weeks and seemed permanently stoned from the cheap and abundant grass. "He's with me, he's with me!" Hunter shouted to the desk clerk, putting an arm around Steadman. "Don't worry. He's sane, just confused."

Hunter grabbed Steadman and pulled him toward the front door. "You can stay with me," he said. "I have an extra bed. But in the meantime we have to go out to this nightclub and pick up Cardoza's credit card. He left it there last night. God what a night!"

The three piled into a Russian car that Hunter had rented and began a harrowing ride through the streets of Kinshasa. If Steadman was shocked by the city he saw on the way from the airport, he was even more shocked by what he saw now. Hunter explained that the city was divided into twenty-eight "zones." This one appeared to be the lowest. Steadman remembers crumbling buildings, wrecked cars sitting on the sidewalks, and big snakes crawling in the storm drains.

Hunter screeched to a stop in front of a row of block buildings. Cardoza ran inside. In a few seconds he came out with a puzzled look on his face. "It's gone!" he said.

"You mean your credit card?" shouted Hunter.

"No. The nightclub is gone. There is nothing in the building. No chairs, no booths, no booze,not even a bar. The place is empty to the walls!'"

"Holy shit!" muttered Hunter. "Let's get the hell out of here!"

The trio drove silently back to the hotel, where Steadman took his bags up to Hunter's room. There were two beds, a stunning river view of the Zaire river, and an enormous bag of grass—about forty to fifty pounds—that Hunter had purchased for one dollar per pound. "Grass was legal. It was the heavenly thing about Africa for Hunter," recollected Ralph, "cheap and plentiful drugs."

After a few minutes there was a knock followed by someone sticking his head in at the door and asking for "medicine."

Hunter filled the man's pipe and sent him on his way. Over the days leading up to the fight, this scenario was repeated many times as Hunter became known as the official "medicine man" of the press corps.

Steadman pulled a bottle of Glenfiddich whiskey from his luggage and poured a couple of drinks. They watched the river and talked about Zaire.

Hunter said, "Why should I come all this way to watch a couple of niggers beat the shit out of each other? What do I want to do that for?"

He had not interviewed either fighter—not even Muhammad Ali, whom he regarded as one of his idols along with Fidel Castro and Bob Dylan—and had not even been out to their training camps. He saw George Foreman walking the corridor of the hotel with his dogs, but he didn't try to meet him. Other members of the fight entourage, colorful figures like the big round Bundini Brown and the electric-haired Don King, didn't interest him either.

"For the next week, he just did nothing," said Steadman. "Totally and absolutely nothing. He was more interested in looking for cocaine. In fact, all he did was look for cocaine."

Steadman set about doing his job. He made in all twenty

charcoal drawings, dark flights of fancy that included Foreman and his dogs, Muhammad Ali hanging onto the bottom of an airplane trying to escape, a strutting Bundini Brown asking a ticket taker "How many asses you put in them seats, man?" and "Mandelli man," a fat black American businessman who comes to the jungle to meet his ancestors.

Hunter gave Steadman an image he turned into a drawing. One day they were sitting beside the pool, Hunter puffing away on a joint, when an airplane flew over towing a sign that read, "President Mobutu welcomes you to Kinshasa." Hunter chuckled, "Hell Ralph, I'd like to hire one of those fuckers. But my sign would be 'Black is Weird,' and I'd tow it over Mobutu's palace."

It became increasingly obvious to Steadman that there would be no text for the drawings to accompany. Hunter was hardly taking notes and often didn't even carry his notebook.

Hunter wiled away his time consuming drugs with Cardoza, who had taken to calling him "M'Bele" and fondling tiny carved black hands that hung from a gold chain around his neck. When they got rowdy in the hotel bar and were stared at by other patrons, Cardoza would reach for Hunter's neck and shake the hands at the people, putting a hex on them and laughing like a witch. Hunter loved it.

With all the drug use came creeping paranoia that the Mobutu government would not let them leave Zaire after the fight, but would keep them captive. Sometimes Hunter sat in the lobby and talked about a giant torpedo being built in the Republic of Congo, across the river, to be launched at Kinshasa. Hunter repeated this story to anyone who would listen, but no one bought the rumor.

Hunter signed his personal checks with the name "Martin Bormann." He talked about renting a plane and flying across the river to Brazzaville where he was sure the Nazi war criminal could be found. He even had Bormann paged several times at the Intercontinental, which amounted to the name being written on a blackboard and carried through the lobby by a bellhop.

The other journalists and photographers ran around constantly between the two camps, covering the fight as though it were a political campaign. Although disturbed by Hunter's lack of note taking, Steadman expected Hunter to pull out of it and write something. After all, no one expected Hunter to actually cover the events he attended. So if he spent his days smoking dope and powdering his nose with one coke dealer or another, it didn't matter as long as he could remember what he had done and write about it. Steadman reassured himself that Hunter had a plan.

The fight was held at 4:00 A.M. on October 30. That morning Steadman scrambled around the hotel looking for Hunter, only to find him floating naked on an air mattress in the pool, scattering marijuana all over the surface of the water.

"What the hell are you doing?" shouted Steadman. "The fight starts in an hour!"

"I gave the tickets away, Ralph," said Hunter, a certain melancholy in his voice. "I told you, I didn't come all this way to watch a couple of niggers beat the shit out of each other."

Steadman panicked. "What do you mean? I've got drawings to do! I've got to see it and feel it!"

"Sorry Ralph," said Hunter, casting more weed and watching it get sucked down the drain of the pool skimmer.

Steadman ran upstairs and desperately tried to call President Mobutu. One of his assistants came on the line and Steadman smoothly explained the problem. "I don't want free tickets," he assured. "What I do want is to watch the fight with President Mobutu, you know, draw pictures of him while he watches the fight."

There was a pause at the other end as the person spoke to

someone in the room. "The president does not wish you to do this," came the reply. "We are so sorry."

Maybe it was the best anyway, thought Steadman. He imagined what it would have been like had he been allowed to watch the fight with the president. Maybe Mobutu would not like his drawings and would tie him up and hang him from the ceiling.

"I always thought this story could have been as good as the Kentucky Derby piece," he reflected. "It was similar in a lot of ways. But he couldn't do that. The newness had gone out of Gonzo. He couldn't do the same trick again, where he just pulls a story from his notes. I guess he didn't want to do that, anyway. But in the end he couldn't have if he'd wanted to, because he wasn't even taking notes."

For Hunter and Steadman, the Zaire adventure didn't end when Ali beat Foreman in eight rounds. Hunter wanted to leave the next day. There were ugly rumors that Mobutu's government was thinking of detaining journalists. Then there were rumors that Ali was desperate to get out of Zaire and that he would commandeer that day's flight to New York, forcing everyone else off the plane and throwing the airline's travel schedule into chaos.

Hunter insisted that Steadman go back to New York with him instead of waiting for the flight to England. Steadman explained that he didn't have a travel visa for the United States. "You don't understand, Ralph," declared Hunter. "We must flee. You can get the visa when you get to the United States. If you don't get out of here now, you may never leave!"

Paranoia swelled to new dimensions in Steadman. "I began to think that what he was saying was true. Maybe they wouldn't let me out." He packed his bags and followed Hunter to the airport. Even though he did not have a ticket for the New York flight, there was enough confusion in the boarding process that he was able to slip through the gate and get a seat.

Hunter's paranoia sustained itself through stops in Lagos, Accra, Monrovia, and Dakar, where he was convinced that he was going to be removed from the flight and detained. In each of these stops, Hunter and Steadman, who was now as paranoid as his partner, attached themselves to the American pilot who told airport officials that the two trembling creatures with him were members of the crew and should not be subject to the usual passport checks.

"I don't know if Hunter was just feeling drug paranoia or what," said Steadman. "But he genuinely felt that we would have been arrested if we had stepped off the plane, and forced to languish in jail somewhere. That's what he told the pilot, who wanted to know why we were walking with him. He said, 'We are bona fide journalists and I think we'll be thrown into jail if we are forced to go out here with the other passengers.'"

Had the passport checks occurred, they would have shown that Steadman did not have a visa for the United States, and he would have been detained until the next flight to England.

There was more Gonzo when the plane arrived at Kennedy Airport in New York. Because of Steadman's visa problems, he was forced to wait for the next flight to England in a bar he dubbed "the Limbo Lounge." Hunter said he would return to the lounge after he cleared customs with his own luggage. When he came back he was furious. A pair of elephant tusks he was trying to smuggle into the country had been confiscated by customs and stored in a temporary holding area.

Hunter had taken great pains to get these tusks to the United States. He had bought them for $300 in the Kinshasa marketplace, somehow convincing the merchant to take an American Express traveler's check that he signed "Martin Bormann." Then he'd lashed them tightly together with cords he'd cut from the lamps at the Intercontinental Hotel. After smuggling them onto the plane in

Zaire and somehow having them make it through four countries, he wasn't about to give them up now, back in the land of the free.

"You stay here, Ralph," said Hunter. "I'm going to get those tusks back. I'm not leaving those bastards here."

Five minutes later, Hunter came jogging around the corner, the tusks tucked tightly underneath his arm. He shoved them beneath the pile of baggage that sat next to Steadman and continued running, hiding in a phone booth. In less than a minute, customs officials came jogging around the corner after him. They searched the "Limbo Lounge" and then continued scouring the rest of the terminal for a man with two tusks. After a brief search, they gave up. Hunter returned to the table with Steadman and had a beer to celebrate his victory over the customs department.

When he got back to Aspen, a letter arrived from U.S. Customs asking for a twenty-seven dollar import fee, which was all they wanted from the start. "He could have avoided all that Gonzo by just paying the fee and taking them with him," said Steadman. "But Hunter didn't listen because he was just too paranoid."

Hunter produced no fight story for *Rolling Stone*. Steadman did twenty drawings but the editors deemed them too "dark and rough" and decided not to use them without a story by Hunter. With the final expenses totaling somewhere around $25,000, the Zaire escapade had to be one of journalism's most expensive mistakes.

In late 1974, Wenner offered Hunter a $75,000 book advance to produce a 1976 version of *Fear and Loathing on the Campaign Trail* for the magazine's book division. Hunter wasn't especially interested in doing another campaign book. He was still worn out from the last campaign and had expressed some fear of being typecast as a political reporter, albeit a Gonzo one. But the money was good and Wenner was forceful. When Wenner flew to Aspen to negotiate a contract that included a third of the advance up front, Hunter could not refuse.

Hunter kicked back on his porch and waited for the advance to come. When it didn't come, he called the magazine and found out that the book division had been sold. His contract had been canceled and the money would not be forthcoming.

Hunter was furious. He made some angry calls to Wenner and wrote him an irate letter. Finally he decided never to talk to Wenner again.

A few months later, in March 1975, the phone rang as Hunter sat glued to the TV set watching the evacuation of the Da Nang air base in Vietnam. On the phone was Wenner, asking Hunter if he would like to go to Saigon as the *Rolling Stone*'s war correspondent.

Vietnam, a high-powered mix of fear and loathing, violence and paranoia, seemed perfect for Hunter. He suggested to some of the *Rolling Stone* editors that the experience of being a war correspondent was what he had trained for all these years. He left for Saigon.

What he found far exceeded his preparation. The American-supported regime of South Vietnam was in its death throes and the citizens of Saigon were in total panic. Eventually many of them would be executed or sent to Communist "re-education" camps. Even strong drugs could not cut through the grim atmosphere.

Hunter tried to whoop it up with bar girls and black marketeers, but they had become frightened and wired and only made him more nervous about being there. He spent most of his time holed up in his room at the Hotel Continental.

Shortly after arriving in Saigon, Hunter called the home office. One of the editors told him that Wenner had taken him off retainer, an act that amounted to losing his staff benefits, including health and life insurance.

Hunter panicked and called Paul Scanlon. Even though the

former managing editor was now a senior editor, he still carried substantial clout at the home office. He talked to people in the business department and had them reinstate the benefits without Wenner's knowledge.

Neither Hunter nor Scanlon knew that, shortly before Hunter had left for Saigon, Wenner had asked Tom Baker, a *Rolling Stone* vice president, to purchase a life-insurance policy on Hunter that would make the magazine a lot of money if the Gonzo journalist were killed. Baker was shocked at the request but did what he was told. As Hunter hunkered down in the world's most dangerous spot, Wenner had the most to gain, whether he wrote a story or died.

Hunter had some interesting adventures over there. In Saigon, one day, Hunter wanted to test the range of some walkie-talkies he had purchased in Hong Kong. Even though he had been warned not to go out after curfew, he strode out of the hotel and began jabbering into the headset to a person in the lobby as he walked down the street and around the corner. Suddenly the person he'd been speaking with heard gunshots over his headset as Hunter's line went dead. Everyone was sure Hunter had been killed, but soon he came walking back in, sweating and swearing that somebody had tried to kill him.

As the North Vietnamese closed in on Saigon, their field artillery sounding sharp and clear as it hit near the city, Hunter ate crab salad with Murray Sayles, the *London Sunday Times* correspondent. The two drew circles and arrows on a map of Vietnam, marking the location of the advancing North Vietnamese and Vietcong troops.

Hunter thought about staying in Saigon after the take-over. In May '75, he wrote a letter, "Confidential Memo to Colonel Giang Vo Don Giang," published in *Songs of the Doomed,* asking the conquering hero for an interview. "I'm not an especially good typist," the letter said, "but I am one of the best writers currently using the English language as both a musical instrument and a political weapon."

Other correspondents with whom Hunter hung out were clearly perplexed and worried about evacuation plans. In the end, Hunter left the country well ahead of many of them.

He had sent about two pages of paranoid telexes from the war zone. Scanlon cleaned them up the best he could and ran them with a 4,000-word story by Laura Palmer, a free-lance war correspondent who had braved Vietnam until the end, escaping on a helicopter from the roof of the American embassy and writing the piece on the USS *Blueridge* as it steamed for a safe port. "When I saw what Hunter sent, I crashed Laura's piece into the issue," said Scanlon. "Hunter never even acknowledged that it ran."

A few years later, Scanlon included Palmer's story in *Reporting: Rolling Stone Style* (1977), an anthology he was editing. Wenner bumped it from the book. He didn't want a constant reminder that Hunter had failed again.

When Hunter returned from Saigon, he resigned from the magazine and asked that Wenner remove his name from the masthead. He told the *Washington Post* that he would only write for *Rolling Stone* under certain circumstances—and to cover the '76 campaign. Other than that, he'd had it with Wenner and was "tired of haggling" about expenses. "It's a marvelous situation," one of the editors told a *Post* reporter, "the world's worst employee working for the world's worst boss." Wenner refused to take Hunter's name from the masthead.

Hunter only produced one article on the '76 campaign. "Jimmy Carter and the Great Leap of Faith," which came out in *Rolling Stone* in June 1976, describes a trip Hunter made to the University of Georgia Law School in Athens, in May 1974.

Hunter's account begins with his arrival at Carter's mansion, disheveled and drinking a beer; he barely makes it past the disbelieving state trooper for a breakfast with the governor.

Hunter writes how he became a fan of Carter's on that visit when Carter spoke to the one hundred fifty or so "heavyweight" alumni present at the law-school luncheon. The speech came at the end of a long program of talks and comments. Repeatedly Hunter had needed to return to his kit bag in the Secret Service car, where he filled a water glass with Wild Turkey.

Hunter might have missed the speech entirely had not one of the Kennedy staffers told him that "this whole end of the room smells like a distillery" and asked him to settle down and listen to the proceedings. That was when Hunter clicked on his tape recorder and began listening.

He later called it "a king hell bastard of a speech," one that ranked up there with the great oratory of America. Carter struck an especially resonant chord with Hunter when he talked about analyzing the structure of the drug penalties in the state of Georgia and eliminating laws that consider alcoholism or drunkenness a criminal offense.

Hunter gave his Jimmy Carter story the subtitle "Fear and Loathing on the Campaign Trail '76: Third-Rate Romance, Low-Rent Rendezvous." Much of the article's first two thousand words dwells on the identity of "Castrato," a knife-wielding fiend who roams the streets of Coconut Grove, Florida, cutting off the testicles of dogs.

The Law Day speech, which Hunter refers to throughout his story, was supposed to run after the story but was killed at the last minute due to space.

The article appeared under a cover line that horrified Hunter: "An Endorsement, with Fear & Loathing." Hunter told staffers that he wrote about candidates, he didn't endorse them. Wenner, who wanted to swing his weight to the Democratic candidate, argued that the article was clearly an endorsement by Hunter.

Hunter went up to New Hampshire to cover the primary, but he couldn't connect with it. He was drinking a lot more; that, combined with his notoriety, made it difficult for him to follow the rigorous schedule of a campaign. Two days after the primary was over, he returned to Aspen.

He told reporters that *Rolling Stone* had too much "celebrity shit" in it and didn't interest him anymore, that he had always wanted to write fiction, and that was what he was determined to do. "When you deal with Jann," he told one reporter, "you think of the worst possible results of what you are doing, and the best possible results, and a lot of the time you end up with both."

What was his novel in progress about? "It's about Texas and gun-running and the American Dream," he told the reporter. "That's what I've always been interested in: whatever happened to the American Dream."

Harriet Fier made the most persistent attempts of any managing editor to get Hunter back into the pages of the magazine. She used every method at her disposal: sweet talk, cajoling, threats. She even ran the following notice in the "letters to the editor" column:

> Attention all you readers who are constantly on our back about where the hell Dr. Hunter S. Thompson is. Please write to him yourself and tell him to get off his ass and start writing again: c/o Woody Creek, Colorado 81656.

The pleading worked. Under Fier came Hunter's first real tour de force in years, "The Banshee Screams for Buffalo Meat" (December 1977), a darkly sentimental ode to Oscar Zeta Acosta, the "300-pound Samoan attorney" of *Fear and Loathing in Las Vegas,* believed dead.

The idea for the piece was very much Fier's. She and several of the female editors in the office had long wondered if Hunter could write about anything that wasn't gift-wrapped in paranoia. "We used to talk about it all the time," said Fier. "Wouldn't it be great to see Hunter write about sex, or relationships, or people, or just himself rather than his monolithic paranoia."

When Fier mentioned this kinder, gentler approach to Hunter, she believed that no one had ever talked to him about it before. They batted a few ideas around and hit upon a sort of eulogy for Acosta— Hunter called it a "Requiem for a Crazed Heavyweight." The piece ran in the magazine's tenth-anniversary issue and was heralded as Hunter's return to journalism, a notion that he quashed at every opportunity. (The piece was later anthologized as "The Banshee Screams for Buffalo Meat" in *The Great Shark Hunt.*)

The piece was far more sentimental than any Hunter had written before. "When the great scorer comes to write against Oscar's name," wrote Hunter, he will record "more mercy, madness, dignity and generosity in that overweight, overworked and always overindulged brown cannonball of a body than most of us will meet in any human package even three times Oscar's size."

After covering the life and legend of his friend, Hunter seemed almost embarrassed to have shown affection. "DO NOT COME BACK OSCAR! Wherever you are—stay there! There's no room for you here anymore. Not after all this maudlin gibberish I've written about you . . . . So BURROW DEEP, you bastard, and take all that poison fat with you!"

Until this piece came out, no one had realized just how important Oscar had been to Hunter. "The thing about Hunter was that he never got personal," said Felton. "He is a great observer of humanity and the world, but he didn't have much of a clue about himself. With the Oscar piece, I think some of his deep personal needs started to come out."

The piece attracted the attention of Art Linson, a Hollywood producer of two films, *Car Wash* and *American Hot Wax*, who was looking for a vehicle with which to launch a directorial career. He saw the story of Oscar as a way to examine "the twisted legend of Dr. Hunter S. Thompson."

Why would Hunter sell so inexperienced a filmmaker the rights to the Oscar piece? "Shit, I did it for the money," he later said. "I was selling options to my work all the time. I've optioned *Fear and Loathing in Las Vegas* a shitload of times. *Playboy* even ran a short piece about how Larry McMurtry was working on the screenplay. I don't know if that was true and I don't really care. People would pay me ten to fifteen thousand dollars for a six-month option and I gave it to them. I never thought they would make the film. One guy in London bought the option to *Fear and Loathing* and told me how he was going to nail the hands of alligators to the top of a bar to film the scene where everyone turns into reptiles. That was sicker than anything I could come up with, I told him. But I sold him the option because I knew it wouldn't get made. I thought the same thing was true this time, but I was sadly mistaken."

Linson and screenwriter John Kaye produced a script; the title was *Where the Buffalo Roam.* Linson got Bill Murray to play Hunter and Peter Boyle for Oscar. A group of Chicano filmmakers and actors protested that Boyle was not Chicano, but the part was not recast.

Before the film was made, the script made the rounds of *Rolling Stone*, where editors were shocked because of its irrelevant content. Steadman mentioned to Hunter that a portion of the film was to be shot on a chicken ranch. "Fucking chicken handlers in a film about me . . . this is ridiculous," agreed Hunter. Steadman and

Hunter came up with the idea to rename the film *The Death of Fun.*

The script so offended Felton and Fier that they made a personal appeal to Linson. They met with him one afternoon at the Plaza Hotel with Hunter and Bill Murray, who appeared to them to be ambivalent about the script. "Linson was smart," said Felton. "The first thing he did was put out a bunch of cocaine to get everybody friendly. Then he put these shades on Bill and took a polaroid of him. He looked so much like Hunter that we knew he was going to do the movie, no matter what the script looked like."

There was talk that the script would change when shooting started. When Fier was on the West Coast working on a project with another writer, she spent some time on the set watching endless retakes of scenes as Linson struggled to capture the right angles. Ralph was there too, making drawings to illustrate a book that would be published if the movie became the hit Linson hoped it would be.

Linson gave Fier a copy of the new script. "Every other page was pink or blue or green, which meant it was different from the original script, which was white," said Fier. "In the end it didn't even resemble the script we had read in New York. It may even have been more ridiculous, but I couldn't tell. I had totally lost track."

Hunter, in Hollywood while the movie was being made, was carted around by producers and agents and made to feel like a spectacle. "People would invite me to parties and then treat me like a playtoy," he recalled in a 1980 interview. "They would kind of nudge each other and say, 'Here's that nut Thompson.'. . . I go to ICM where I am assigned an agent, who assigns me a studio who assigns me a director who screws things up. Right now Hollywood is screwing me with everything including Studebaker springs. And on top of it all, that piece of shit movie will be shown for the rest of my life!"

The movie was a flop, panned even in *Rolling Stone*, where Hunter's longtime editor and friend David Felton wrote that Linson and Kaye had ignored almost every part of the truth about Hunter and his relationship with "The Brown Buffalo." Instead, they relied upon their imaginations, "hacking out an embarrassing piece of hogwash utterly devoid of plot, form, movement, tension, humor, insight, logic or purpose," and reducing Hunter's life and times to a Three Stooges routine. Felton allowed in the article that Linson may have captured the most telling picture of Hunter just by making the film. "For only a drug-crazed greedhead would sell his name to such a cheap piece of exploitation. Hunter received $100,000."

One critic conceded that "Bill Murray's portrayal of Thompson is just loony enough to frequently amuse us—at least those of us already familiar with the Thompson legend."

The movie spawned a new type of Thompson follower, non-readers who see Hunter as a drug-abusing boozer out looking for a good time, not as a writer. "They think I'm the guy in the movie, not the guy I am," he complained. "They're frightening."

Dave Hacker tells of a visit he made to Owl Farm with his family. They arrived at about eleven in the morning. Peacocks were roaming around the front yard. Sandy intercepted them before they reached the front door. The last time she had seen Hacker was when she and Hunter returned from South America in the midsixties.

"Hunter's asleep," she whispered. "He goes to bed about seven or eight in the morning and doesn't get up until three in the afternoon. If you want to wait, that's fine. But he's rigid about his sleep. He won't be disturbed."

They all went inside and lounged around until about three, when Hunter came out of the bedroom. Sandy went to the kitchen to fix him a sandwich. It was clearly a routine. "She seemed to be there to serve him," noted Hacker.

Hunter paused by his "chemotherapy chair," a high-backed easy chair with speakers on either side and panels in the arms that lifted up to expose compartments that contained chemical stimulants. "Here's the stuff I use to help me appreciate music," he said.

He talked to Hacker for a couple of minutes, then became clearly irritated that his meal wasn't ready. "Sandy," he roared, "where's my goddamn sandwich!" He was going toward the kitchen when his pet myna bird, in an iron cage, muttered, "You dumb son of a bitch."

"Hunter stopped and then, just like he had gone berserk, he started beating on the cage and cursing at the bird," said Hacker. "We thought he was doing it as a joke. But then he just kept beating on the cage and yelling, 'You fucking bird, you fucking bird.' The beating seemed to go on forever, but it probably lasted about a minute. It was a rather startling display of outrageous, uncontrolled anger directed at this colorful bird."

Breathless, Hunter returned to the "chemotherapy chair" and began to eat the sandwich Sandy brought him. When the women and children went out on the porch, Hunter talked to Hacker about the source of his frustration. "I don't think I have anything else to say in my writing," he lamented.

Hacker was shocked to hear such a candid remark. "Hunter, why don't you take all this wonderful stuff that you've been writing and think of it in fictional terms," he offered. "That's what Hemingway did. Take the factual stuff and think of it in terms of a novelist."

"I can't do that," complained Hunter. "I can only react to what's happening. That's all. I can only write about what's happening."

"Bullshit," declared Hacker. "You may feel at the moment that you've exhausted yourself. You have had a pretty busy life and done a lot of things. But that doesn't mean that you're at the end of the line. At least try some short stories."

"That's not me," he objected. "I couldn't do that. I have never tried it and I couldn't do it."

Hacker suggested that trying was better than just "sitting and watching your acreage appreciate." But Hunter said that it was over for him.

"Anyway you look at it, he had been living so intensely for ten or twelve years that it didn't surprise me that he'd reached this point," said Hacker. "But it was tough to see him with no plans, just existing."

When Hacker returned home he wrote to Hunter, restating his belief that Hunter should try his hand at fiction. Hunter never replied.

Hunter's response to everyone who wondered where "his head was at" may be in the Author's Note to *The Great Shark Hunt*, a massive collection of his works published by Simon and Schuster in 1979. He talks about how it feels "to be a 40-year-old American writer in this century . . . compiling a table of contents for a book of my own Collected Works. . ."

I feel like I might as well be sitting up here carving the words for my own tombstone . . . and when I finish, the only fitting exit will be right straight off this fucking terrace and into The Fountain, 28 stories below and at least 200 yards out in the air and across Fifth Avenue.

Nobody could follow that act.

The piece is signed and dated "HST #1, R.I.P. 12/23/77."

.   .   .

A friend tells a story that illustrates how Hunter's attitude toward sex outside of marriage changed over the years. In the early sixties, Hunter was shocked at the reckless abandon with which this man ran around on his wife. "Jesus Christ," said Hunter, "I can't stand all this sexual stuff you are going through. You screw everything that walks."

"Many years later, in the seventies," said the friend, "Hunter called me at about four in the morning and made as close to an apology as I have ever heard him make. He said, 'You know that sexual thing I complained to you about? Well I think you were right all along. I've been in a rut.' After that he hit the ground running, chasing women until Sandy couldn't take it anymore."

Gene McGarr tells a story of Sandy catching Hunter in a ski condo with another woman in the late seventies. She stood outside and shouted for him to come out. When he didn't reply, she yelled until most of the people in neighboring condos were up and looking out the windows. When he didn't reply this time, she threw rocks through the windows until he sheepishly appeared.

Groupies on the college lecture circuit wanted to experience the kind of Gonzo action that Hunter didn't write about. He was usually more than willing to accommodate them. Female staff members at *Rolling Stone* had trysts with him and then called him in Woody Creek to reminisce. Sometimes Sandy listened to their calls on other telephones, and then launched into tearful accusations that Hunter could not deny. Several times he promised to clean up his act and stop the Ginger Man routine. But he went on anyway.

Not long after leaving Saigon, Hunter went to London to see Ralph Steadman. The first thing he said when he got off the plane was, "I need some coke and a warm body to hang on to. Can you get them for me?"

Ever accommodating, Steadman did his best. He introduced Hunter to a young woman in the art community who took care of all Hunter's needs. That was the first day of the trip. Things went downhill from there. "Hunter in London," sighed Steadman, "was like a whale in a fish tank."

The pubs closed at odd hours, preventing Hunter from having a steady supply of alcohol. A coke dealer who met Hunter at the Chelsea Arts Club tried to rip him off by selling him something akin to milk sugar. Hunter made a scene that almost got Steadman kicked out of the club. "Why are you introducing me to these weird, cheap fucking people?" Hunter shouted at Steadman after he tested the man's wares. "What the fuck are you trying to do to me?"

Later that same night, as they were about to drive away from the club, Steadman saw a woman friend whom he wanted to introduce to Hunter. For Hunter, it was love at first sight. "I think that's the woman I have wanted all my life," he said after making arrangements to meet her later.

The romance was short-lived. "She called him after that," said Steadman, "worrying after him like some women do. 'Stop fucking with my brain. Leave me alone,' he told her. And that was the end of that love of his life."

Another woman Steadman found Hunter moved into the Brown Hotel with him. They ran up an enormous tab. By the end of the week Hunter wanted nothing more to do with her. Hunter skipped out on the bill and has never paid to this day.

Hunter couldn't stand London, so Steadman offered to let him stay with his family at Old Loose Court, his home in Kent. Hunter paced around all night, a habit that kept Anna, Ralph's wife, on edge. Hunter tried to calm him down by taking a strong dose of valium, which didn't work. He continued to pace until Sadie, Steadman's daughter, refused to take her coat off when she came home. Drug dealers showed up at odd hours, as did photographers, journalists and hustlers whom Hunter and Steadman had met in Zaire.

Finally Hunter realized the disruption he was causing. He locked himself in his room and slid a note underneath the door: "Okay, I'll stay in my room. Cancel all interviews. Nevermind, cancel everything. Forget everything. It was a dumb idea to come here in the first place."

When Hunter got back to Woody Creek, Sandy found herself fielding calls from English women who wanted to talk to her husband.

Sandy stuck with Hunter until 1979. She typed, transmitted stories on the telefax wire and functioned as a social secretary, managing the flow of characters who came and went at Woody Creek. Then, finally, she left Hunter for a man from the neighboring town of Carbondale. Hunter was devastated by her departure.

"He had this idea about his marriage that was sort of old-fashioned," said a long time friend. "While he might have been unfaithful and was busy having his own adventures, he looked at Sandy's loyalty to him as being absolute. When she had the affair it really blew Hunter out. He suddenly began acting like the victim, as though she had betrayed him."

Shortly after she left Hunter, Sandy and her boyfriend visited Paul Semonin in San Francisco, where he owned and operated the Ice Pick art gallery. Semonin was shocked to see Sandy with another man. She had always bent over backwards to make it work with Hunter. On the rare times that Semonin asked her about the strain Hunter's abuse put on their marriage, she said she had learned to accept the rough edges and work on them.

"It was her rationalization that she thought she could soften them," said Semonin. "Her strategy was to be nurturing, to take all the abuse and come out on the warm side of it. She had always kept at it pretty faithfully."

Finally, she told Semonin, she just got worn down by Hunter. The verbal abuse had become too much. Semonin had seen plenty of that when he visited the Thompsons at Woody Creek.

"Hunter would go out of his way to find something wrong," said Semonin. "Typically I would hear, 'There's no more grapefruits,' or 'there's no more whiskey,' or 'you were supposed to mail this piece of correspondence.' It would be things ranging from the basic to the trivial, but they would trigger in Hunter this kind of over-response. He would go into this rage that had a verbal intensity and a charge behind it that made it very intimidating. He wouldn't do that only to Sandy or other women, he did that to men, too. The difference was that other people could just leave or tell him he had gone too far. Sandy just had to bear with it and hope that it would eventually go away."

She told a friend that the verbal abuse was bad, but the physical abuse was worse. Finally it was the whole picture with Hunter that drove her off. The closeness just wasn't there.

"His sensitivity and sharpness had a closeness to it and an intimate quality that was valuable," reflected Semonin. "But that would get wiped out with this radical hell-raising. It seemed to me as though he was protecting himself from some side of his personality, and all this hell-raising is some kind of angst that allows him to do that. There is a boundary, a point where he feels he is becoming emotionally bound and he feels threatened by that. His individualism, his posture about being a superman, is rooted in this social distancing from people, causes, community and family. Instead of being a good husband, Hunter just decided to stay a superman."

8

THE WORLD OF FITNESS (1980-1990)

In spring of 1980 I wrote to Hunter asking him if he would be interested in covering the Honolulu Marathon for *Running*, a magazine owned by the Nike Shoe Company and edited in Eugene, Oregon, "the track capital of the world." I described the marathon as a "Gonzo gathering of Body Nazis," a reunion for those "truly compulsive" about their fitness, or at least so "seriously guilty" about something that they saw running twenty-six miles as the only sufficient way to do penance. I pointed out that this was a way for him to revive his image in the literary world without writing for *Rolling Stone*.

His reply arrived on May 28. He mentioned his $10,000 fee and a $10,000 fee for his "executive assistant" Laila Nabulsi. He also asked about calling in Ralph Steadman, and suggested that, if I arranged for him to win the marathon by placing a manhole forty yards from the finish, we could make money on a sure bet.

I picked up the telephone and gave him a call. The phone rang at least ten times before it was scooped up and rolled around like rocks bouncing in the maw of a steam shovel. "Too early," growled the deep, guttural voice at the other end.

"Of course," I said to myself. It was 10:00 A.M. in Aspen.

I called back at 2:00 P.M. The phone was lifted from the receiver and dropped back down. At 4:00 P.M. I called again. There was no answer. At 5:00 P.M. I called and got an answering service. I left my home number. At 2:00 A.M. Hunter returned my call. "I thought it might be a little late for you but what the fuck? If we're going to work together, you might as well get used to the hours."

I sat at the kitchen counter and tried to make notes of the conversation: "total expenses for total coverage . . . why the fuck would you trust me? . . . anyone who advocates running twenty-six miles deserves to get screwed . . . if we glorify them, more will do it . . . you're not some kind of crank, are you? . . . these Nike guys must be acid heads . . . I need a fucking vacation anyway . . . are you sure they'll pay for this?"

As a way of keeping Hunter interested in running, I mailed him a pair of Nikes—top-of-the-line, state-of-the-art running shoes with gun-metal gray uppers and air soles. I thought a man fond of high tech and the latest fashion would fall in love with these shoes. I was wrong. Two weeks later a letter arrived explaining in detail why the shoes ate shit.

I called Hunter and made plans to visit Woody Creek.

I was driven from the Aspen airport by a cab driver who was extremely excited to be taking someone to the mountain lair of Aspen's "bad boy." He said he had taken people to John Denver's house and even to Andy Williams' place before his wife Claudine Longet "shot and killed that skier" (Vladimir "Spider" Sabich). But he had never been to Hunter's house, although he had read some of his books, and had even seen the movie, which he liked. Did I think Hunter would be out shooting his .44 today? Would the cab be surrounded by angry, drooling Dobermans?

At Owl Farm, there were no sounds of gunfire and no Dobermans. Peacocks roamed in and out of a caged area on the wooden porch of a rustic log cabin. A pair of metal vultures kept watch from ten-foot poles. Laila Nabulsi, a petite, dark-haired beauty, met me on the porch. She introduced me to Cannibal, a baby peacock that had pecked a hole in the shell of his brother's egg shortly after he was hatched. I asked about the famous Doberman pinschers. "He finally decided they were too messy," said Laila. "Peacocks aren't as messy, and of course they don't bark."

Hunter was on the telephone, talking to an editor at *Esquire* magazine in his abrupt staccato way that makes him sound like a baritone machine gun. "I know, I know, it's not exactly what you wanted . . . But it's pretty damn good . . . No, it's fiction . . . There's about forty pages. . . ."

He put his cigarette in an ashtray on the coffee table and shook my hand. Then he picked up the cigarette again and finished his phone conversation, after which he got Laila started telefaxing the forty manuscript pages to New York on a primitive, noisy, and painfully slow machine.

The blare of three television sets added to the noise. They sat next to one another, all tuned to the network news. The three anchormen talked seriously about some Middle Eastern situation. On the coffee table were cigarettes, a joint, assorted pills, a bottle of Heineken beer, a glass of Wild Turkey, and an iced glass of whiskey. As we spoke, Hunter took hits from each of them in turn.

"*Esquire* wanted me to do a piece on the invasion of the boat people," explained Hunter. (The boat people were Cubans fleeing to Florida to get away from Fidel Castro.) To cover the "invasion," Hunter and Laila had spent a month at the Miami Hyatt, racking up a hotel tab that exceeded $15,000. Instead of interviewing the boat people, Hunter had spent most of his time racing around the high seas in cigarette boats.

"The story was so heavily covered by television and newspapers that I didn't think I had anything to add," said Hunter, taking a drag from a cigarette, then another from a joint, followed by a gulp of beer. "So I thought I'd offer them part of this novel I'm working on."

Called *The Silk Road*, the novel-in-progress related the adventures of Gene Skinner, a former Vietnam helicopter pilot who decides to make a profit by charging five hundred dollars per head to smuggle refugees in his speed boat. (Excerpts from the novel were later anthologized in *Songs of the Doomed*.)

"I'm trying to figure out a way to use journalism as a springboard to fiction instead of using journalism as a way to make money," Hunter said, pacing and consuming. "There's no way I could make enough money in journalism unless I wrote all the time. You simply cannot make enough money at it. And you never have time to finish anything, you never have time to polish anything, you never have time to wrap it up."

He made a pass at the table, expertly hitting on every substance without spilling a drop or flicking an ash.

"I think Hemingway was right about journalism," continued Hunter. "He said, 'It's a good thing as long as you know to get out of it in time.' I think I stayed in it a little while longer than I should have. It's easy to do though. All you have to do is answer your phone and you can get stuck in journalism forever." In his introduction to *Generation of Swine* he had written, "I have spent half my life trying to get away from journalism, but I am still mired in it—a low trade and a habit worse than heroin, a strange seedy world full of misfits and drunkards and failures."

He mentioned that recently he had received an offer to do a book on the decade of the seventies and what it would mean to the coming decade of the eighties. The offer had included a $90,000 advance. Hunter had turned it down. "Nobody should ask that kind of question and nobody should try to answer that right now," he declared.

He said he wanted to write fiction, "especially since I don't know how much time I have."

"Time?" I asked. "What do you mean, 'time?'"

"Time left in my life," he said, matter-of-factly.

At five in the afternoon Laila suggested that we go out for dinner. Hunter took almost two hours to change clothes and get out the door. First he changed from his shorts and T-shirt into khaki pants and a shirt. Then he changed hats, searched for cigarettes and a Dunhill lighter, and loaded his pockets with enough illegal substances to spend the rest of his life behind bars. Finally Laila shouted, "You're worse than a goddamn woman!"

Hunter froze and glared at her. "I guess it's time to go," he growled.

We took Hunter's ancient Volvo and drove the winding road to a rough-hewn restaurant on the main street of Basalt, a tiny cowboy town north of Woody Creek. The manager knew Hunter and gave us a table near the bar. Hunter had a margarita, two glasses of wine, two double Wild Turkeys, and several bottles of beer and continued to function in a normal fashion. At one point he produced a small rock of cocaine from a shirt pocket and Laila made powder and two rows with a razor blade on her pocket mirror. Hunter snorted both rows. The manager came over and told him it was too crowded to do that.

It was late when we left the restaurant and took the winding mountain roads that led back to Woody Creek. We picked up speed until the Volvo was rattling along at nearly eighty miles per hour. When we came to a series of tight switchbacks that called for heavy braking and steering, Laila got scared. She curled up on the floor of the back seat and began screaming at the top of her lungs for Hunter to slow down. "Hunter, goddamn it! Hunter!" I was petrified.

The fear in the car drove Hunter to new madness. While

wrestling the car through the turns, he reached for the dash and shut the lights off. Suddenly we were hurtling through the mountains with nothing but the faint glow of moonlight to guide us. Laila continued to scream. I pleaded for my life. Hunter began a litany of muttering.

"This is what happens to the goddam tourists and old people who come up here. They drive through these mountains at night and suddenly their lights go out . . . they don't know where the hell they are. . . . They run off the road into the creek . . . and drown . . . or they hit a deer and wreck on the highway. . . . Feel that? The way we slipped? Well in the winter there's black ice. Hit that and you end up in the mountains and don't get found till spring."

Guided by moonlight and Hunter's memory, we made it to Owl Farm. "Hell," said Hunter, "what's the problem? I do it all the time."

The next morning while watching Pat Robertson's "700 Club" we worked out the details for the Honolulu trip. He insisted on two things: "Everything is cash in advance" and "you can't in any way imply that I was laying low from journalism but now I'm back doing the same old thing."

Later I heard that *Esquire* magazine had rejected Hunter's fiction piece and the editor who had assigned him the boat-people article suffered grave retribution. Having signed Hunter on for an all-expenses-paid trip to Hawaii, I decided I'd better enlist the help of Ralph Steadman to keep Hunter under control.

I got Steadman's number from Hunter. When I called, the man at the other end of the phone sounded as polite and stilted as an English butler. I explained the assignment as well as my concern about whether Hunter would do the job.

"I would say that you have something to worry about," agreed Steadman. "Hunter has been known to fall through lately. Remember, he hasn't published a story to speak of in about eight years."

Steadman went on to discuss the large number of stories in which Hunter hadn't produced because he'd failed to get the editorial attention he needed. "Of course, attention isn't all he needs," added Steadman. "Sometimes he doesn't do the job even when he has all the help you would think he should have."

I was prepared to give Hunter all the attention he needed, but exactly what kind of attention were we talking about?

"It's sort of like following a how-to book," said Steadman. He gave me a five-point plan guaranteed to get the most out of Dr. Gonzo:

1. "Make certain that everything gets paid in advance [airplane tickets, hotels, rental cars] since he is more afraid than most of not having his expenses paid."

2. "Talk to him every day or at least try to. You may not be able to reach him, or he may be asleep or not want to be disturbed, but try to talk to him about the story every day. He has to know that the story is important, that you depend on it. If he thinks it's not the first thing on your mind, he might just give up."

3. "If there's work to be done on the story, don't let him go back to Aspen. It'll never get done if he goes back home. Bring him to Eugene and lock him in a hotel room. Promise him something good when the story is over, but try not to let him out of the room unless there's a fire. And stay with him and make him work."

4. "Fulfill his needs. Alcohol, drugs, and room service are necessary to his motivation. Be prepared to provide all of them."

5. "Never try to drink as much as he does or take as many drugs. The editor hasn't been made who can keep up with Hunter's substance habits. You'd be better off not to drink or

do anything at all around him. If he even thinks you are trying to keep up with him he will start pouring it on and you might find yourself waking up dead."

"And there's one other thing," added Steadman. "The most surefire way of getting him to produce a story is to send me along. We're the right chemistry and I'll make him work."

I signed Steadman on, but I remained concerned that Hunter would use my offer for a getaway and never produce anything. He had mentioned that he was eager to go because he was in the middle of a "savage divorce."

According to Bill Dixon, Hunter's divorce attorney, Sandy was trying to force a sale of Owl Farm. Even when Hunter offered to buy her half, she refused, insisting that the farm be sold so that neither one of them would be able to live there. Dixon argued that Owl Farm was important for Hunter's ability to produce future income. He hired a Library of Congress researcher who pulled together all references to Woody Creek in Hunter's writing. He even amassed all the clips of *Doonesbury* to show the court that part of Hunter's valuable public persona was tied to the farm. In the end, Hunter kept Owl Farm. Juan stayed in Aspen, living with a friend.

Once Hunter got to Honolulu, I received a constant stream of calls from *Running* magazine staff members about his behavior. "Man, these people are looking at me like I'm the anti-Christ," he said, "but once they get used to having me around, they seem to like me."

Don Kardong, a contributing editor to *Running* and a marathon runner, had dinner with Hunter in a Polynesian restaurant. Hunter thought the lanky runner was acting "superior" and the friend he had brought with him was acting too "preppie." At the end of the dinner, he raised himself drunkenly from the table, swigged some lighter fluid into his mouth and sprayed it over the open flame of his cigarette lighter. A ball of fire rose to the ceiling, singeing the palm leaves that hung down as tropical decoration.

"He called it a 'Gonzo fireball,'" said Kardong. "It almost set the place on fire."

Before he could tank up for another fireball, the manager and a battalion of waiters collared him and requested that he leave. When I mentioned the incident later, Hunter said he'd done it because "they were acting like a couple of Stanford graduates." Which, in fact, is what they were.

Hunter's plan of jumping out of a manhole and running the last forty yards to win the race were dashed by John Wilbur, a former professional football player, now an assistant football coach at the University of Hawaii, who told Hunter he had tried a similar stunt the year before. "He jumped into the race in front of his house which was almost two miles from the end," said Hunter, "and was passed by three people between there and the finish line. Even after twenty-four miles they still had more speed in them than a fresh and fast football player."

Hunter and Steadman ended up watching the race from the back of the radio press van, which moved at between eleven and twelve miles per hour, just ahead of the front runners. It was, he said, "something like being the rabbit in a dog race."

When the press van reached Wilbur's home two miles from the finish line, Hunter and Steadman jumped off and joined Wilbur on the roadside. A light rain kept the streets wet and magnified the sound of the runners' feet as they struck the pavement. "They're as fine tuned as a Wankel rotary engine," Hunter commented. "They don't bounce or waste energy, they just flow."

After the first hundred runners breezed by, the rhythm changed. The next runners were panting and groaning. A lot of them had "hit the wall," the point were a runner's energy is used up and the runner feels as though he or she has hit something large and unmovable. The sound in front of Wilbur's house became a virtual "hell broth" of moans and slapping feet.

"Then came the real weird ones," observed Hunter, "the ones you see dragging their feet along the road in the evenings." Watching these stragglers brought out the meanness in Hunter. He, Steadman, and Wilbur taunted, "Fall down! You're already dead on your feet! Run, run, you geriatric slobs. I've got $100 on you! Hey, fat boy, wanta beer? Hey baby, wanna dance? Go for it! Only twenty more miles to go!"

Up to this point the runners had been cheered on by the crowd. Some scowled or raised a fist at the yahooing trio. Some ran to the center of the road to avoid them. One ran right at Hunter and panted, "You son of a bitch! If I wasn't trying to make a good time, I'd kick your ass!"

Steadman drew a sign that said "Race Cancelled Due to Nuclear War." They stood beside it until it was announced that Duncan Macdonald, a local doctor, had won the race in a little over two hours, fourteen minutes.

After a few days, the Gonzo team developed a working headline: "The Charge of the Weird Brigade: A Rude Visitor's Guide to the Honolulu Marathon and other Hawaiian Nightmares: Run Fast, Dive Deep and Die for No Reason at All on the Kona Coast."

The Kona Coast figured in the headline because they had moved their base of operations to the big island of Hawaii and rented a house in the town of Kona.

If one is to believe the local chamber of commerce, there is no place closer to paradise than Kona. Hunter and crew expected to get plenty of sun and do some marlin fishing, snorkling, writing, and illustrating.

The house they rented sat on a narrow strip of land between the highway and the ocean. The day after they arrived, the ocean

began "acting up," as Steadman put it. The surf became dangerous, aggressively slamming into the rocks and sometimes reaching
into the house itself. "We have nothing but savage surf here,"
reported Hunter on the telephone.

The bad weather drove Hunter and Steadman inside. Steadman
produced sketches at a rapid rate. He was "focusing on some of the
psychological drives that make people do what they do." In one of
the pictures, five emaciated runners are "carbo loading" at a table
heaped with spaghetti, forking it into their gaping mouths in such
large portions that it is impossible to tell whether the food is going
in or coming out.

Hunter pinned Steadman's images around his typewriter for
inspiration. After a few days of thought, planning, bad surf and
substance abuse, he had an idea where the story was going.

The surf, said Hunter, was "like having seven wolves outside
your door." Boulders were being thrown into the pool along with
enormous black crabs and sometimes even fish. Steadman fell off
a rock and was laid up with shooting pains in his back. Rescue
squads were called out daily to save people swept away by the
surf.

"Hawaii is a big lie," said Hunter. "This place eats shit in 175
different ways. These cocksucking bastards, these lying pigs. They
should be destroyed, these fucking islands should be blown up and
destroyed. I'm going to devote the rest of my life to the destruction
of the tourist industry in these fucking islands. This is a very
cheap, ugly and truthless way of life. Everything they have told us
about Hawaii is a lie! The lie is effective and the tourists come. I
think Reagan has told us more truth than these bastards!"

Within a week, the first draft of the piece was finished. Hunter
called on Sunday and left a message on the answering machine:
"Hello, you bastards. . . . You better keep staff on hand at these
critical moments. This is Hunter out in—where the fuck am I?—

Kona. We're sending off thirty-seven pages plus all the drawings plus a lot of other shit today. And I'm not sure just how it will go, whether we'll fly it or send it by train. We'll call in with a waybill number. Laila is typing it now, since it's not entirely finished. The jumps and breaks need work, but it's a fucking monster article. A monster."

When I heard the message on Monday, I called Kona. Steadman answered. "Yes, by God, it's on the plane. You've got a big package coming. It's a real coup." He warned me not to let Hunter get back to Aspen, to bring him to Eugene and not let him out of my sight until he was finished.

Hunter got on the line. I told him I wanted him to come to Eugene. "I'll definitely come up there," he promised. "This thing needs a lot more work."

Before coming to Eugene, Hunter and Laila stopped off in Los Angeles. Laila was a good friend of John Belushi's wife, and they stayed at Belushi's house. While leaving the house one afternoon, Hunter rammed his rental car into the remote control gate at the end of Belushi's driveway, damaging his car and disabling the gate.

While in Los Angeles, Hunter and Laila spent a couple of wild nights with Bill Murray and his girlfriend Mickey, whom he later married. One morning, to get that "high, fine smell of cordite into the air," Hunter lit a roll of ten thousand Black Cat firecrackers in the hallway of Murray's house. The explosions started out sharp and clear as the gray haze of gun powder fogged the room. Then they became muffled as the shards of paper from exploded fire-crackers piled up. Soon there was just a leaping pile of paper on the floor that sizzled and smoked as the explosions continued.

Hunter was wildly enthusiastic. Bill and Mickey were not. When the explosions stopped, Mickey packed a bag and left, swearing to stay away until Hunter was out of the house. Hunter and Laila left for Eugene the next day.

I got Hunter a suite at the Valley River Inn. He and I didn't leave the hotel for five days. He didn't even leave the room. I brought in an IBM Selectric from the office and stacks of typing paper. Room service was alerted that Hunter S. Thompson was staying at the hotel and sometimes required special attention. Anything he wanted he could get in his room without setting outside the door.

In accordance with Steadman's instructions, I promised Hunter a "treat" when the story was completed. If all was finished by Friday, we would get together with Ken Kesey for drinks. After years of battling the legal system in the San Francisco Bay area, Kesey now lived in Eugene, his home town.

Hunter's piece contained a brilliant analysis of the running boom and why he considered it "the last refuge of the liberal mind."

> Run for your life, sport, because that's all you have left. The same people who burned their draft cards in the Sixties and got lost in the Seventies are now into *running*. When politics failed and personal relationships proved unmanageable; after McGovern went down and Nixon exploded right in front of our eyes . . . after the nation turned *en masse* to the atavistic wisdom of Ronald Reagan . . . . The time has finally come to see who has teeth, and who doesn't . . . . Which may or may not account for the odd spectacle of two generations of political activists and social anarchists finally turning— twenty years later—into *runners*.

Hunter introduced Gene Skinner, the protagonist in the fiction he had tried to peddle to *Esquire*. Skinner shows up in Honolulu to take pictures of the marathon. He meets Hunter at the airport in a GTO convertible and immediately asks him why he is covering this event as a journalist. "I thought you quit this business," he says.

"I did," wrote Hunter. "But I got bored."

I divided the story into thirteen sections and arranged them on the floor in two rows. We hovered over the sections, talking about the strengths and weaknesses of each one. About half the sections were in good shape and needed little more than a brushup editing. The remaining sections needed more significant work. Some seemed disconnected from the rest of the manuscript and needed a bridge to close the gap and make the story more coherent. We wrote what was needed on a plain piece of typing paper and inserted it in the gap on the floor. Some sections were unreachable, even with a bridge, and were thrown out. At the end of about three hours, we had agreed on the direction of the story.

After a room service dinner of club sandwiches and Heineken beer, Hunter got to work.

Music was part of his working mantra. He carried with him a complete sound system—speakers, tape player, and tapes. He liked to play the same tape over and over again, hour after hour. While writing *Fear and Loathing in Las Vegas* he played the Stones' *Beggars Banquet* album so many times that he wore out one tape and had to buy another. For the marathon gig, he had a fresh copy of Ry Cooder's latest.

The television was on. A half dozen drinks were lined up from room service. A second cigarette was lit. A joint was rolled. Pills came out of a leather bag. The typewriter was switched on.

Output on that first night wasn't great. He stayed with it, gazing at white paper until inspiration arrived and then exploding with a couple of "hot damns" or "fucking A's" that were followed on the page by a torrent of words. Sometimes he ripped the page out of the typewriter, wadded it up, and threw it in the direction of the wastebasket a few feet away. Other times he praised his effort with a "yes" or "now you're golden" and set the page on the typing stand's pull-out shelf.

By Friday morning, after seventy-two hours of almost steady work, it was clear that my fears about Hunter were unfounded. Although we were both exhausted and Hunter was stumbling over his words due to the high level of drugs and alcohol in his bloodstream, he had finished a 10,000-word article that magazine editors all over the country would covet.

The room was a shambles. No maid had been allowed in for three days. At least two dozen bottles of Heineken lay around in various states of emptiness, along with trays of half-eaten club sandwiches and french fries, glasses of Wild Turkey, crumbled typing paper, ashes and butts.

"I didn't think I had it in me," Hunter half-joked. "The difference between this gig and some of the ones that didn't work out is that you stayed with me and kept me on track. That's the problem with New York publishers, they just want to give me assignments and then leave me alone. They don't realize that I require special attention."

He took a sip of coffee. "I'm tired of dealing with big publishers and big movie studios, big everything. From now on, I'm only dealing with independent publishers and producers. The big outfits aren't as much fun."

I was beginning to have significant gaps in cognition, yet sleep seemed impossible. I found it hard to believe that Hunter could carry on at such a burn-out pace.

"Well, stress kind of sneaks up on you," he said. "It's like the surf, you suddenly find yourself in it, and you can't get out. I got my first death warning from a doctor during the campaign in 1972. This doctor in Aspen, a specialist from the Houston

Medical Center, gave me about a year to live. He said my life-style was affecting tension and hypertension, and anxiety and abuse of my body and all that. He said that if I kept it up a year I'd be dead."

"Did you slack off?" I asked.

"I did a bit," he said. "I went back to him every six months for a baseline. But I work a certain way and I can't give that up."

I went to my room and took a nap. Later, as promised, we drove over to the VFW Hall to meet Ken Kesey. Hunter hadn't seen Kesey in about twelve years. Both of us were jittery from lack of sleep. Hunter had an especially bad case of "speed shakes" from all the amphetamines and coke. We ordered a couple of beers in the Vet's Club bar and waited for Kesey.

"You know, Kesey almost convinced me to stop writing at one time," recalled Hunter. "In LaHonda when he was making those films with the Merry Pranksters about their bus trips, he told me that writing was an archaic form of expression. He thought I should make a film about the Hell's Angels and forget the book."

Hunter's chemical sweat was profuse by now and his jitterishness had slipped into high gear. As Kesey neared the table, Hunter jumped to greet him and swept a glass onto the floor. "I can see what you've been into," said Kesey.

Drinks were ordered and Kesey loosened things up by presenting Hunter with a plastic vitamin jar full of psychedelic mushrooms. Hunter showed his appreciation by extracting one and biting off a piece of the cap. He washed it down with a swig of beer. "I have something for you," he said, handing Kesey a package of firecrackers he had smuggled from Hawaii.

They talked about the Hell's Angels and how Kesey had tried to befriend them long after Hunter had given up. "It even reached the point where I finally gave up on them," said Kesey. "They just wouldn't be nice."

They also talked about the frightening aspects of fame, a subject that had obsessed Kesey since the recent murder of John Lennon. "The crosshairs of fame move around," said Kesey. "And you can sure feel it when they are on you."

"I know what you mean," agreed Hunter. He mentioned a quote the producers had put on the movie poster for *Where the Buffalo Roam*: "I don't advocate the use of drugs, alcohol and violence— but they've always worked for me." He'd fought to have that quote removed. "Things like that create the Billy the Kid Syndrome. People come gunning for you," said Hunter. "They come up and say, 'Hi, I'm Sam Smith from Kansas. Want to fight?' It's gotten so as soon as someone approaches my table to introduce themself, I just reach for the catsup bottle."

Hunter expressed surprise that the two of them hadn't died years ago. He said he never thought he would see his thirtieth year, that he would die of a drug overdose or be killed violently in a car accident. He had always lived his life assuming he would die early. That accounted for the fact that he was always running out of money. "Why would I save anything if I'm not going to be around to spend it?" he asked. "The problem is, I keep outliving my money supply."

After three drinks, Kesey put on his leather peasant hat and announced that he had to pick up his daughter at school. We went out to the curb where Kesey had parked his enormous 1966 Pontiac convertible. Kesey gave Hunter a final handshake and climbed into his car. "I'll see you again pretty soon," shouted Hunter. Kesey started the car and we walked away.

"Here you go, Hunter!" shouted Kesey. We turned to see him throwing the lighted package of firecrackers at our feet. Kesey put the accelerator to the floor as we danced in a cloud of cordite.

"You old hippy! You fucking burn-out!" shouted Hunter.

About three weeks later Hunter and I had a terrible blowup. It was my fault. A "politically correct" editor at the magazine was upset about some of Hunter's language and changed several of his expressions to ones she found more benign. She changed "god-damn race" to "beastly race," and the exclamation "Jesus" to "geeze." "Shit," as in "kicking the shit" out of someone, became "tar." "Bastard," as in "look at that bastard run," was now "guy."

At one point in the story, Hunter is talking to his fictional friend Gene Skinner about a black man who pushes a stewardess off a cliff. He wrote, "All of a sudden this crazy nigger just runs up behind her and gives a big shove." She changed "nigger" to "guy." At another point, she completely eliminated a sentence in which Hunter describes a black marathoner as "the fastest crazy nigger in the world."

When I talked to the editor about the revisions later, she pointed out that the story was laced with racism. Repeatedly in the piece Koreans and Samoans are painted as raping, mugging thugs who run brothels and live like animals. She said that when Hunter called blacks "niggers," that was more insensitivity than she could tolerate.

The censorship drove Hunter wild. He tried to reach me as soon as he received a photocopy of the galleys. "What the fuck do you think you're doing?" he shouted. "Who the fuck changed my 'fucks'? And I sure as hell don't say 'geeze.' If people read me saying 'geeze' they'll think I've become a goddamn born-again!" Changing "niggers" made him craziest of all. "I could sell this fucker to Jann Wenner tomorrow," he yelled. "He's dying to get something out of me. Change it—or I'll have my fucking lawyer on you."

I tried to explain that the edits had slipped by me and I was glad he'd caught them. But I also suggested that he might want to remove some of the racist slurs in the story.

"Why the fuck would I do that?" he asked, speaking so fast he was tripping over his words. "I am a bigot. I'm what they call a 'multibigot.' A multibigot is different from a 'unibigot.' A unibigot is a racist. A multibigot is just a prick. I don't necessarily like any group or type or any identifiable race, creed, or color. They all deserve mockery and shame and humiliation. I suppose I can even include myself. So change it fucking back."

I tried to smooth things over, but Hunter could not be calmed. He angrily passed the telephone to Laila, who went through the galleys page by page to make sure everything was changed back. She seemed abrupt and unfriendly, not her usual self.

"What are you so upset about?" I asked.

"Hunter's pissed, so I'm pissed," she growled.

"That's liberated," I said.

"Look," she declared. "I'm Hunter's dog. When he says bark, I bark."

"Charge of the Weird Brigade" came out to mixed response. Many of our readers were incensed that we would publish an "obscene" work or have a noted "drug addict" writing on such a pristine sport as running. About fifty letter writers threatened to cancel their subscriptions (but to my knowledge none actually did). At the same time, many readers wanted more marathon coverage from Hunter. "It's nice to have a literate nonrunner's opinion," wrote one reader. "Even though he's nuts, I really enjoyed him."

Several magazine editors called to congratulate me on landing a piece by Hunter. "Many have tried, few have succeeded," said one editor at *Rolling Stone*. Several others called to see if I would try to get a piece out of Hunter for their publications. Even Wenner was impressed with Hunter's resurrection. While on a trip to New York, Hunter took the cover to Wenner's penthouse. According to Laila, Wenner was "jealous beyond belief."

"He stole the cover," said Laila, "which is what Hunter wanted him to do as sort of a sharp stick in the eye to remind him that he could still work. Then Jann wanted Hunter to come and write something about John Lennon, another obituary piece. Instead, Hunter gave Jann a lecture about how morbid the magazine had become with so much stuff in it about death. Then he wrote a memo to the staff about morbidity and how to polish its image. His idea was to have the back page become the 'Black Page,' which would be nothing but a listing of that week's suicides and their reasons. He wanted it devoted to people who had died of pills and loneliness, and wanted it called 'DOD: Dead of Despair.'"

On March 3, 1981 I received from Hunter a letter on *Running* Magazine stationery. He offered to do a series of marathon articles—Paris, New Zealand, Bangkok—for a flat fee of $25,000 plus "decent shoes, if possible." High-style global marathon coverage, he called it. Unfortunately, although the idea was intriguing, we never developed the series.

After "The Charge of the Weird Brigade" came out, Alan Rinzler, a vice president at Bantam Books, contacted Hunter and Steadman to see if they wanted to turn the piece into a book. Rinzler thought the theme "why do they lie to us?" was a strong one for the eighties, since the truth was on the slide all over the world. He wanted Hunter to write about 200 more pages, for which Steadman could create some color drawings.

As book editor for *Rolling Stone*, Rinzler had worked with Hunter over ten years before. He believed Hunter could pull it off. He offered $90,000, to be split equally between the two collaborators.

Hunter and Steadman went back to Hawaii to continue their research on the Great American Lie. They linked up with a charter boat owner who captained a trip in which they were tossed on high seas while Hunter struggled with the deleterious effects of mescaline. Since the Hawaiian tourist business promises blue sky and intense pleasure, the trip provided grist for their theme.

At the end of the second trip, Steadman had enough to produce the illustrations for the book, but Hunter hadn't gotten anywhere. Back in Woody Creek, Hunter called Steadman. "We need to have another go at Hawaii. I don't have enough. I need to go back and get some more."

Steadman packed his bags. The two flew to Hawaii, but that still wasn't inspiration enough for Hunter. Once again, he couldn't get rolling; they returned home after a couple of weeks. Back in Woody Creek, Hunter called Steadman in England and told him, "We need to go to Washington. There's a connection there to our theme. 'Why do they lie to us?' can probably be answered in Washington."

For two weeks Hunter and Steadman hung out in the Hyatt Regency in Washington. They received a steady stream of visitors—journalists paying homage to an idol, politicos hoping to wrangle their way into some of his copy, and drug dealers.

At the end of the two weeks, Steadman had just about reached the end of the first third of his $15,000 dollar advance, and Hunter still hadn't started. Through his agent Lynn Nesbit, Hunter convinced the Bantam editors that he and Steadman should have another third of the advance. Traveling is expensive, he explained, and they had undertaken three trips when they had originally expected to take only one. "It's a bigger assignment than we thought. You guys are getting off easy."

The editors went along with Hunter's rationale.

Hunter went back to Aspen. But working there has always been a struggle for him. Too many friends and diversions make it hard to concentrate. John Belushi showed up to party for a few days. They spent hours listening to punk rock tapes so Belushi could capture the aura of the genre. Belushi was writing punk songs of his own. He carried a tape recorder, singing into it and playing it back, trying to hone his routine into some kind of act.

One morning two Woody Creek residents encountered Belushi on the road in front of Hunter's house. He was ambling like a disoriented bear, confused and slightly angry.

"Can we give you a ride?" asked the driver.

Belushi got in the back seat. His eyes were half closed and bloodshot. As his head lolled from side to side, his eyes kept falling out of focus. The man who was driving noticed white powder on Belushi's face and a stream of snot dripping down his nose. "I had to leave," Belushi explained, motioning back to Hunter's house. "I can't keep up with that guy."

The couple felt sorry for Belushi and took him home. There, after a few sips of coffee, he fell asleep until late afternoon. Then he went to dinner with the couple, after which he asked them to drop him off again at Hunter's house.

Meanwhile Laila called Steadman and asked him to come and help Hunter get down to work. Steadman checked in at a local motel. He began producing drawings, pinning them up around Hunter's living room so Hunter would have images to pique his imagination. Every day Steadman showed up at Owl Farm with new drawings, but still Hunter didn't get to work.

"You've got to do it, Hunter," Laila yelled, pacing the room and blowing streams of cigarette smoke. "You've got to start writing."

"I can't do it," said Hunter, resignation in his voice. "I need to have all the drawings first!"

One morning Steadman arrived early. No one was up except Jones the cat. Belushi was lying fully clothed on a small sofa in the living room. For a moment Steadman thought he was dead. He was just plopped there, a motionless mountain of flesh with an unhealthy pallor. Around him were piled food, audiotapes, empty beer bottles, remnants of drugs. Steadman relaxed when he saw Belushi take a deep breath. Then he sat down and drew a portrait of Belushi debauched.

When he had more than forty of Steadman's drawings, Hunter started writing, a scene here and an anecdote there. The pages he sent to his editor were in such poor shape that Bantam decided to call in Ian Ballantine, who had published *Hell's Angels*.

Ballantine didn't like what he saw. The book was more than a year late and Bantam was $90,000 in the hole. He thought the editor had made a mistake in giving Hunter the remainder of his advance. The manuscript was short, and there was no continuity. Some of the scenes were good and funny, but they were connected to nothing. The only thing that kept the project interesting was Steadman's art. Dark and angry voodoo gods, thunderous waves, exhausted runners, crazed surfers, marlin fishing scenes— arranged in the proper order, they told a story by themselves. Ballantine decided to use the art like a clothesline for Hunter's words.

Over the next several months, Ballantine flew to Aspen four times. He set down some ground rules for his meetings with Hunter. He didn't mind alcohol, he said. But he didn't want Hunter to drink more than a few beers while they were working. He also would not tolerate any drugs. As soon as Hunter brought out any pills or chopped a line of cocaine, Ballantine would be gone. Also, no more money. Hunter agreed to the terms.

Ballantine showed up driving a rented car and wearing a business suit "so I would look like a man who knew something about making money." He wanted it clear that he was not there to be exploited.

Hunter and Ballantine went to work. It took much of the day to get Hunter in the right mood. This usually involved the two of them talking about a section of the book; sometimes it meant just hanging around while Hunter got into a groove.

Hunter would concentrate for a few minutes, then jump up from the table and pace wildly around the house. Sometimes he wrote two or three different scenes and then couldn't remember their order. As Hunter wrote on, he made huge and senseless jumps in logic. After a few hours, he was shot. He involved himself in what Ballantine called "evasive behavior." Although he clearly didn't want to write, it also seemed as though he couldn't write. He got flustered and distant, unable to put his words down on paper or even adequately get them out of his mouth. When that happened, Ballantine knew they had reached a dead end for the day.

Hunter then would head for the liquor cabinet and start drinking beer and vodka, one right on top of the other. Ballantine would pack up and return to his hotel.

"There was no reason to push it," said Ballantine. "Hunter could concentrate for just so long and then he would be gone. He would starting drinking as a defense of his lack of concentration. Plus it scared him into wanting to be drunk."

Ballantine later said that he thought Hunter was brain-damaged from too many drugs and good times. He was sure medical science could prove it.

In the end, *The Curse of Lono* had to be composed of many elements. There were Steadman's excellent drawings. There were excerpts from *The Last Voyage of Captain James Cook* by Richard Hough. In fact there is almost as much writing done in this book by Hough as by Hunter, and the joke around Bantam was that Hough should have received a third of the royalties. Hough was included because Hunter did not write enough text to equal even a thin book. Additional padding was provided from the writings of Mark Twain and William Ellis.

Ballantine had the book printed on a heavy stock to add some weight and to better reproduce Steadman's art work. The result was a book that had the feel of a greeting card. "I wanted to use the shortness of the book to its advantage," explained Ballantine. "People in publishing often don't understand the greeting card aspect of a book."

The Curse of Lono met with brisk sales and generally enthusiastic reviews. Perhaps the most subdued review was Charlie Haas's in the *New York Times:*

> Comparisons between *Fear and Loathing in Las Vegas* and Hunter Thompson's new book are inevitable. . . . But the differences between the books are as striking as the similarities. . . . *Lono* is not nearly the sharp entertainment that *Fear and Loathing* is, and Mr. Thompson, wanting to reflect a different moment in time, may not want it to be. The Gonzo manner seems down to a formula at times, and, most disappointingly, the fantasies that provide vicarious vindication in *Fear and Loathing* seem bilious and undirected here.

Patricia Holt of the *San Francisco Examiner* was more laudatory in her review: "Following an absence of many years, that great gonzo journalist and professional dope fiend, Hunter S. Thompson, is back with another dose of fear and loathing, this time projected from the land of (to him) faraway paranoia. Hawaii." She compares Hunter's writing and Steadman's art to *Doonesbury:*

> Remember those languid little circles that used to rise like bubbles around Uncle Duke's head whenever he had abused himself with yet another substance? Well, these are back as originally conceived by artist Ralph Steadman . . . as if to remind us that fear and loathing is *for certain* a constant and abiding factor in everyday life.

Hunter's hometown paper, the *Louisville Courier-Journal,* gave the Terror of Louisville a pat on the back: "If you're addicted to Hunter Thompson, you'll probably find *The Curse of Lono* fun to read. . . . If it's your first Thompson, you're in for a strange experience."

On college campuses, Hunter became an even bigger draw than before. In 1984, the year *Lono* came out, he delivered a performance an average of once every other week. That came to almost $200,000 in speaker's fees. To date, the book has sold about 200,000 copies.

In the middle of the night in May 1984 my deep sleep was shattered by the ringing of the telephone. "Better wake up the drug dealers, I'm coming to town," barked Hunter. "I'm speaking at the University of Oregon. Better tell Kesey. Maybe he can scare up some of that stuff that Hitler used to stay awake in the bunker and we can go all night."

He apologized for not speaking to me since *The Curse of Lono* came out. "The last idea you had turned into a book," he said. "Nobody has been able to do that in years. Do you have any other ideas?"

I actually did have a subject that would be perfect for Hunter to research. It was Hunter himself. I had never fully understood why he was so physically fit. Here is a man who smokes several packs of cigarettes a day, drinks alcohol in the quantity that people in Weight Watchers drink water, a man who snorts cocaine on a daily basis along with whatever mind-numbing, heart-thumping, blood-pressure-raising pharmaceuticals he can get his hands on.

Once Steadman had let it slip that Hunter was a "secret health freak," running as many as nine miles at a shot, but only at night. "Is that true?" I had asked Hunter.

"Well," he said, "I used to do that but not any more. I used to like doing it because there is a good feeling about being in touch with your body and the road. It's like music. I used to run the roads of Aspen or do push-ups, but now I go off and play volleyball with strangers. It would ruin my reputation if people thought I was involved in any kind of health activities."

In fact, Hunter was in great physical condition. He was able to play paddle tennis for six-hour stretches and swim great lengths without apparent cardiac repercussions.

It didn't make sense. It went completely against all the abstinent, low-fat, Jane Fonda truths America had lived with for the last five years.

Wouldn't it be interesting, I thought, to subject Hunter to a voyage of discovery through the world of fitness? We could start at Dr. Kenneth Cooper's Aerobics Clinic, a sweaty substance-free compound in Dallas. They could run Hunter through a battery of physical tests that would show how fit he really was. Then we would go on for five weeks at the Pritikin Longevity Center, where even fat is considered a controlled substance.

After Pritikin, Hunter would visit exercise physiologists, geneticists, cardiologists, and other body experts to discover the role of genetics and upbringing in fitness and longevity. He would have to undergo more medical tests—biopsies, blood tests, treadmill tests, and so forth. Then he would visit various bodybuilders, triathletes, marathoners—athletes so compulsive about their fitness that they work out several hours each day—and study their driving compulsions. He would dabble in some diet and exercise regimen. In the end, he would return to the Cooper Clinic and be retested to see if his level of fitness had improved.

It was, I thought, the perfect idea for the fitness-obsessed eighties.

The morning after Hunter's speech at the University of Oregon,

I told him about my idea. I proposed to call the book, *The Rise of the Body Nazis*. "Any book with Nazi in the title is my kind of book," he said. I ran through my outline.

"Holy shit, they'll pay me a quarter million for that one!" he grinned. "And they'll have to! I don't know if I can go without cigarettes, let alone the other stuff, for five weeks."

"You can always cheat," I reminded him.

"That's it! That'll help the story," he declared, jumping up and pacing the room. "I'll sneak cigarettes! I'll go to this Pritikin center and sneak out with other inmates to smoke."

Hunter chattered excitedly about the cruelty of the fitness movement and how it took pleasures away from people and left them fit but unhappy. "You don't ever see runners smiling, do you?" he asked. "I didn't see one goddam happy marathoner the whole time I was in Hawaii."

He reveled at being the fly in the ointment of fitness. "Write this up as a memo and send it to some publishing houses," he said. "They'll jump at this one. But what ever you do, don't let Jim Silberman see this."

I was puzzled. Silberman had been his friend and editor for almost twenty years, beginning with the hardcover *Hell's Angels*. Why not send it to him?

"Because I owe him a novel and I'm about a year behind the deadline," said Hunter. "If he sees this he'll go nuts. Oh, and don't send it to my agent, either. She wants me to get the novel done. She won't like this."

I promised to write up a proposal.

In the end, *The Rise of the Body Nazis* didn't work out. I did exactly what Hunter told me not to do. I sent the proposal to a Simon & Schuster editor who loved the idea. He presented it to a committee of editors so they could make an offer. One of the editors was Jim Silberman. He had already given Hunter

$125,000 from a $250,000 advance for a novel, and the manuscript was a year overdue.

Silberman called me a few days after the meeting. "You tell Hunter that if he writes this book I'll go to the courts and take his ranch away!" he said.

"You tell him," I replied.

"No, you tell him," demanded Silberman. "He won't talk to me. I was dumb enough to give him $125,000 and now he won't talk to me because he knows I want that book."

"Why don't you take this book instead?" I suggested.

"Because I don't want this book," he shouted. "I think this is an irresponsible thing for you to do. Don't you know this could kill a person like Hunter?"

I laughed at the notion that an overdose of health could kill anyone. "Are you serious?" I asked.

"You'd better believe I'm serious," he said. "You better tell him I'm dead serious about the farm, too!"

Later that day I told Hunter about the conversation with Silberman. He emitted a low whistle over the phone. "I didn't know he really expected that novel so soon," he said. "I guess that shoots this idea in the head, doesn't it?"

"I guess so," I said. And it certainly did.

In 1985 William Randolph Hearst III, grandson of the man who was the model for Citizen Kane, had hopes of reviving the *San Francisco Examiner*'s failing circulation and brought in Hunter Thompson as a columnist. He paid Hunter $1,500 per column.

Many of the *Examiner*'s straight reporters considered Hunter's columns an expensive joke. He wrote about an elderly Chinese woman who claimed to have been Richard Nixon's mistress and gave a detailed account of the affair; he rehashed newspaper articles and satellite TV; he told about his girlfriend Maria Khan being tattooed. Rumor has it that Maria, a recent graduate of an

Arizona journalism school, wrote several of the columns when he froze up.

In 1988, Silberman published *Generation of Swine,* a collection of *Examiner* columns Hunter had put together with his *Examiner* editor and friend, David McCumber. Subtitled *Gonzo Papers Vol. 2: Tales of Shame and Degradation in the '80's,* it found its way onto the bestseller list. It got poor reviews, but the faithful bought it anyway.

Hunter never did finish the novel for which he was contracted to Silberman. To cover the outstanding advance, Hunter went through his files with McCumber and collected odd pieces, letters, memos, excerpts from his three unpublished fiction manuscripts, including *Prince Jellyfish, The Rum Diary,* and *The Silk Road.* Silberman published the anthology, titled *Songs of the Doomed: More Notes on the Death of the American Dream: Gonzo Papers Vol. 3,* in lieu of a novel. The plot of the anthology took an unexpected turn.

"Shortly before this book went to press," Hunter notes in the guise of the "Editor," "we were stunned and profoundly demoralized by a news bulletin out of Aspen." Hunter was "arrested on nine felony counts and three bizarre misdemeanor charges of brutal sex and violence."

A final twenty-five page section of *Songs of the Doomed,* "Welcome to the Nineties: Welcome to Jail," contains documents about Hunter's lawsuit. A second "Editor's Note" introducing this section explains that Hunter's lawyers filed motions against the publisher, and that *Songs of the Doomed* had to be made up "despite the author's objections and bizarre motions filed by his attorneys in courts all over the country."

"The Case" began when a porn film producer named Gail Palmer-Slater sent videos and letters to Hunter. One of the videos was "Shape Up for Sensational Sex," a kinky fitness tape that she'd produced. One of the letters was a greeting card that said, "Sex is a dirty business but somebody's got to do it." Included was a handwritten note that said, "We could have a real good time."

Palmer-Slater followed up her mailings with a personal visit to Hunter in February 1990. She claimed that she wanted to purchase the rights to *Fear and Loathing in Las Vegas*. He told a *High Times* Magazine interviewer that "she wanted me to help her start a boutique and mail-order business for marital aids and dildos—sex toys. She wanted to become the Ralph Nader of the sex business."

They had a few drinks and, according to Palmer-Slater, mountains of cocaine were snorted by Hunter and two of his friends. Palmer-Slater says he became angry because she wouldn't join him in the hot tub, and showed his displeasure by pinching her breast. He says that she got "sloppy drunk" and tried to prevent him from calling a cab to get her back to her hotel. When she tried to grab the phone away, he put his hand on her chest and pushed her away. "That was the sexual assault," he told *High Times*.

She told her side of the story to a friend in Los Angeles, who called the police in Aspen. Late that evening, a member of the district attorney's office called Palmer-Slater's hotel room. He got her husband, Dr. Charles Slater, a Michigan eye doctor. "I made it quite clear that we didn't want to do anything, that we wanted it to quiet down," said Dr. Slater. "But the D.A. said, 'no, we can't do that. This guy's a wild man and he's going to get carried away sometime and really hurt somebody. Now's our chance to really nail him.'"

Five days later seven investigators from local district attorney Milt Blakey's office raided Hunter's house. They searched the place for eleven hours and came away with almost a gram of coke, thirty-nine hits of acid, marijuana, blasting caps, and dynamite. This led to an eight-count indictment, dated April 6, 1990, that included charges of sexual assault and possession of controlled substances and incendiary devices.

Six months before the incident, police had attempted to seize a machine gun from Hunter when he'd fired it at a porcupine. Before that, they had cited Hunter for pulling a shotgun from his golf bag at an Aspen driving range and trying to shoot a golf ball out of the air.

Beyond the police blotters, stories about his bad behavior toward women were well known. One ex-girlfriend told a friend that Hunter had become angry with her for talking too long to a man at Woody Creek Tavern, ripped her clothing off, and thrown her outside the house and into the snow where she could easily have frozen to death had she not been able to sneak into the house after he'd gone to sleep.

Hunter fired his first attorney and hired Hal Haddon and Gerry Goldstein, members of the National Association of Criminal Defense Lawyers. He was determined to make it a Fourth Amendment issue.

The assistant D.A. apparently couldn't make the charges stick. He dismissed the case on May 30.

Hunter claimed to have spent almost $150,000 defending himself. Friends ran a full-page ad in the local papers asking for contributions to the Hunter S. Thompson Defense Fund. Porn-film producers Jim and Artie Mitchell drove all the way from San Francisco with a car full of buxom women, some porn stars themselves, and paraded through the streets in support of their friend. If the trial went on, the Mitchell brothers promised to turn the streets outside the courthouse into a circus. Some feel that it was the threat of having a porn parade descend on Aspen that really led to the dismissal of charges against Hunter.

A few months later, Jim Mitchell shot his brother Art to death. Business at their O'Farrell Theatre in San Francisco was bad and money from films like "Behind the Green Door" was running out. Why Jim shot his brother isn't totally clear. His drinking may have had something to do with it. Hunter went to Jim's trial to provide moral support. One good turn deserves another.

On August 22, Hunter's lawyers filed a Notice of Intent to bring a $22 million civil lawsuit against the D.A. for "Malicious Prosecution, Gross Negligence and Criminal Malfeasance." Hunter plans to write a book about the whole affair. His working title is *99 days: The Trial of Hunter S. Thompson.*

"Publishing Dr. Thompson has never been an easy job," notes his editor in *Songs of the Doomed.* "We lived in his shadow and endured his terrible excesses—clinging always to the promise that he would sooner or later make sense of his original assignment: *The Death of the American Dream.*"

In "Still Gonzo After All These Years," a January 1991 *Louisville Courier-Journal* interview with Roger Cohen, Hunter alleged, "I don't even have time to abuse myself these days. I'm an addictive personality, but I'm also addicted to functioning. I consider myself essentially a roadman for the boys upstairs, the lords of Karma."

ACKNOWLEDGMENTS

All told, I interviewed more that 100 people in researching this book, among them bankers, writers, editors, music teachers, artists, actors, lawyers, publishers, farmers, college students, professors, convicts, ex-convicts, reporters and grade-school teachers.

Some of those sources have chosen to remain unnamed. To them I offer a note of appreciation for the help they gave. Unauthorized biography is the truest form of history, and they acknowledged that by their participation.

Some don't mind being thanked out loud. Among those are Anne Beneduce; Roscoe C. Born, one of the founding editors of the *National Observer*; Ian Ballantine, founder of Ballantine Books and Hunter's first publisher: Judy Booth Lord; Don Cooke; Dave Hacker, who worked with Hunter during his tenure at the *Observer* and kept in touch with him for years afterwards; Archie Gerhardt, Hunter's high-school economics teacher; Joe Hudson, a first-rate sculptor and a resident of Big Sur; Steve Isaacs, dean of journalism at Columbia University in New York City and a Kentucky neighbor of Hunter's; Susan Peabody Barnes, Hunter's first girlfriend;

Clifford Ridley, a former *Observer* editor; Clifford "Duke" Rice, Ralston Steenrod; T. Floyd Smith; Sam Stallings, Jr.; Bernard Shir-Cliff, who first discovered and mined Hunter's talents for the book world; Warren Hinckle, former co-editor of *Scanlan's Monthly*, where Gonzo started; and Sidney Zion, the other co-editor of that fine, bizarre, yet short-lived magazine.

A number of Hunter's friends from Louisville, Kentucky provided insights into Hunter's Gonzo childhood. Most helpful in this regard was Gerald Tyrrell, whose humor and perspective were greatly appreciated.

Counted among the Louisville crowd is Paul Semonin, who shared memories of his long friendship with Hunter, one that began in their wild youth and saw years of important change for both of them. Semonin is now a historian, and it showed by the way he doggedly tracked down facts when I asked him questions about the good doctor. He allowed me to use photos from his personal collection and provided an excellent analysis of the cultural motivations behind some of Hunter's fictional work. His help was invaluable.

Gene McGarr was also a source of many great stories about Hunter, especially from his years in New York, where Hunter searched for an outlet for his work and struggled to fine a job in journalism. McGarr stayed close to Hunter for several years after the two of them worked together at *Time* magazine. McGarr's memories of Hunter remain fresh and provided crisp insights in what made him tick.

The *Rolling Stone* years were wonderfully recreated by a number of people who were there, including David Felton, who was Hunter's first editor there. Now a producer at MTV, Felton kindly provided memories of those drug-crazed years. Harriet Fier talked at great length about her dealings with Hunter. Paul

Scanlon, former managing editor of *Rolling Stone* and a current assistant managing editor of *GQ*, was generous with his time and memory. Charles Perry, now the restaurant critic of the *Los Angeles Times*, had the rare pleasure of dealing very closely with Hunter as *Rolling Stone's* chief copy editor. Not only did Perry tell about the time he spent around Hunter in those heady years, but he also gave me free access to taped interviews he did with Hunter while working on *The Haight-Ashbury*, his excellent history of the counterculture in the freewheeling San Francisco of the sixties. There were other sources at *Rolling Stone* who chose to remain anonymous. These years were intense times for everyone at that magazine—memorable, exhausting, terrific, and hellish. They were at the cutting edge of the counterculture, back when that edge was sharp and cut without impunity. No one makes magazine like the *Rolling Stone* of the sixties and seventies anymore, but maybe someday they will again.

Ralph Steadman was a tremendous help. Not only did he produce the cover for this book, but he also contributed greatly of his time, allowing me to interview him for several hours about his somewhat tangled and mysterious relationship with Hunter S. Thompson.

On the editorial front there are a number of people to thank, namely Suzanne Ironbiter and Elizabeth Hock, editors extraordinaire; Marian Cole, Cornelia Guest, and Nyda Cutler, who kept the facts straight; and Neil Ortenberg, publisher of Thunder's Mouth Press, who is certainly at the vanguard of those new publishers who carry no fat and move like lightning. I appreciate Neil, even when I shouldn't, and hope there are more books for both of us.

My wife, Darlene Bennett-Perry, was also a great help in writing this book. Not only was she a source of moral support, but she spent days in university libraries and on the telephone, assembling the public record on Hunter. I thank her lovingly for both of these. She is the best wife a man could have.

Finally, I owe far more than I care to say in print to my agent, Nat Sobel. In Nat I have no greater friend and no better critic, a valuable combination that is hard to find.

INDEX